READINGS IN MEDICAL SOCIOLOGY

edited by

SARAH CUNNINGHAM-BURLEY

and

NEIL P. McKEGANEY

TAVISTOCK/ROUTLEDGE

London and New York

To our mothers, Dorothy and Elsie
and for Rebecca Louise

First published in 1990 by Routledge
11 New Fetter Lane, London EC4P 4EE

Simultaneously published in the USA and Canada
by Routledge
a division of Routledge, Chapman and Hall, Inc.
29 West 35th Street, New York, NY 10001

Typeset in Baskerville
by Pat and Anne Murphy, Highcliffe-on-Sea, Dorset
Printed and bound in Great Britain by
Biddles Ltd, Guildford and King's Lynn

British Library Cataloguing in Publication Data

Readings in medical sociology.
1. Medicine. Social aspects
I. Cunningham-Burley, Sarah, *1957*–
II. McKeganey, Neil P. *1955*–

Library of Congress Cataloging in Publication Data

Readings in medical sociology / edited by Sarah Cunningham-Burley
and Neil P. McKeganey
p.   cm.
Bibliography: p.
Includes index.
1. Social medicine.   I. Cunningham-Burley, Sarah.
II. McKeganey, Neil P.
RA418.R376   1989   362.1'042—dc20   89-6324 CIP

ISBN 0-415-00832-8
ISBN 0-415-00833-6 (pbk)

CONTENTS

v

FIGURES AND TABLES

LIST OF CONTRIBUTORS

Kathryn Backett is currently a research fellow at the Research Unit for Health and Behavioural Change, University of Edinburgh.

Michael Bloor is a research sociologist at the Medical Research Council's Medical Sociology Unit, Glasgow. He also teaches at undergraduate level in the Department of Sociology, University of Glasgow.

Michael Calnan is a Senior Research Fellow at the University of Kent.

Sarah Cunningham-Burley is a research sociologist, currently working at the Medical Research Council's Medical Sociology Unit, Glasgow.

Neil Drummond is currently a research fellow at the Health Services Research Unit, University of Aberdeen.

David Hunter is currently Director, Nuffield Institute for Health Services Studies, University of Leeds.

James McIntosh is currently a lecturer in Social Policy and Administration at the University of Glasgow.

Neil McKeganey is at present employed as a medical sociologist at Glasgow University's Social Paediatric and Obstetric Research Unit where he is conducting a study of injecting drug use and HIV infection.

Christine Mason is a lecturer in the Department of Community Medicine, Ninewells Hospital and Medical School, Dundee.

Kenneth Mullen works at the Medical Research Council's Medical Sociology Unit, Glasgow, and is also involved in undergraduate teaching of Medical Sociology at Glasgow University.

Maureen Porter is currently an honorary research fellow in the Department of Sociology, Aberdeen University, having just completed a study of contraceptive decision making for the Family Planning Association.

ACKNOWLEDGEMENTS

We would like to thank all the contributors for their part in the development and completion of this volume. We would also like to thank Heather Gibson of Routledge for her help and encouragement. Margaret Dobbs, Irene Hind, Kim McIndoe, Jean Money, Gill Sinclair, and Eleanor Rattray have all kindly helped at some point in the typing of the manuscript. We would also like to thank Irene Hind for her work on the indexing.

INTRODUCTION

SARAH CUNNINGHAM-BURLEY

and

NEIL McKEGANEY

In this edited collection we have tried to bring together a range of papers based upon current or recent empirical work within the medical sociological field. Of course, there is nothing startlingly original in the idea of an edited collection on recent work. Two of the most widely cited volumes, for example, are those edited by Wadsworth and Robinson (1976) and Tuckett and Kaufert (1978). Both of these volumes, however, were based upon work carried out in the early seventies and, in some cases, earlier than that. Since there have been recent new textbooks in medical sociology (Morgan *et al.* 1985; Stacey 1988), it seemed to us that there was the scope for a new edited collection of original papers, some of which were based upon areas of long-standing interest to medical sociologists, such as professional – client relationships, and others based upon more recent developments within the medical sociological field; for example, investigations of the organization and management of health care.

Medical sociology has a strong empirical tradition. Horobin, in a review essay 'Medical Sociology in Britain: true confessions of an empiricist' (1985), wrote:

> medical sociology over the past two decades has been characteristically discontinuous and piecemeal. But it has also had a healthy bias towards practical issues largely because of its uneasy symbiosis with medicine and its separation from academic sociology. It is fashionable to criticize this research output on grounds that it lacks theoretical or conceptual sophistication, takes capitalism for granted or simply that much of it is trivial. I believe that such criticism conveniently ignores the dynamics of the research process and in its condescension fails to give due credit for the considerable

proportion that it is interesting and meaningful. I am content to let a thousand flowers bloom even though I would personally only water some of them.

(Horobin 1985: 104)

We hope this collection reflects the strength and diversity of this empirical tradition, with contributors reporting on recent projects. Some chapters provide quite detailed descriptions of the research process (Neil McKeganey; Sarah Cunningham-Burley; Kathryn Backett; Kenneth Mullen); while others consider the relationship between their topic area and medical sociology in general (Maureen Porter; David Hunter). While all the contributions contain work of interest to policy makers and health practitioners as well as sociologists, a few are more oriented towards a social problems/policy perspective than others (Neil McKeganey and David Hunter). Some of the work is on-going (for example, Neil McKeganey and Kathryn Backett), while others report completed projects (for instance, Neil Drummond and Christine Mason and Michael Calnan). The bias in this collection is towards qualitative research: in one volume we could not hope to do justice to the total range of medical sociological research, and we have no contributions which explicitly address the inequalities in health debate which has dominated the 1980s since the publication of the Black Report (Townsend and Davidson 1982). However, two chapters focus on differences in health-related beliefs between middle-class and working-class groups (Kenneth Mullen and Michael Calnan).

It has been a concern of medical sociologists virtually from the conception of the subject itself to explore the various ways in which matters of health and illness are influenced by the social context in which they occur. In the first section of this book we have focused upon selected aspects of that context. In Chapter 1 Michael Calnan considers the inter-relationship between perceptions of food and health across middle-class and working-class households. This is a particularly important area to research at a time when the individual is being held increasingly responsible for his or her own health and well-being. Although Calnan finds a good deal of overlap between the two social groups in terms of their perceptions of good and bad food, and in their identification of diet as important for health, there remains much that divides them in terms of their perceptions of particular foods, their understanding of different diets and in their food purchasing. While the middle-class group emphasized a balanced diet, the working-class group were more concerned with whether a meal was filling. Calnan also notes that there was a greater discrepancy between beliefs and practice amongst the working class, and offers suggestions about why this is the case.

In Chapter 2 this concentration upon the social context of health and illness is addressed in terms of another long-standing interest of medical sociologists: namely, in the patient's compliance with the medical practitioner's advice. Looking at the way in which diabetic patients manage their condition in terms of the shifting priorities within their everyday life, Neil Drummond and Christine Mason are able to examine the basis for much of the disparity between the patients' accounts of their illnesses and those produced by medical practitioners. Although the latter often assume that health will occupy a particularly prominent place in the patient's hierarchy of values, as Drummond and Mason point out health is only one of a number of factors competing for the individual's attention and resources. In this chapter Drummond and Mason also raise questions as to the nature of sociological analysis and of the way in which the interview setting itself can structure the sort of accounts individuals produce of their life. This is a topic which other contributions to the volume also address (Kathryn Backett and Sarah Cunningham-Burley).

This interest in the social context of health and illness is further explored in Chapters 3 and 4, where the focus is upon health beliefs and behaviour within the family. In Chapter 3 Kathryn Backett begins to explore the notion of family health. In this respect Backett can be seen to be correcting an over-concentration upon illness rather than health amongst many medical sociologists. Importantly, at a time when health promotion is becoming increasingly salient, this chapter explores the whole concept of 'family health culture' and begins to look at the manifold ways in which families seek actively to promote health. Like Calnan, Backett found that beliefs and practices were complexly related. Although her respondents had accepted much of the current orthodoxy about health, these ideals were not always accomplished at a day-to-day level. Backett's chapter is additionally welcome in its concentration upon middle-class families, which have been under-researched in favour of a concentration upon working-class families. Finally, like Drummond and Mason, Backett raises questions pertaining to the methodology of eliciting people's views on matters that are often very sensitive and highly emotional.

Also using qualitative techniques, Sarah Cunningham-Burley, in

Chapter 4, provides an examination of beliefs and practices relating to children's illnesses within the family. Concentrating on illness rather than health, the chapter complements Backett's work. Although focusing on illness, the analysis draws on the concerns, beliefs, and practices of the mothers interviewed, in order to understand how they recognize, construct, and explain illness in their children through a process of monitoring and interpretation. Illness was in fact only one explanation or outcome for a range of behaviours and states which the mothers routinely noticed in their children. Health, illness, and normality were closely related, and the chapter explores the concepts of normality and normal illness, as used by the mothers, as well as their theories of causality.

The next two chapters focus on issues which are potentially detrimental to health: namely, drug and alcohol use. One of the most recent developments in the medical sociological field has been in respect of AIDS-related research projects. In the absence of a vaccine protecting people against contracting the AIDS virus, behavioural changes on a large scale are the only viable means by which the spread of infection may be curtailed. It is entirely understandable, then, that along with a range of other professionals, sociologists should have become involved in the growing field of AIDS research. In order to reflect this we have included a chapter by Neil McKeganey, which looks at one of the highest risk practices for contracting and spreading HIV infection; namely, injecting drug use. The chapter reports on a current ethnographic study of injecting drug use in the community, and associated risks. McKeganey not only explores the extent of drug use within his study locale but looks specifically at the sharing of unsterile injecting equipment. Not only did he find an environment in which drugs were commonplace, he was also able to explore the social context of needle sharing: such activities have to be understood as part of a culture of sharing and mutual support — a culture that extends beyond drug users. McKeganey discusses both the policy implications of this, and the relationship which a social problems perspective has to sociology more generally.

Whilst society at large generally frowns upon the topic of drug abuse or misuse, it tends not to include in this the socially acceptable drugs of alcohol and tobacco. Indeed, as Kenneth Mullen shows in Chapter 6, there is a good deal of ambivalence in people's attitudes towards alcohol. He found ambivalence about women drinking, drunkenness, and the nature of personality change through the consumption of alcohol, although not about alcoholism. There is a dearth of literature on men's health beliefs. By interviewing men in-depth about their views on alcohol, Mullen was able to explore the contradictions in an individual's beliefs, as well as the differences between social groups. This chapter complements that of Calnan since, like Calnan, Mullen examines these attitudes across working-class and middle-class divisions. For example, the men from the manual group were more likely to mention the influence of social circumstances on drinking behaviour.

One of the areas of most long-standing interest to medical sociologists has been that of the relationship between professionals and clients. This is an area which has undergone a good deal of development recently as medical sociologists have sought to employ the writings of Michel Foucault to explore the nature of current professional practice. Whilst much of Foucault's writings concentrate on the processes of perception and surveillance within clinical practice, as Michael Bloor and James McIntosh show, Foucault's ideas can also be employed to analyse areas of professional practice as diverse as therapeutic communities and health visiting. Their analysis is innovative in using fieldwork data, rather than documentary materials, in adopting a Foucaudian approach. They focus not only on surveillance, but also on concealment, and produce a typology of client resistance in the context of local techniques of surveillance.

Also, in the section on the professional client interface we have included a chapter by Maureen Porter. It is probably fair to say that the area of reproductive health-care consultations has been the subject of more sustained critical sniping from patients' pressure groups and the medical profession itself than any other medical specialty. It is also probably true to say that quite a few medical sociologists have, themselves, been in the forefront of demands for a more consumer-oriented mode of practice. It is appropriate then to consider critically the extent to which reproductive health consultations have changed in the face of such concerted criticism. Drawing on a range of studies she has conducted, Porter shows that the gains for this criticism have been far from universal, and such changes as have occurred have not always done so as a result of criticisms levied. As Porter points out, however, it remains far from clear whether the criticisms that have been made express the wishes of the majority of female patients or those of a vocal minority.

Finally, we have included in the collection a chapter by David Hunter on the topic of health-care organization. This is a topic which, as Hunter rightly points out, has received scant attention from medical sociologists even though it is an area where medical sociological expertise could be profitably employed. Hunter first seeks explanations for medical sociology's weak contribution in this area: some of these relate to medical sociology itself, and some to the wider socio-political environment in which research is conducted. He then draws on his own empirical work on community care policy to illustrate the importance of a sociological approach in providing explanations for the diversity of provision across Britain. Hunter concludes his chapter with a call for sociologists to become actively involved in the whole arena of organizing and managing health care. In the light of continued organizational change in health care, this should certainly be heeded.

Part One

THE SOCIAL CONTEXT OF HEALTH AND ILLNESS

FOOD AND HEALTH: A COMPARISON OF BELIEFS AND PRACTICES IN MIDDLE-CLASS AND WORKING-CLASS HOUSEHOLDS

MICHAEL CALNAN

Evidence from epidemiological studies suggests a strong association between food consumption patterns and a number of major diseases (Doll and Peto 1982; European Atherosclerosis Society 1987). These findings have resulted in the issuing of guidelines for a 'prudent' diet by a number of bodies (Department of Health and Social Security 1984; Health Education Council 1985), which have been adopted by health authorities (Unit for Continuing Education 1983) and professional groups. However, it is less clear that the public has been influenced by these guidelines and there is little evidence of marked changes in dietary behaviour, particularly in social classes IV and V (Ministry of Agriculture, Fisheries and Food 1987).

The few ethnographic and small-scale sociological studies which have been carried out on eating practices suggest that the public do feel that diet is an important factor in the maintenance of health (Pill 1985). However, beliefs about what constitutes a healthy diet (Calnan 1987) do not appear to correspond to the orthodox scientific view of the 'prudent diet'. Some of the scientific concepts are not referred to, whilst others have been interpreted in ways which do not correspond to the suggestions contained in these reports.

The aim of this chapter is, drawing on new evidence collected from a qualitative study carried out in 1986, to examine lay beliefs about food and health in greater depth. However, before this study is described in more detail, it is important to outline briefly some of the different sociological and anthropological approaches to food consumption as these will help to throw light on how the study data are interpreted. Sociological approaches to patterns of food consumption have taken a number of different forms. There are those which have examined patterns of food consumption (preparation, cooking and taking of meals) in the context of the social organization of the household. For example, Murcott (1986) argues that to attempt to get a sociological grasp of domestic food habits, behaviour and choices, it is necessary to examine the social relationships within which eating habits, food preparation, food purchase and cooking are located and to understand the social organization in which they occur. For a sociological analysis of food consumption, she suggests it is necessary to ask questions about autonomy, control, power, the exertion of sanctions in the relevant social relationships, and to examine the belief systems and ideology which overlie them. Using this approach Murcott (1986) argues that, while women still do most of the cooking and are responsible for food preparation, in the performance of this type of work they are constrained and influenced by various factors such as the competing demands of other tasks including paid work, which restricts the amount of time available to carry out food preparation and so on. In addition, married women appear to provide meals according to the tastes and preferences of their husbands rather than themselves.

Another sociological approach is less concerned with the distribution of resources and the division of labour within households than with the way in which food consumption is influenced by outside material constraints. For example, Blaxter and Paterson (1982), when discussing patterns of food purchase amongst a sample of mothers with low incomes, show how shopping is limited to the range of foods available in small local shops and the mobile shop. Anthropologists have also examined eating habits in their social and cultural context, although they have tended to view dietary patterns as a product of culturally defined rules and codes of conduct. These rules shape the times and settings of meals, the content of meals and the order in which dishes are served. For example, Douglas and Nicod (1974) in a study of the structure of working-class meals showed that meals were highly structured events and that the meals themselves contained careful combinations of foodstuffs. These authors concluded that any attempts to change these patterns of food consumption for nutritional reasons would have to take into account the rules that structure these patterns. Douglas (1975), in a later paper, shows how the language of food consumption reflects the boundary system in social relations and social events. For example, with those people to whom one is close and intimate, such as friends and relatives, food is *shared*, whereas in the case of people who are more distant socially it is acceptable to invite them for 'drinks' or some more formal event.

Helman (1986), while also interested in the inter-relationship between culture and eating habits, has focused more directly on food and health and how folk models about food relate to health. He has formulated a classification of the inter-relationship between culture, health and illness which employs the following five categories of food-stuffs:

1 Food/non-food	e.g. edible or inedible food
2 Sacred/profane	e.g. clean or unclean or natural/artificial
3 Social food	e.g. symbols of prestige
4 Parallel food classifications	e.g. balance between hot and cold foods as in humoral theory of physiology
5 Food as medicine/medicine as food	e.g. food to restore balance

This very brief overview of different sociological and anthropological perspectives on food consumption clearly suggests that food has a significant social role and that patterns of food consumption are intimately related to the social relations in society. However, there are also indications that food is of considerable importance in lay models of health and illness. This has been borne out in more recent empirical research. For example, Charles and Kerr (1985), in their study of the formation of eating habits and attitudes towards food within families, found that mothers frequently referred to the concept of a 'proper meal'. The proper meal fulfilled the dual functions of ensuring that children eat properly and healthily every day and of teaching them about the social forms and social relations which characterize eating patterns within families. For example, a proper meal was one that the family sat down and ate together. It was also one where the meal was cooked. The Sunday 'dinner' with its joint and two veg. was regarded as the proper meal *par excellence*.

'Cooked meals' were also prominent in a sample of working-class women's perceptions of good food. Once again this referred to a specific pattern of meal preparation, consisting of roast meat and gravy with potatoes and other vegetables. The study by Pill (1985) showed that, although diet was held to be of little relevance in the causation of illness, it was thought to be important in maintaining health. This view was also found in a study carried out by the author

(Calnan 1987), which compared the health beliefs of samples of middle-class and working-class women. This study showed that, for both social classes, having a good diet and carrying out regular exercise and fitness were seen to be the key elements in maintaining health. The conception of a good diet was analysed in more depth and showed some similarities and differences between the groups. The importance of fresh foods, particularly fresh vegetables and fruit, as against artificially packaged foods was emphasized by both social classes. The middle-class groups were particularly concerned about the constituents of diet (low fat, high fibre) and this was reflected in the emphasis that was placed on a balanced diet. In contrast, the working-class women saw a need to have 'good food' on a regular basis. Good food was defined in terms of a cooked meal with meat and two vegetables including potatoes or chips. Having three 'square' meals in a day was a popular description of a healthy diet amongst the women.

The aim of the qualitative study described here is to follow up in more depth some of the concepts, such as a 'balanced diet' and 'square meals', which emerged in the previous study (Calnan 1987). However, rather than focus on health beliefs in general, this study focuses only on patterns of food consumption. This chapter concentrates on the perceived relationship with health. The study collected information about variations in patterns of food purchase, preparation, cooking and eating habits, and the chapter will examine how people's beliefs relate to their food and eating practices. A comparison was made between professional and working-class households to examine the influence of social and economic circumstances.

RESEARCH METHODS

This exploratory study focused on a small number of households from each of the social class groups (social classes I and II and social classes IV and V). Factors other than class which may also influence patterns of food consumption include educational background, employment status, marital status, and age. However, the scale of the study limited the investigation to a specific type of household that contained two married adults or heterosexual adult couples living as married. These households were sampled from information gathered in a community survey which covered a representative sample of people on the electoral register in a local district in south-east England. The

12

group of individuals who were sampled were white married women aged 20 to 35 years, where at least one member of the family was working. Social class was defined according to the occupation of the woman if she was working, or the occupation of her husband if she was not. In order to take into account educational background, only women from social class IV and V who had left school before age 16 were included, whereas in the social class I and II group only women who left school after sixteen were included. Household and family income is notoriously difficult to estimate and to collect data upon. However, an attempt was made to collect data on this topic through asking the interviewee to indicate into which band the income coming into the household per week fell. The findings showed that on average the income in the working-class households was between £100 and £200 a week and the average household income for the middle-class households tended to fall between £200 and £300 a week.

Letters were sent out to potential respondents to ask if they would like to take part in the study, and the final sample of interviewed people consisted of twenty-one from social class I and II and sixteen from social class IV and V. The latter groups proved more difficult to contact and complete an interview with than the former.

A detailed interview schedule was developed and piloted. Ideally we would have liked to carry out interviews with both partners, although the limitations of resources allowed us to focus the interview only on the person in the household who took the major responsibility for food purchase and preparation and serving of meals. This was usually the woman, although where the man took the major responsibility for at least one or more of the activities such as food preparation, an interview was also carried out with him. However, throughout the interview, emphasis was placed on eliciting information about the way other members of the household influenced decisions about food consumption.

Two trained interviewers were used: we were concerned not only ensuring that the interviewers became skilled in carrying out tape-recorded interviews but they were fully informed about the areas and concepts that we were interested in and also understood the rationale behind each of the questions.

The interview schedule was divided into five sub-sections, and questions focused on:

1 food purchase, with a detailed set of questions of what foods were bought in the past week and why;
2 food preparation and cooking;
3 serving of food and meal times;
4 health beliefs and food consumption;
5 socio-demographic factors and social and economic circumstances.

Each of the thirty-seven completed interviews transcribed and presented here are the data on food consumption and health beliefs (4) and food purchase (1).

RESULTS

Maintaining health

As I have noted, evidence from ethnographic research has shown that the public feel that diet is one of the major elements in the maintenance of health (Pill 1985; Calnan 1987). However, as this sample represents a younger age group than those used in previous studies, it is important that beliefs about health maintenance are also examined here rather than that we move straight into analysis of food and health.

Table 1.1   Lay health beliefs about the maintenance of health by social class (rank order of frequency)

Middle class (Social classes I and II)	Working class (Social classes IV and V)
Diet	Exercise
Exercise	Diet
Active mind	No smoking
Sleep	No excessive use of alcohol
Lack of stress/working	Hard work
Fresh air	Lack of stress/working
No excessive alcohol use	
No smoking	
Hard work	

Table 1.1 shows the range of activities which were believed to be important in the maintenance of health for both groups of women. Diet and exercise were still seen to be the key to the maintenance of

health although there was a slightly different emphasis in the two groups. Eighteen of the twenty-one middle-class women interviewed mentioned that diet was important in maintaining health, and twelve thought that exercise was important, followed by three who referred to health as having a stimulating life and active mind. In contrast, thirteen of the sixteen working-class women in the sample felt that exercise was important, and twelve said diet was important. The next categories, such as 'No Smoking', were only referred to by one respondent.

The middle-class respondents, when discussing diet, tended to talk in terms of a 'balanced' diet, for example,

'Well, a balanced diet, a little exercise, as much sleep as you feel you need and not overworking.'

'Well, balanced diet and plenty of exercise.'

The other common way of describing diet used by both groups, but particularly the working-class woman, was in terms of eating properly, having the right foods, or having the right quantity. This was how two working-class women expressed their views:

'To eat properly and exercise and to walk instead of going by taxis.'

'Exercise, fresh air, eating properly, that's it generally.'

The later sections will investigate in more detail what the terms 'balanced diet', 'eating properly', and 'eating in the right quantities' actually mean. However, first it is important to consider briefly what underlies lay beliefs about health maintenance. Logically, the key to understanding health maintenance should lie with lay beliefs about health (Williams 1983). Previous studies have shown that lay concepts of health contain a number of different elements (Calnan 1987), one of which describes health as being 'active and fit'. The emphasis on exercise in the maintenance of health clearly links with this. Concepts of health were explored in this study (although they cannot be discussed here in any great depth) and being fit and active was an element frequently referred to by both middle- and working-class respondents. Here are two middle-class respondents:

'To feel energetic and be able to exercise without feeling unfit . . . to be well, I suppose.'

'Being very rarely ill. Being fit to be able to do what you want to do physically.'

Or, as the working-class women suggest:

'I suppose being fairly fit and agile and able to get on with things and not sort of puffing and blowing and coughing and sneezing all the time.'

'Being fit, not having colds all the time, flu and that sort of thing — basically being healthy and being fit to swim and do things you enjoy without finding it tiring.'

The relationship between perceptions of health and the maintenance of health through diet is not simple. The idea of food as a 'fuel' to keep people energetic and active and get them through the day may be important, explaining the emphasis on quantity and regularity. However, the idea of a balanced diet may be more closely linked to theories about the control of illness, such as maintaining immunity from disease. Or it may be linked with a type of biological explanation which sees a balanced diet as a means of keeping the body functioning in a healthy manner.

A series of more specific questions were then asked about food and health, beginning with:

Some people when they think about food and diets use certain words to describe them. What do you think about the idea that there are:
a) Good and bad foods or diets
b) Healthy and unhealthy foods or diets?

Good and bad food

Each of the women was asked about their ideas of good and bad food (diets). The distribution of responses are described in Table 1.2 and analysed by social class. Both groups agreed that good diets should be based on 'fresh' goods, particularly 'fresh' fruit and vegetables. For example, this middle-class respondent stated:

'I would say all fresh food is good and processed food I don't believe is. I mean these ready made meals I don't believe in. I don't believe in fish fingers or frozen things — you never know what's happened to them. It's all right going to Safeways and getting them off the shelf, but where have they been before that?

16

Table 1.2   Perceptions of good and bad food by social class
(rank order of frequency)

Middle class (Social classes I and II)		Working class (Social classes IV and V)	
Good	Bad	Good	Bad
Fresh food (e.g. fruit/ vegetables)	Processed vegetables/fruit	Fresh vegetables/ fruit	Fatty foods
Moderate amounts of each	Sweet food	Potatoes, greens, meat	Chips/fried food
Balanced	Fatty/fried food	Balanced	Sweet/sugar
Meat/veg/fruit	Cake/sweets	Natural foods	Additives/ preservatives
Dairy products	Fast food	Low fat	Convenience food
Not too much	Refined food	Don't think about it	
	Dairy products/ high cholesterol	Debatable	
	Coffee	Depends on individual	

You know I would rather go into a butchers and see what's what and say well I'd like that piece please. I'd rather do that because I can see what I'm getting. And then if anything's wrong I have only myself to blame. Fresh foods are more nutritious. Well they have not been preserved and I don't know I suppose it's the fact I can see what I'm buying and also to me it tastes better. There's more taste in them.'

The working-class women concentrated more on fresh vegetables than fresh fruit:

'Yes, obviously fresh vegetables, and more, I think they are better than tinned vegetables. Well because you are preparing them yourself. They've got nothing else added to them. I mean they might have chemical or whatever when they've put them on in the field, you can't win can you. You don't put preservatives in peas that you shell rather than in a tin of peas, there's sugar and salt and what not in tinned food and frozen and the dried foods are not too good for you. I suppose they could do harm, I mean if you didn't have a mixture, if you just lived out of a tin or out of dried packets and just ate all of these, I suppose they could, yes.'

The other definitions of 'good' food which were particularly prevalent amongst the middle-class women involved having a moderate amount of each food and a 'balanced' diet. These examples illustrate these two types of concern:

'My husband maintains there are no such things as a health food. There are foods that are perhaps better for you and I think everything in moderation.'

'There probably aren't bad foods, but there are bad diets, I think. All food is good for you, it's a question of balance isn't it? I mean if you get the balance wrong that's a bad diet, basically. If you have a reasonable amount and a reasonable balance of food.'

Such concepts were not as prevalent amongst the working-class women where more emphasis was placed on having potatoes, greens and meat. For example, this working-class respondent talked about 'good' and 'bad' food:

'Junk foods such as chips all the time — very fatty foods give spots — good foods — well in the summer I like salads and that sort of thing or a good main meal, potatoes, greens and that sort of thing and meat of course next.'

Some of the working-class women also identified the importance of 'natural' foods, as the following dialogue illustrates:

A: There is definitely bad diets.
Q: What would you call a bad diet?
A: Well like I said about my sister eating junk food all the time and I think that is because it doesn't do them any good and I think that she is realizing that now because she is coming up for sixteen and she is getting quite chubby and she wants to lose weight, so I said, if she stopped eating all this junk food and ate some fresh vegetables. You see I don't think it is good for them and most of the time you don't know what's in this junk food anyway.
Q: What sorts of things worry you about what's in junk food?

18

A: Well in beefburgers — I don't eat them because they have got fat in them and I don't think there is anything worse than finding a lump of fat when you are eating. The same with sausages because they have got a lot of fat and the colouring as well. Flavourings as well, I mean hardly any of it is natural.

Q: And you think that is bad for you?

A: Yes I do.

Q: In what way?

A: Well like with John now he is all right but just before I had June — no it was after I had June, because I ended up taking him to the Doctor because I couldn't cope with him, he ripped all the wallpaper off and he ruined this table, we had to have it stripped down and re-varnished. He smashed all the table in, he smashed our glass doors on our wall unit. He has ruined everything in the house, he's broken. He used to run round and round the room shouting and punching me and swearing at me. If I took him in a shop he would have tempers and throw himself on the floor and I think when Kelly was two weeks old he gave her a black eye and he had bitten her toe just after I brought her out of hospital. I took him to the Doctor's and he said 'Have you thought about additives?' He didn't tell me anything about them he just said had I thought about them and a friend of Jim's, across the road, lent me a book and when I read the book it had everything he was eating was just full of additives. So one day, he used to eat a lot of 'Penguins' [biscuits], he had been good all morning and he had a 'Penguin' and in about ten minutes he started rushing about so I looked up the additives in it, checked them in the book, and some of the additives in them it said could cause hyperactivity in children so we just stopped at that. He slept in our bed for six months, couldn't sleep in his own room.

The two groups of women differed in the types of food that they considered to be bad. While both groups agreed that sweet foods and fried foods (chips) were bad, processed or prepacked food was the food that the middle-class women most frequently referred to as being bad whereas working-class women referred to fatty foods. Here are further examples of this difference in emphasis. First the middle-class respondents:

'Processed foods, canned foods and ready made things, I can't really see how things that have got a lot of chemicals to preserve them added to it are going to be as good for you as a fresh vegetable. I'm not saying it's bad for you. I just don't know, but you know I just can't see that it can be as good.'

'Fresh food has a better taste and I suppose knowing that they probably contain more vitamins and just the fact that they do taste better is really . . . I do think a certain amount of dairy products are good for you, despite the amount of publicity against them.'

Second, the working-class respondent:

'Bad foods are things like chips and fried bread and fried eggs, everything like that, but good foods I class as grilled things and things that aren't too fatty. That is what comes straight into my head. Convenience food is bad, like keep going to the freezer and the same fried shelf.'

There was, therefore, some agreement between the groups about what constituted good and bad food or diet, although overall the working-class women were more critical of this type of question than the middle-class women. For example, one working-class respondent suggested that food was not a priority:

'I don't know really. I don't take that much notice of food in that way. I suppose if it weren't good for you I would eat it or buy it whatever but there would have to be something wrong with it, I think, for me not to buy it.'

And another said that she tried not to think about it:

'Well I suppose there must be, but I tend to try and not to think about it too much because I like what I eat and that's it you know. I don't tend to ponder on whether or not it's doing me any good or any harm. Because I think if you get too much like that you'd be frightened of eating anything.'

In terms of popularized scientific knowledge about food and health, three types of message seemed to have been accepted. One of these was the dangers of consumption of fatty foods, although it was unclear how far the message had been accepted, particularly as it relates to dairy products and saturated fat. The term 'cholesterol' was mentioned by only one (middle-class) person. The second message was about sugar and sweet things, and the third was about artificial colourings, preservatives, and additives. The following quotation from a working-class woman illustrates these messages clearly:

> 'Well I've come to the conclusion that if we didn't eat what people tell us are bad for us, we'd probably starve anyway. So I think balance it out, you know, don't eat too much of this, that or the other, just a little of what you fancy . . . sugar is bad, for teeth and weight. . . . I do buy orange with the no-added sugar and things you know. I think it's the preservatives and things as well that it's got in it, you know — all these preservatives are bad, and the colourings and trimmings are bad for the children. I thought, well I'll cut out as many as I can.'

Healthy and unhealthy foods

A similar pattern of responses emerged from both groups of women when asked about their understanding of 'healthy and unhealthy foods'. Table 1.3 shows the differences and similarities between the two social class groups. Once again, having a 'balanced diet' and 'eating in moderation' were particularly important for the middle-class women, whereas of greatest importance for working-class women were 'fresh' vegetables.

Table 1.3 Perceptions of healthy and unhealthy food by social class
(rank order of frequency)

Middle class (Social classes I and II)		Working class (Social classes IV and V)	
Healthy	Unhealthy	Healthy	Unhealthy
Balanced diet	Fried food/chips	Fresh foods (veg, fruit, meat)	Sweet and sugar
Moderation/ don't overeat	Sweet food/cakes	Moderation/ balance	Dried foods
Fresh food	Sugar	Varied diet	Fried foods/veg
Well-prepared food	Salt		Additives
	Red meat		Too long in fridge

Fried foods and sweet foods were seen as the major source of bad health by both social class groups, as the following quotations illustrate:

'I think there are some foods that are healthy and some that are not. I tend to think of things with a high fat content — things like chips, sauces that have a lot of cream or butter in them aren't as good as things which have less fat because they give you a heart attack I suppose. I did do A-level biology years ago and I think carbohydrates and fats are easy to immediately store and harder to break down . . . fresh fruit would be of more benefit.' (middle class)

'Fried foods are unhealthy but I would eat them but I don't think they are good for you. Mostly chips because they have got fat in the potatoes — fat is unhealthy — mostly on the TV when you see the documentaries, I like watching those.' (working class)

Finally, in both sets of women there were hints of scepticism at the 'continuous health messages' about food, although the scepticism appeared to be most pronounced amongst the working-class women:

'Well, they say that the sweet stuff and creamy stuff is unhealthy but I mean we still eat it even though they tell us, well if we listen to everything that they said about food I mean, none of us would eat anything, I don't think, because there is something in everything isn't there? Well there must be, otherwise we could all be ill. I think if there was something bad in there, surely we would all have something wrong with us.'

'I don't know, it's very hard to say because food goes in fads. You know, one minute something is dreadfully unhealthy for you, the next minute it's great, you know, and you must have it. I probably think that any indulgence of any particular type of food probably is unhealthy, whereas a more balanced, you know, bit of everything type, that is going to be better.'

Respondentes were then asked what they thought was meant by (a) a 'balanced diet', (b) a 'square meal', and (c) a 'proper meal'. These were the terms which had emerged as important in a previous study which appeared to be related to social class.

A balanced diet

The notion of a balanced diet seemed more familiar to the middle-class women although, as we shall see, the other terms were more familiar to the working-class women. Table 1.4 shows the range of categories used by the different social classes to define a 'balanced diet'

Table 1.4 Definitions of a 'balanced diet', 'square meal', and 'proper meal' by social class (rank order of frequency)

Middle class (Social classes I and II)	*Working class (Social classes IV and V)*
BALANCED DIET	
Mixture of proteins, calcium, vitamins	Mixture of all types of food
Mixture of foods — less fatty foods	Fresh vegetables and meat
Right quality of food — not too much nor too little	Mixture of vitamins, proteins, etc.
	Regular meals
	Right foods and diet
	Don't know
SQUARE MEAL	
Meat/veg and sweet, sometimes with starter	Meat and two veg and sweet
Substantial meal	Substantial meal
Filling meal	Filling meal
Nutritious meal	Cooked meal
Balanced diet (vitamins, etc.)	Balanced diet
Cooked meal	Quick/convenient meal
Meat pudding	Don't know
Everything on your plate	
PROPER MEAL	
Meat and two veg	Meat and two veg
Three course meal	Cooked meal
Planned meal with right ingredients	Filling
Cooked meal	Healthy food
Nutritious	Three course meal/out
In between balanced/square	Don't know
Don't agree	

along with their frequency. The familiarity of the concept for the middle-class women is illustrated by the fact that the vast majority of women defined the term in a similar way: the range of categories expressed by this group was restricted to three. By far the most common of these categories used by the middle-class women was one which described a 'balanced diet' as a mixture of different types of biochemicals. There are four typical responses:

'A mixture of proteins, vitamins, calcium in the diet to keep your body functioning and keep your mind alert and keep you going.'

'It's having all the goodness from every amount of food. Your protein, your carbohydrates, your vitamins, your minerals.

A balance of those things adds up to a more balanced diet isn't
it?'

'I think it's the amount of protein, carbohydrates and fat and
different types of food that you have with it, taken over each day.
You need vitamins. I mean there are some things that you have to
take in everyday. I think it's Vitamin C that can't be stored, some
things can be stored, so it's a balance of that.'

'A portion of nutrients that you need, so fresh fruit because of
vitamins, and also vegetables. Carbohydrates like bread and cakes
comes in to that as well. Proteins — that's cheese, eggs and meat.'

Clearly, the mixture of biochemical constituents which should be in a
'balanced' diet varied from respondent to respondent, although there
were some which were common, such as vitamins and proteins. The
second category of response articulated by the middle-class women
emphasized the balance of foodstuffs, as the following examples
illustrate:

'A balanced proportion of vegetables, meat, fish, cheese, eggs . . .
that kind of thing.'

'Making sure you have fresh vegetables, fresh fruit, milk and
cheese all in your daily diet.'

'I think it's not having too much of one type of food really. I mean
it can't be very good for you, if all you eat is wholemeal bread. I
mean wholemeal bread is good for you, but if you have too much
it's not going to do you any good. So I think it's just having the
right amount of the right things — I think it's a fair amount of
fresh food. If you stick to fairly fresh vegetables and fruit what have
you . . . I don't think you could go far wrong.'

This second category, then, involves an emphasis on getting the right
balance of foodstuffs, particularly from vegetables, dairy produce,
and meat. The third category was articulated by just one of the
respondents, and it involved interpretation of the notion 'balanced
diet' in terms of the right quantity of food:

'Whatever suits you physically . . . if you're overweight, you've
got to tone it down, if you're underweight you tone it up.'

Table 1.4 shows that the working-class women, although using some
of the categories adopted by the middle class, offered a wider range of

categories. This wider variation reflects the greater difficulties the working-class women had with the concept of a 'balanced diet'. Certainly many of the women began with 'I don't know' and 'I suppose'. Common definitions of a 'balanced diet' used by the working-class women included a mixture of biochemical elements; for example:

'Well, you get your proteins and your minerals and your vitamins in equal amounts that should be in your diet. A normal amount rather than going up and down with one or the other, trying to keep them all regular.'

The definition also included a mixture of different types of food:

'Balanced diet — you're going to have a bit of veg, a bit of fruit, maybe a bit of meat if you're not vegetarian in your diet — cereal if you go through a day's eating you know, from your breakfast until your tea — balanced over the day.'

There were, however, other categories which were exclusively referred to by the working-class women. One of these was the provision of specific meals with fresh vegetables and meat; for example:

'Something that gives you a bit of everything really. Like with a main meal, your greens are good for you, and that sort of thing . . . fresh vegetables and a balance between vegetables and meat.'

The other two explanations tended to emphasize temporal aspects of balancing food intake. One of these suggested 'balance' meant regular meals such as: 'Well, three good meals a day', and the other was a balanced intake over the day: 'I suppose a balanced diet is eating the right foods in the morning, at lunchtime and in the evening, to keep it on a level, like they say you're supposed to eat.'

In summary, the middle-class women appeared to be more familiar with the concept of a balanced diet than their working-class counterparts, and there was more agreement amongst them about what the term meant. 'A mixture of biochemical constituents' was the definition commonly used by the middle-class women, whereas the working-class women used a range of categories which included ideas about balancing the quantity as well as the content.

A 'square' meal

In contrast, the middle-class women found that a 'square meal' was more difficult to explain than their working-class counterparts. In the middle-class women's accounts there was more frequent use of the terms 'I suppose' and 'I don't know'. The following response illustrates this uncertainty:

> 'A good square meal. I don't know, it conjures up a Lancastrian with roast beef, that's what it conjures up for me. It would not be particularly healthy but nourishing and you would be filled afterwards.'

The combination of a meal that contained meat and two veg and was filling or substantial were the two types of explanation which were common amongst both social groups (see Table 1.4), although the former was more prevalent than the latter. However, the meat and two veg usually needed to have been preceded by a starter and followed by a sweet. These two extracts illustrate the view from a middle-class and working-class point of view respectively:

> 'Potatoes, vegetables, meat, two veg and a sweet to follow I suppose.'

> 'I should think if you start with something like soup if you think of a three course meal or grapefruit to start with and then your meat and vegetables and maybe a little bit of stodge for pudding, just to fill you up.'

A square meal for both groups seemed to imply a full meal with more than one course. The middle-class women, however, seemed to be more critical of the concept, and suggested that it was a rather old-fashioned term. For example:

> 'It's a lot of stodge with gravy tipped over everything. Well I suppose it ought to be a filling and satisfying meal which has all the right food constituents in it but the phrase sounds like a warming kind of meal. Well there is no reason why a healthy meal shouldn't be that. It makes it sound as if it's lots of potatoes, lots of suet pudding or something like that.'

> 'When I was a child, I suppose a square meal was meat and two veg and a pudding. What it would be now I don't know, because I think people are more adventurous really in cooking. I'd like to think a square meal was one that we all sat down to . . . something that satisfies everybody I suppose.'

The working-class women also tended to describe a 'square meal' in terms of having something 'substantial' and 'filling' but included a meal that was cooked or hot. The following illustrate this approach:

'Well, I call what Jim has is a square meal, what he has when he comes home. The rest is just like our snack.'

'Having one main meal of the day, one hot meal. You can have snack meals and that but if you have a main meal then that is a square meal to me.'

Apart from the meal being cooked, a square meal was also described as being a main meal by the working-class women:

'One of my meals, like tonight's sausage, mash and beans, because I say that is our square meal because we don't have another meal, something substantial.'

'I would not like to say, because my meals, I would not call a square meal because I don't have a square. . . . I only have the one meal, then my one meal consists of whatever we're having but I suppose somebody else, their square meal could be twice as much as I've got on my plate.'

Finally, the working-class women also tended to see square meals as 'healthy' meals or as being good for you, which appeared to be contrary to the middle-class viewpoint:

'It would be a healthy meal like meat, vegetables and potatoes not like eggs, bacon and chips.'

'Meat and vegetables, fruit and a drink. Something that will keep you going but is good for you.'

'A square meal is one that is doing you good and sort of fills you up.'

In summary, while both middle-class and working-class women gave a similar range of definitions of the term 'square meal' it appeared to be a term which the middle class found more problematic and of which they were more critical than the working-class group. Certainly the latter group suggested that it was more likely to encourage health than the middle-class group.

A proper meal

The women were asked how to define a 'proper meal' after they had been asked about a 'balanced diet' and a 'square meal'. While the last two were clearly different concepts for both groups, a 'proper meal' seemed to overlap with a square meal, as the distributions of categories of response in Table 1.4 clearly indicate. Having a cooked, filling meal with meat and two veg was an explanation which was common currency amongst both groups, although the term 'proper' did appear to add something extra for both groups. For the working-class women it appeared to imply a 'healthy' meal:

> 'Well a proper meal you would not have any pudding, you'd just have a piece of fruit for your pudding, you wouldn't have any tinned fruit and ice-cream or anything like that, you'd just have the fruit . . . just eat the things that are good for you.'

The following extract shows that the word 'proper' also conjured up the idea of 'healthy' for the middle-class women:

> 'Yes, well I've used that, I mean I often say that you see about the children, you haven't had a proper meal today. And yet Eleanor might have chosen to have something like a boiled egg and a piece of toast and Marmite. She probably would have got as much as she needed from that and wouldn't really need what I've eaten. I suppose something that has got vegetables and potatoes in some form . . . you see I mean the same thing, meat and two veg not necessarily the meat bit. She'll have got what she wants and Amy will have got what she wants too, but I might not consider that they've had a proper meal if they haven't had what I've had.'

In addition the notion of a 'proper meal' also seemed to have connotations of what the professions felt was the right way to eat: 'Soup to begin with, three courses, sit down at the table.'

In summary, a proper meal for both groups had much in common with a square meal, although 'proper' appears to have overtones of being 'healthy' or nutritious. There were also social connotations attached to the term 'proper meal', as it was seen either as a social occasion which the family sat down to or was a special three-course meal which was eaten sometimes in the home or usually a meal that you had out in a restaurant.

Patterns of food consumption

The second part of this analysis examines actual patterns of food consumption in households. Food consumption can be divided into three separate but interrelated components. They are: food purchase, food preparation, and the cooking and serving of food. Each of these stages in food consumption depends not just on which products are purchased but also on how the product is converted into a meal and who eats it. Each of these stages has been examined in fine detail in this study; for the purpose of this chapter the emphasis will be on patterns of food purchase.

Who does the shopping? The answer to this was the same in both groups: namely predominantly the woman. Sixteen of the middle-class women said that they did all the shopping by themselves, and another five said that they shared the activity with their husbands. Similarly, eleven of the sixteen working-class women said they did all the shopping by themselves, and another three said they shared the task with their husband. In one working-class household the woman shared the shopping with her mother-in-law, and in another the husband did all the shopping by himself. Thus, the information about food purchase was mainly elicited from women in this study, although where the man took the major responsibility he was interviewed. However, this was not to say that the tasks and preferences of other members of the households did not influence the selection of food.

The interview, after initial collection of personal details, began by focusing on food purchase, and one of the questions each of the respondents was asked was about the items of foodstuffs which they had purchased in the previous week. To help find out exactly what had been purchased, the interviewer went through a check list of sixty-seven different items with the respondent, although the respondent was given the opportunity to add anything which was not on the list. The respondent was asked if each of the items had been purchased and, if so, to describe it and what it was actually used for (how it was prepared). The major focus of this chapter is on 'food and health' so only the purchase of items which in contemporary 'scientific' writings have been linked with health and health problems will be considered here. These thirty-two selected items are listed in Table 1.5, which also shows the frequency with which each of these items were purchased by social class groups.

The pattern of results shown in Table 1.5 describes the structure and nature of the English diet as a whole rather than highlights differences between groups within the population. Bacon, bread, breakfast cereal, eggs, fruit, margarine, milk, meat, poultry,

Table 1.5 Frequency of foodstuffs purchased in previous week,
by social class

Selected foodstuffs	Middle class Frequency (n = 21)	Working class Frequency (n = 16)
Bacon	15	13
Bran	8	2
Bread/rolls	20	16
Breakfast cereal	18	16
Butter	8	5
Cheese	20	16
Chocolate bars	8	8
Cream	7	3
Crisps/snacks	13	16
Eggs	19	16
Fish	16	11
Flour	16	13
Frozen dinners	—	2
Frozen sweets	6	7
Fruit — fresh	18	15
Fruit — canned	10	12
Fruit juice	15	10
Lard	6	14
Margarine	17	16
Meat	18	16
Frozen meats	9	5
Canned meats	6	6
Milk	19	16
Nuts/seeds	11	8
Potatoes	18	16
Poultry	17	15
Salt	13	13
Sausages	16	16
Sugar	15	16
Sweets	1	7
Vegetables	19	16
Prepared foods	15	8

sausages, sugar and vegetables were bought by the majority of people
in both social class groups. However, some differences between the
groups in the items purchased were evident. For example, bran was
more common amongst the middle-class groups, as were prepared
foods such as pâté. In contrast, lard and 'frozen' dinners were
purchased more frequently by the working-class group.

The picture which emerges from these data is one which seems to
suggest that both social class groups purchase a similar range of

Table 1.6 Frequency of 'healthy foodstuffs' purchased in previous week, by social class

'Healthy' foodstuffs	Middle class Frequency (n = 21)	Working class Frequency (n = 16)
Bread		
Wholemeal/brown	13	1
White	—	7
Both white and brown	8	8
Flour		
Plain	6	13
Wholemeal	2	1
Both plain and wholemeal	8	2
Margarine		
Low in polyunsaturated fats	9	2
Ordinary	5	7
Both low poly/ordinary	5	5
Milk		
Skimmed/semi-skimmed	9	3
Full fat	10	10
Full fat and evaporated	—	2
Powder	—	1
Potatoes		
Fresh	15	11
Frozen	—	—
Both fresh and frozen	3	4
Sugar		
White	5	11
Brown	4	1
Both white and brown	6	2
Vegetables		
Fresh	5	4
Frozen	2	—
Fresh and frozen	12	6
Fresh and frozen and tinned	—	7

foodstuffs. However, this is somewhat misleading: when details about the type of bread, margarine, and so on were analysed, a different picture emerged.

Table 1.6 shows a more detailed classification of what food was purchased, focusing specifically on a selected range of foodstuffs, some of which have been at the centre of debates about what constitutes a healthy diet. As a result of this more detailed analysis a number of quite marked differences became apparent.

The consumption of brown or wholemeal bread was very common amongst the middle class, and all the respondents reported that in the previous week they had purchased brown or wholemeal bread only or in combination with white bread. For example, two middle-class respondents stated:

'Well, either white or wholemeal, because I have a feeling wholemeal is better for you so I tend to buy that. My husband prefers white for toast.'

'Half and half. I usually buy two loaves at a time, brown and white, because I prefer everybody to have brown but it doesn't agree with the children.'

The working-class sample, on the other hand, was split between those who had white bread only and those who had white bread in combination with brown bread.

There was a similar difference in the pattern of flour consumption, where wholemeal flour was more popular amongst the middle-class group and only two of the working-class women reported purchasing it.

Margarine was purchased by the vast majority in both groups, although, as Table 1.6 shows, there was a difference in the type purchased by both groups. Purchase of polyunsaturated margarine was much more common amongst the middle-class than the working-class women although some working-class women did buy it:

'Well, it seems that on every commercial that is saying about their margarines they say it is supposed to be healthier for you, so I started looking at the fuss and all the different sorts of butter and that as well. I find that they have nearly all got it so I have kept to the one that is low in it. Just to be on the safe side . . . this is for spreading on bread and that so I buy that.'

The ease with which the margarine spreads appears to be an important influence on purchase; a middle-class respondent holds:

'It's usually polyunsaturated . . . that's for the table, whereas for the cooking margarine I usually buy a big tube. Now sometimes that's polyunsaturated and sometimes it isn't. . . . I do believe it is right to get polyunsaturated but sometimes you can be influenced by the price, and also well some of them. . . . I tried a brand from Tesco's and it was too hard and that was difficult for spreading so . . .'

Similarly, low fat (semi-skimmed) milk was more popular amongst the middle-class women, although it was seen as an aid to slimming just as much as 'healthy food'.

'Fresh' as opposed to 'frozen' potatoes were favoured by both groups. Those working-class women who purchased sugar tended to purchase white sugar rather than brown. In contrast, brown sugar was more popular amongst the middle-class women, with two-thirds of sugar consumers saying that they bought brown sugar either in combination with white sugar or by itself.

Finally, vegetables were reported as being consumed by most respondents in both social groups. However, there was also a difference here. A minority of both groups said that they 'only' purchased 'fresh vegetables'. The remainder amongst the middle class tended to purchase fresh and frozen vegetables in combination. However, the remainder of the working-class women either purchased fresh and frozen vegetables or fresh, frozen, and tinned vegetables in combination. Thus, this more detailed analysis has uncovered some quite clear differences between the groups, with the middle-class women's patterns more closely following 'official' recommendations about a healthy food than their working-class counterparts.

DISCUSSION

Lay discourses on health and its maintenance contain a number of different substantive elements, but food and diet are among the most significant. This was evident in previous results (Pill 1985; Calnan 1987) and is clearly highlighted in this study. Beliefs about health maintenance appeared to be associated with beliefs about what constitutes health. Food and diet might be seen as important for maintaining levels of energy and providing the resources necessary to keep active and fit to perform daily tasks. However, the middle-class women tended to talk in terms of a 'balanced diet' and 'everything in moderation'. The notion of a 'balanced diet' may have been derived from knowledge about nutrition gained through school. The idea of 'everything in moderation', however, may reflect more general ideas about maintaining equilibrium in all aspects of life.

In contrast to the middle-class women's emphasis on a balanced diet and not eating too much, the working-class women were more concerned about the meal's being substantial and filling, and this was particularly evident when the two groups discussed notions such as a 'balanced diet' and 'a square meal'. Previous studies have suggested (Pill 1985) that the more traditional idea of a 'cooked meal' or a meal consisting of 'meat and two veg' is now a class-biased phenomenon; what is being identified in this study are cultural differences in perceptions. Alternatively, this difference might be accounted for in terms of the influence of material circumstances. Blaxter and Paterson (1982) in a study of socially disadvantaged families found that for the majority of respondents, health was defined in a functional way in terms of the ability to carry out normal roles, such as carrying on working. Working in this context meant physical work either in the home or in paid work. Thus, substantial meals were a prerequisite for being able to get through the daily tasks.

What of the similarities between the social class groups? In my previous study, one of the major ingredients in a healthy diet which was articulated by both social class groups was having 'fresh' food (Calnan 1987). It was suggested then that both groups of women were operating with ideas about diet which were products of periods where there was a shortage of food, such as during the war years and the depression. Fresh food in those days was in short supply. Fresh fruit in particular was seen as a symbol of prosperity. However, with this younger group of women, their concern about fresh food was a product of more contemporary ideas where the shift is away from processed or artificially packaged food towards 'natural' food. Certainly, the data show how food additives are high on the agenda of this generation of women as potential sources of ill health.

Data from the National Food Survey (Ministry of Agriculture, Fisheries and Food 1987) show some marked difference in the type of food purchased between high- and low-income groups, particularly in relation to the types of bread, flour, milk, and sugar which are purchased. These differences were replicated in this small-scale study, and clearly illustrate that the working-class group's pattern of food consumption may be potentially more harmful to health than that of the middle-class group, according to current knowledge. However, it must be remembered that these data reported here only provide a partial picture of food consumption in that they take into account neither food prepared and eaten away from the home, nor the preparation, cooking, and serving of food in the home.

What of the relationship between beliefs and practices? The analysis enables a comparison to be made between social groups' beliefs and practices rather than an individual's beliefs and practices. Both groups tended to justify sweet and fatty foods as particularly harmful to health, whereas fresh food such as fresh fruit and vegetables were seen to be significant in the maintenance of health. Were these beliefs reflected in patterns of food purchase? The answer to this is yes, in part for both groups, although the difference between beliefs and practices was more marked in working-class households. The latter tended to eat more sweets, more white sugar, more lard and margarine containing saturated fats and drink more full fat milk than their middle-class counterparts. Also, although both groups tended to eat fresh food, the middle-class women tended to opt for a combination of frozen and fresh vegetables, whereas the working-class women also tended to buy tinned vegetables.

Further analyses of the data from this study might go some way towards answering why there is a greater discrepancy between working-class women's health beliefs and patterns of food purchase. However, at this stage, only speculative explanations can be offered. First, working-class women's patterns of food purchase may be influenced by beliefs, tastes, and preferences which have little to do with health, and concerns about health are, for whatever reason, not a high priority in deciding what food to buy. Second, working-class women may prefer to buy 'healthy' food for their families but are constrained by obstacles created by other family members, such as dominance of husbands or children's tastes, restrictions on 'housekeeping', or by such 'external' factors as lack of time, energy, finance, and other resources. Third, health education messages may have had an uneven impact so that information about the harmful effects of particular foods has yet to reach or has been rejected by the working-class women. Certainly, there is some evidence to suggest that messages about the health risks associated with the consumption of dairy products has yet to have an impact, particularly amongst the working-class women.

ACKNOWLEDGEMENTS

Thanks go to Paul Fieldhouse for helping with setting up the study, to Jill Rudge for carrying out the bulk of the interviewing, to Barbara Wall and Lyn Roughley for help with the analysis, and to Linda McDonnell for typing the various drafts of the manuscript. This study was funded by a grant to the Canterbury and Thanet Health Authority from the Health Education Authority.

Chapter Two

DIABETES IN A SOCIAL CONTEXT: JUST A DIFFERENT WAY OF LIFE IN THE AGE OF REASON

NEIL DRUMMOND AND
CHRISTINE MASON

INTRODUCTION

This chapter describes the experience of people with diabetes as revealed in a study which was carried out in Dundee in 1985. Before outlining the method used in the study, we need to account for our choice of the phrase 'age of reason' included in the title. In using that phrase, we shall assert that behaviour, specifically concerning issues of health or illness, can be understood as rational responses to a set of perceived stimuli, or constraints. Within this complex process of perception, cognition, and action, whatever course the latter takes is the product of influences from former components. The crux of the argument will concern the idea that patients make decisions concerning their level of compliance with the diabetic regime within a structured context, and in ways that maintain a demonstrable logic, such that each decision, or course of action, can be explained and justified as being beneficial to the patient's condition at that particular time, within his or her own idea of 'benefit'. Furthermore, we shall argue that the rationale adopted by patients differs from that seen by them as informing medical practice, and built into the diabetic regime. The key to understanding this dichotomy lies in the different contextual factors regarded as significant, or meaningful, by patients, and those seen by them as being important to medical practitioners. Our approach, therefore, is intended to describe the patients' view of diabetes in their own terms, and to juxtapose this with their accounts of how that differs from the medical view.

Conrad (1985) has suggested that previous studies on compliance are centred either upon doctor–patient interaction or on patients' health beliefs. Our argument draws principally upon the latter as providing explanations for 'non-compliant' behaviour. Like Fabrega

(1974), we take the view that health exists in a state of competition with other factors deriving from the individual's context. We shall attempt to describe this competition, relating patient-held explanations to their perception of medical knowledge and understanding.

The phrase 'age of reason', however, is not just a felicitous signal of a discussion of rationalism. It also, in its traditional sense, accurately identifies the philosophical standpoint of medical practice. In the historical Age of Reason, principally the late seventeenth and eighteenth centuries, rational thought was seen to be the main instrument by which knowledge was achieved. Intuition was reduced in importance to the minimum, except by the odd sentimentalist. It is from this period, following Bacon's *The Advancement of Learning* (1605) and Newton's *Principia* (1687), that the power of the scientific method, based on the principles of empiricism and induction, and the observation of actual events and their relationship, began to acquire the dominance it maintains now. Hobbes's *Leviathan* (1651) and Locke's *Essay Concerning Human Understanding* (1690) spearheaded the movement of empiricism into the realms of social and political theory. By the mid-eighteenth century, 'Reason' had become so entrenched into the consciousness of the nation that Fielding and others could satirize its more extreme proponents.

The ethos that informs current medical practice asserts a rationale located solidly within this positivist, objectivist tradition. The logic of treatment regimes involves conceptualizations rooted within this way of seeing, of the body as a physical mechanism, disease as the mechanism malfunctioning, treatment as a physical adjustment to the works. Foucault (1967) describes the age of reason as being 'no longer the fatal time of the planets, . . . not yet the lyrical time of the seasons; it is the universal but absolutely divided time of brightness and darkness' (1967: 109).

We contend that the age of reason lives on, founded on monolithic oppositions of black or white, light or dark, right or wrong. Not only does medical practice subscribe to such a view of itself, but patients also hold similar views of practitioners. However, in discussions with people technically classifiable as 'diseased', it can become apparent that this is not the view that patients have of themselves, and that the classical rationalism of medical science is not a universal experience. This is not to say that patients' actions or attitudes cannot be explained or translated as being entirely sensible, careful, and considered; it is merely to suggest that the factors perceived as meaningful by patients may not always be the same as those so regarded by practitioners. Particularly because of the differences between the everyday context and the clinical, the process of rationalization as conducted within patients is different from that within practitioners.

The presence of this non-congruity in patients' perceptions of themselves and of their practitioners became apparent during fieldwork for a previous study which we conducted. This involved eliciting patients' accounts of their compliance with the diabetic regime. Responses tended to recur with a similar message, particularly from respondents in socially disadvantaged areas. One patient in particular articulated it very succinctly: 'It's just a different way of life. What we are, and what the doctors do. Just a different way of life. That's all.'   .

The present study sought to understand the basis for people's perception of 'difference', and how that perception affected their ideas about compliance. We were concerned that the focus of the investigation should be on the experience of living with diabetes in socio-economically disadvantaged areas. This was partly because the perception of patients living in such areas was that they had particular difficulties to cope with which inhibited their level of compliance with the diabetic regime. It was also the case that, in the view of several clinicians in the diabetic department, patients from such backgrounds tended to experience most difficulty in achieving satisfactory levels of diabetic control. Unashamedly, we sought to concentrate on this section of the community in the hope of explaining their attitudes and behaviour regarding diabetes to clinicians. Our task was, effectively, to improve clinicians' understanding of their patients' difficulties, thereby enabling them to tailor more appropriately the diabetic regime to take account of the exigencies of 'real life'. It was also our intention to use patients' accounts to inform a future programme of diabetic education such that it became more meaningful for the patient, in both form and content.

An initial methodological problem concerned the identification of criteria for determining whether patients fell into our target population. This was overcome using a set of tables produced by the General Register Office (Scotland) (GRO(S)), listing the numbers of households in each post-code sector of Dundee having up to six 'indicators of deprivation' (GRO(S) 1983). The indicators were: head of household seeking work, permanently sick, or disabled; head of household of socio-economic group seven, ten, eleven, fifteen or seventeen;

overcrowding; large household (four or more dependent children); single-parent family; household containing only pensionable persons. From these tables, we determined the percentages of households in each sector having at least two indicators of deprivation, and decided to concentrate on those sectors wherein at least a quarter of households had at least two indicators of deprivation. These conformed closely with our subjective experience of the various neighbourhoods in the city.

Our next task was to identify a sample of patients from our target areas. This was achieved by using a recently compiled register of insulin-using diabetics attending Ninewells Hospital out-patient diabetic clinic (Waugh 1987). This generated a sample of eighty-five patients aged between sixteen and forty years inclusive. Previous experience suggested that a high non-response rate would be likely, and we decided to try to interview the whole sample. In the event, interviews were obtained from forty-seven people. Of the remainder, seventeen had moved house and were untraceable, thirteen could not be contacted, and eight people refused to be interviewed.

The interviews were carried out using a semi-structured questionnaire designed to investigate the reciprocal relationship between socio-economic context and diabetic care. The principal issue for investigation concerned patients' experiences of diabetes, both at first diagnosis and at present, particularly with regard to selected features from people's everyday lives: family, work, social life, and leisure. Each interview was audio-recorded and transcribed verbatim. The interviews were rarely difficult. In most cases, respondents spoke readily, and some were extremely enthusiastic and talked at length. At the outset it was emphasized that we wanted their accounts of their experiences, and their opinions. We also made it clear that each interview would remain in confidence so far as the clinicians were concerned. In the main, respondents were interviewed alone, but sometimes this was not possible and the interview had to be conducted in the presence of others, usually the respondent's family. On such occasions the presence of other people was used as an opportunity to obtain accounts of 'living with a diabetic'.

There are obviously restrictions on the quality of information gained from 'one-off' interviews. Unlike Cornwell (1984) or Locker (1981), our research was not structured to provide extensive contact with the subjects of the study over a long period of time. The principal reason for this was the limited duration of funding for the work. It might be argued that, to use Cornwell's phrase, we derived a series of 'public accounts' in which respondents told us the kind of information they thought we were looking for and considered appropriate to relate to strangers, rather than revealing a more deeply held, and perhaps different 'private account'. Nevertheless, it was our clear impression that some forthright talking was going on; that this was seen as a rare opportunity to discuss diabetes openly with someone connected to the hospital but not closely connected to the provision of medical care, and therefore something to be made the most of. In some cases respondents appeared eager to describe their particular approach to the disease, as though the process of being interviewed legitimized what had previously been covert, and gave credence in a public arena to what had already achieved personal justification (cf. Conrad 1985). This apparent honesty by respondents may derive from the manner in which the interviews were carried out. Great care was taken to establish a relaxed atmosphere, in which interviewer and interviewee were engaged in conversation, rather than the latter responding to a series of dry, pointed questions. If appropriate, the interviewer would offer accounts of his own experiences in order to create a situation in which both parties to the discourse were making active contributions. Such interviewer-generated intrusions, however, were done sparingly.

VISIONS OF REASON

On analysis, we studied the ways in which patients' contexts had impact upon their compliance with the diabetic regime, in their perception, searching for features of their experiences described by them as being different from their view of ideal medical compliance.

Such differences were frequent. Their source appeared to lie in the patients' understanding of 'normality', juxtaposed to what they saw as normal within the medical perception. Normality is not an entity that can be described or illustrated directly. However, it is possible to describe its character through establishing some of its visible effects; that is, through establishing the boundaries that surround the concept of the normal and, from there, inferring the content of the space within. This is analogous to the concept of the 'Trace', a sign under erasure, whose meaning can only be inferred through establishing the lack of presence, the gap in a text remaining following the deletion of a sign (Derrida 1976). To describe the significance of normality with

41

regard to the experience of diabetes involves defining the boundaries of the trace. These are represented by constraints, factors that inhibit action.

The idea of normality that informs medical practice, as far as patients are concerned, is strongly influenced by the notion of the body as a physical mechanism functioning without impairment. Following the work of Kleinman (1981), we asked respondents to develop 'explanatory models' for their diabetes, how it worked within them, what caused its initial occurrence and so on. Responses to these questions revealed how strongly the biomedical explanation for disease had been accepted by patients themselves. Almost without exception, patients described their condition using images and vocabulary drawn directly from a clinical rhetoric. For example:

'They think it was something to do with all the upheaval of my first marriage, at that time. That brought it on. Because it's not obesity. I wasn't fat. In fact I was very skinny. And it's not hereditary. 'Cause there's not anybody in my family got it at all.'

It is therefore necessary to describe the principal constraints imperative to the diabetic regime. Diabetes is a condition wherein insufficient insulin is produced in the pancreas to control the level of blood glucose. A massive overload of glucose produces an 'hyper-glycaemic' coma, high levels of toxic ketones, and ultimately death. Hyperglycaemia represents one constraint on normality, within the shared perception of medical science. In opposition to this, across the trace of normality, lies an area in which a dramatic reduction of blood glucose has occurred, 'hypoglycaemia': the body, eventually, dies through lack of energy. These, obviously, represent the extreme limits of normality within the medical perception of diabetes. Within the space between these constraints, medical science has generated the concept of the optimum blood glucose level, at which the amount of energy being put into the body is exactly matched by the amount being expended through work. Figure 2.1 illustrates the developing trace of diabetic normality in the gaze of medical science.

There are three further major constraints resulting from the concept of optimum blood glucose levels. Energy intake is the first. Levels of blood glucose increase with the amount of food consumed, and certain foods produce more glucose than others. Diabetics are encouraged to moderate their intake of foodstuffs with a high carbo-hydrate content. Furthermore, the consumption of food with a high

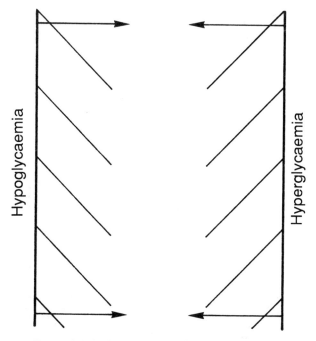

Figure 2.1   Trace of diabetic normality in the gaze of medical science — I

fibre content prolongs the transformation of carbohydrate into glucose, easing the establishment of optimum levels. Therefore there exists a dietary constraint that consists of recommending the intake of low carbohydrate food and eating a high fibre diet.

The second constraint is represented by the use of insulin. This is the catalyst that allows the release of energy stored within blood glucose for consumption by the body. Without insulin, that energy cannot be used. It would seem that blood glucose could be maintained around the optimum level, irrespective of carbohydrate intake, by increasing or reducing the insulin dose. To an extent, this is what occurs. Patients monitor their blood glucose levels, either by blood or urine testing, and adjust their insulin dose accordingly. Unfortunately, artificial insulin may adversely affect the macrovascular system. There is therefore concern in the medical gaze to keep the intake of insulin to a minimum. Also, a prolonged higher intake of insulin combined with a high carbohydrate consumption leads to the energy being released but transformed into fat, unless the energy is consumed through exercise.

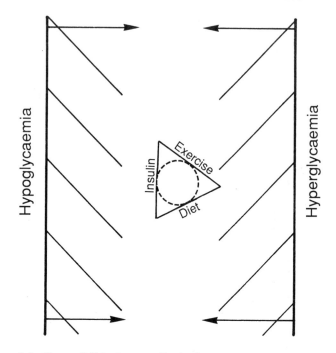

Figure 2.2 Trace of diabetic normality in the gaze of medical science — II

Thus the third constraint, exercise, is an integral component of the trace of diabetic normality, and together with diet and insulin, surround the space in which optimum blood glucose levels are located, defining it, and are themselves located within and defined by the concepts of hypo- and hyperglycaemia. We can now construct an image of diabetic normality in the medical perception with greater completeness, as in Figure 2.2.

Therefore the normality of the diabetic regime, in the gaze of medical science, recognizes a series of constraints that are essentially physiological. It is mechanistic and objectivistic, responding to conventions whose significance is rooted in scientific determinism, in a 'black or white' interpretation of reality. It is highly reasonable, in the classical sense of the eighteenth century.

We must now consider the question of 'normality' as seen from the perspective of the diabetic patient, and describe the constraints that he or she recognizes as imperative and the underlying rationalism that is applied in response to these constraints. Since diabetes is the

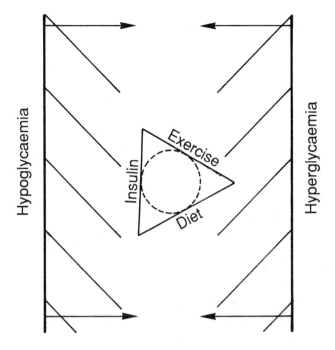

Figure 2.3   Trace of diabetic normality in the gaze of the patient — I

name for a physiological condition that is recognized as such by patients, part of the normality of daily living includes a set of physiological constraints similar to those asserted by medical practice, but not identical. Hypoglycaemia is noticed by the patient almost immediately upon his or her blood glucose level reducing below the normal, non-diabetic level. Therefore the position of the hypoglycaemic constraint is virtually identical to that recognized by medical science. Slight hyperglycaemia, however, is less noticeable. Furthermore, raised blood glucose levels do not entail such an unpleasant experience of illness as does hypoglycaemia, and physiological complications of chronic hyperglycaemia tend to arise after a period of time usually measurable in years rather than weeks.

Within the gaze of the diabetic patient, then, the space of optimal blood glucose level is substantially wider, extending into the region of clinical hyperglycaemia, as described in Figure 2.3.

The relationship between the immediacy of hypoglycaemia and the distant prospect of hyperglycaemic complications has powerful implications for levels of diabetic control maintained by patients. One respondent said:

> 'Feeling fine. But I'm not sticking to my diet again. See, I've always had the problem, when I stick to my diet really well, and the control's perfect, I always feel nervous. I always feel on edge. Dinnae like driving, dinnae like washing windows. . . . Always feel like I'm about to keel over. That's probably one of the main reasons I've never stuck to my diet.'

His decision to ignore the dietary regime and, incidentally, frequently to avoid taking insulin, follows a logical pattern. Strict control is too close to the onset of hypoglycaemia, making him nervous, frightened of passing out. Maintaining higher blood glucose levels prevents such a state of anxiety. It represents, in his terms, a rational response to a perceived constraint. Patients' accounts of their dietary compliance, or lack of it, frequently asserted a similar process of cost-benefit analysis:

> 'I don't stick to my diet. I eat what they're having. I can't afford to muck about. I know what I can have without making myself ill.'

> 'I don't stick to it. Anything, absolutely anything. I tend to have a lot more carbohydrate than they recommend, but I may put in a bit more exercise than most diabetics would. I dare say I have a higher intake of insulin as well.'

> 'Have I got to speak the truth here? The diet was terrible. And it still is terrible. And to be honest, I don't keep strictly to my diet. Because really, if I had to keep to that diet all the time, I think I would be, well, I don't know where I'd be, I think I'd be climbing the walls.'

Such accounts indicate that patients can produce justifications for both their attitude and behaviour that imply a reasoned assessment of their condition. Furthermore, it becomes apparent that the constraints recognized by them as imperative are more diverse than those recognized by practitioners and include family relationships, self-image, and emotional equilibrium. Each of these can become actively instrumental in dictating the course of diabetic self-management. The 'trace' of normality begins to develop, as illustrated in Figure 2.4.

The immediate constraint of 'diet' is itself altered and deflected by more distant factors deriving from the patient's context. In order to

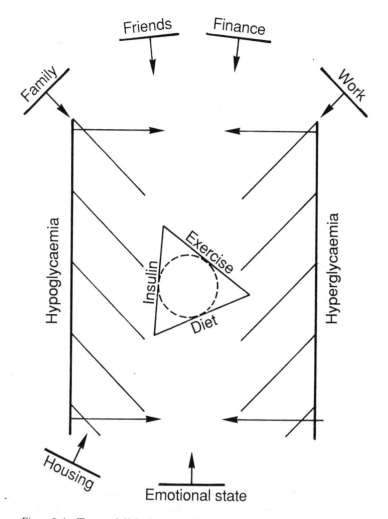

Figure 2.4 Trace of diabetic normality in the gaze of the patient — II

emphasize this process, we can focus, for example, upon 'finance' as an imperative constraint (one that is particularly important amongst our respondents), and recount their articulations of a rationalized approach to accommodating financial restrictions into their conception of normal diabetic life.

'Mairi' lives with her two-year-old son, having been separated from her second husband for six months. She is entirely dependent on social security, 'supplementary benefit for myself and my child', she said, reiterating the declaration made on the application form:

> 'I'm still paying up the HP for carpets and everything, because all you get from social security is only enough to carpet one room, and it's just the thin stuff, cheap. So at the moment I'm paying a debt, HP, through a clubbie. And it was £700 but I've managed to get it down to £400. Which is still an awful lot. And then my husband was a bit of a rogue. . . . He went and left me with a lot of debt, and spent a lot of money. . . . Plus the telephone bill. So I am finding it very, very hard.'

By putting part of her allowance aside to pay off her debts, Mairi has £10 a week left:

> 'For both of us. And that's for domestic stuff as well as food. And if I'm needing anything for John. . . . A lot of things are expensive. Like the fresh orange juice. I'm supposed to drink that rather than the other orange juice. And it would be good if I could afford it. I mean, it's 49p. And I would need about two of these cartons a week. Things like that. . . . At the moment I'm trying to get a vacuum cleaner. I'm trying to think about getting a gas heater fitted for this winter, for up the stair, because it's like Jack North up the stair, it's really terribly cold. And I mean in his room, I've got a Dimplex heater, I mean that's why my electricity's going round like this. [She spun a finger in the air.] My room, I don't bother.'

'Steve', three years out of school, unemployed, lives by himself in a local authority bed-sit, reeking of age and decay. Until recently the building was sheltered housing for the elderly. Now it is being converted for young, single people. He talked about the problems he had keeping to the diabetic diet:

> Finance is the main one. I get an allowance from social security, it's only about £2, it doesn't help much. First few days after I get my giro, fine, can control it well. But from today [Tuesday] leading up to Friday when I get my giro, I just eat rubbish, whatever I can get my hands on. Rolls and chips and things like that. Cheap things . . .

ND: What would you eat over the weekend?

Just proper food, not junk. Mince, tatties, that kind of thing.

ND: Why didn't the money last?

Get £20 a week, because I get my extra allowance. But loads of debts. They came up and took the TV away yesterday because I've not been paying it. And I never got a furniture grant when I first got the place. I don't know why that was. So I took out *that* [nodding toward a sofa bed] on credit, and I owe people money, so I've just got to pay off my debts with whatever I've got left. That's what it goes on. When they ask why I'm not keeping to my diet and I say it's because I can't afford to eat properly, they just say things like, 'Well, the solution to your problems is — you'll need to eat better', you know? Just say I can't. They just say, 'Eat better and you'll get well.' See they dinna really understand. It's a bit annoying, but there's nothing really I can do about it. I dinna think they believe us.

'John' works part-time on a Manpower Services Commission scheme. He says it is hardly worth his while, since he loses supplementary benefit as a result. He lives with his wife and three children in a house on the edge of the city. He spends a lot of time decorating his house and fitting it out. One of his children suffers badly from eczema: 'Most of the time, fine. But if the kids are needing shoes or something, my diabetes goes all to hell. I think more about them than I do about diabetes.'

In each of these cases, the presence of acute financial restrictions creates a need for decisions to be made as to the allocation of resources. There is no *a priori* reason why 'health' should be placed at the head of the list. Nevertheless, there is evidence in the texts quoted above to suggest that, from the patients' point of view, practitioners assume that it ought to be their main priority, thereby establishing the rules that inform the concept of 'compliance', and transform it into an issue as concerned with power as much as with well-being: 'Have I got to speak the truth here?', 'They just dinna believe us.' In 'Steve's' case, his decision to concentrate on his indebtedness rather than eat 'properly' was interpreted by clinic staff as fecklessness, not as a legitimate response to circumstances, made by an individual with a measure of self-determination.

In the patient's gaze into normal living, the physiological constraints are substantially modified, with both their power and

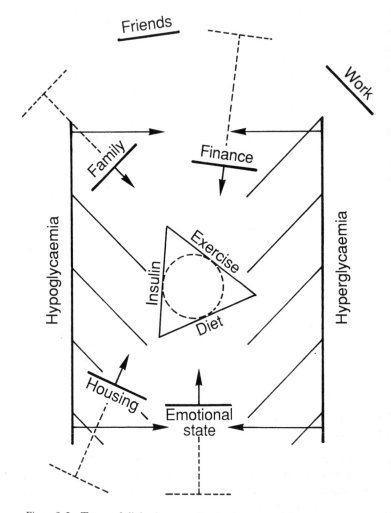

Figure 2.5 Trace of diabetic normality in the gaze of the patient — III

meaningfulness changed by their interaction with other constraints that derive from each patient's socio-cultural context. This is illustrated in Figure 2.5.

Whilst the principal physiological constraints remain, they are far less rigid, susceptible to deflection by factors deriving from external, 'non-diabetic' normality, and possibly even rendered entirely ineffectual. Patients' accounts of this process, however, reveal that it is not random: dietary non-compliance, for example, does not occur solely as the result of an idle whim on the part of the patient (though of course it may) but, rather, systematically, as part of the competition that exists between the various constraining factors. The configuration of these imperatives is highly individualistic, and subject to dramatic transformation over time scales of unpredictable duration. Whichever imperative is perceived as most meaningful results from a process of decision making that reflects the context of the individual at one point in time, occurring in relation to the patient's gaze into normality, a condition that integrates a range of imperatives: social, emotional, financial, and historical, as well as physical and physiological.

Evidence for this individualized conception of diabetic normality can be gleaned from patients' accounts of their use of practitioners. A substantial number of respondents saw the principal value of the diabetic clinic as a 'trouble-shooting' device, useful only when the patient perceived a problem with his or her own quality of self-care:

'If you're feeling there's something wrong you need some place to go to find out what to do, if you're not sure of yourself.'

'I know what I'm trying to do. I'm fairly, well, I'm not bad at keeping control. I'm not saying I'm perfect, but, unless I've got specific problems, and I'm needing someone to answer them, I don't really see what the clinic's doing for me.'

One respondent cited the failure of the clinic to take account of her particular situation which for her made the clinic ineffective:

'What can they tell you in five minutes, that you've been doing for years? To me, this five minute thing, fair enough, they've got your blood and what have you, but to me, they're not seeing you in your natural circumstances.'

It is our contention that the analysis which people make of the competition between imperative constraints, the 'weighing-up' that precedes the selection of a course of action, contains a rationale that can only be realized by understanding the setting of the patient in a context, and his or her understanding of that setting. This kind of 'patient-centred' rationalism has been discussed elsewhere (Williams 1984). If such a view is accepted as legitimate, non-compliance cannot be interpreted as a failure by the patient to accord with the demands of a therapeutic regime whose function is to promote his or her health and well-being, but rather as the failure of the regime to accord accurately with the patient's own perception of his or her state of health. In the particular case of diabetes, for example, one would conclude that, were the diabetic regime to have been constructed by a patient whose socio-cultural context was informed by a set of norms and values derived from a 'working-class' tradition, then 'diabetic normality' would entail dietary requirements that were less concerned with limiting carbohydrate intake, and viewed higher doses of insulin with equanimity. The medical perception of the health risks associated with such a regime is the result of conventions of 'healthiness' derived from what is essentially a 'scientifically derived' set of values and norms. None of the respondents claimed to be even attempting to control their diabetes as rigorously as their physicians recommended. But the degree to which they conformed or not varied as circumstances changed around them: there were periods when their control dramatically increased; for example, just before being reviewed at the clinic.

In our interpretation of patients' accounts of the exigencies of life with diabetes, we have sought to establish the existence of a system informing actions of compliance or non-compliance with the regime as presently established. We have not, however, analysed the process whereby that rationale is constructed. We need now to attempt some account of the deeper structure, of the process that underlies the apparent rationality of the patient's response.

Throughout this chapter, there have been some clues as to how this process might be realized. Two terms in particular have been adopted — the 'trace' and the 'gaze' — drawn from post-structuralist theory. The trace is the gap in a text that implies meaning. The normality of diabetes, for both practitioners and patients, cannot be described directly; it can at best be inferred from its relationship with neighbouring structures. The gaze has been used to describe the process of making sense of the trace, not a direct 'seeing', but a half-sight, a combined act of recognition and comprehension, of bringing the experience and history of the viewer into the act of cognition. In literary terms it is the act of reconstructing texts in the light of subjective experience, an aspect of the 'role of the reader' (Eco 1979), a role that is active, positive, and intrusive.

The ambiguity of these terms is deliberate. They are used as metaphors to imply the existence of concepts that language cannot successfully define, in defiance of a logical analysis. Their import is fundamentally aesthetic, intended to communicate the sensation of experience, both sensual and intellectual, rather than defining the experience. The interplay between the individual and his or her context is similarly complex. The experience of diabetes can be only partially, and unsatisfactorily, explained through attempts to describe patients' decisions relating to their self-care as the result of an apparently cerebral 'cost-benefit' analysis. It would be convenient if patients' decision making could be linked to a series of contextual constraints, to a series of causal relationships. But it seems more likely that patients' responses to perceived constraints are realized through their making a set of aesthetic responses to their context, not to an intellectualized, cerebralized rationalism.

There are good reasons for doubting a cerebral rationalization. The delineation of patient decision making as 'rational' works only retrospectively. It may release information about how a patient got to his or her present state of diabetic control, but it will reveal nothing about his or her future condition. Furthermore, the apparent linear sequence of the causal relationship, of one decision occurring in the light of an antecedent constraint, does not fit happily with actual experience. In their accounts, constraints tended to become imperative for patients in clusters, not singly: financial difficulties and emotional pressures, for example, tended to act on patients simultaneously, such that they were actively responding to the total set at once, not to each constituent in a diachronic sequence. Under such circumstances, responses are likely to be informed by the aesthetic appreciation of 'what feels right', rather than 'what does logic determine to be right?'.

Despite the simultaneity of encroaching constraints, patients' accounts often portray their experiences as though they made decisions in a linear sequence. This may be a result of the data being collected through the use of the interview method. When interviewees described events, their act of speaking necessitates the ordering of memories, ideas, accounts of action, or description of feeling. The apparent rationale of interview texts may be a reflection of the linear character of speech; the requirement to articulate clearly, to communicate a lucid, believable account, not necessarily an accurate one. As described by Potter and Mulkay (1985), interview texts may have more to say about the conventions of communication in their structural relationships than they do as ostensive articulations of thought and action. As Young (1981) puts it, the relationship between what a patient says and what he thinks, knows, and feels is problematic.

At the core of this problem is the fact of sociology being a linguistic discipline, frequently relying upon a highly artificial form of discourse, 'the interview', for its raw material. We have suggested that the process underlying decisions to comply or not with a therapeutic regime is essentially aesthetic. Can sociology develop either a theory or methodology to investigate such a concept? Perhaps one of the most enjoyable features of sociological research is its catholic nature. Over recent years, sociology has embraced ethnography (Locker 1981; Cornwell 1984), communication theory (Silverman and Torode 1980), poetics (Brown 1977), cultural anthropology (Kleinman 1981; Geertz 1975; Fabrega 1974), and more recently, discourse analysis (Potter and Wetherell 1987) and text analysis (Williams 1984). The shift in emphasis from 'behavioural science' to more qualitative, interpretive approaches implies that sociology is indeed well placed to investigate patients' aesthetic experience. We would argue that, if a more realistic account of the patient's condition is to be given, then such an investigation is vital. Returning to Foucault, it is necessary for medical sociology to move out from the relative banality of the age of reason, and address the intensely subtle complexity of the 'lyrical time of the seasons'.

ACKNOWLEDGEMENTS

We thank Dr Ray Newton, Consultant Physician, Diabetic Department, Ninewells Hospital, Dundee, for his constant support and encouragement; Dr Norman Waugh, Tayside Health Board, for frequent technical advice; and above all, the people who agreed to talk to us. This study was funded by a grant from Nordisk (UK) Ltd.

Part Two

HEALTH BELIEFS AND BEHAVIOURS IN THE FAMILY

Chapter Three

STUDYING HEALTH IN FAMILIES: A QUALITATIVE APPROACH

KATHRYN C. BACKETT

A theme of increasing importance in medical sociology is that of understanding health beliefs and behaviours within the social contexts in which they develop. One such context is everyday domestic life.[1] This chapter reports on a qualitative multi-interview study in progress in 1989 in Edinburgh. First, the study is outlined and its rationale described. The relevant conceptual and methodological issues characterizing research into both 'health' and 'family' are discussed. The techniques of grounded theory development which the study employs require the researcher to reflect upon the interaction between methods and the production of data. Another section therefore addresses those methodological issues which have arisen during the fieldwork. In the final section substantive material is presented concerning the concept of a 'family health culture'. This illustrates the important role to be played by qualitative research in conceptual clarification.

INTRODUCTION

There is now a wealth of data which delineate at the population level statistical associations between, for example, social class, age, marital status, sex, and aspects of physical or mental health. However, analysis of population trends does little to clarify the social processes which lie behind the figures at the individual or family level. Also, much of this information has been gathered using survey methodology. In epidemiology and medical sociology alike such surveys have been dominated by the biomedical paradigm, which usually implies biologically based disease models of behaviour. This tradition is reflected not just in the kinds of methodologies used, predominantly quantitative, but also in the nature of the topics selected for research, predominantly pathogenic. Thus, much valuable data now exist about patterns of disease, etiology, risk factors, illness-related behaviour, living conditions, and ill health. Relatively little attention has, however, been paid to salutogenesis, or, as Antonovsky has put it, 'Why do people stay healthy?' (Antonovsky 1979: 35).

One attempt to acknowledge the importance of social context for understanding health-related behaviours has been the introduction of the somewhat vague concept of 'lifestyle'. At present, however, lifestyle research seems flawed, essentially because of its tendency to focus more on individual behaviours than on social processes. The suggestion of links between ill health and an individual's lifestyle has led to accusations of 'victim blaming' (Crawford 1977). Arguably, lifestyle seems to have been incorporated into health research as some kind of abstract mediating variable which can appear strangely detached from the actual processes of daily life. In addition, at the empirical level, lifestyle has tended to be operationalized as the sum total of health-related behaviours, most often the 'holy four' (McQueen 1987) of diet, drinking, smoking, and exercise. As such, lifestyle again seems separate from the social conditions and circumstances of which it must be seen as an integral part (Dean 1984).

Therefore, both conceptually and methodologically, a strong case now exists for a more grounded approach to understanding the social processes underlying the observed statistical associations between demographic variables and health. The sociology of family and primary relationships offers a considerable resource since it incorporates strong interactive and psychodynamic traditions (Blumer 1969; Burr, Hill, Nye, and Reiss 1979). Often this work has been most revealing when it examines family members facing a 'problem' or special circumstances with which they are not equipped to deal in a 'taken-for-granted' manner (Jackson 1956; Burgoyne and Clark 1983). Another significant influence is that of feminist critiques of the family which have emphasized the existence of gender-based power relationships within domestic groups (Barrett and McIntosh 1982). These critiques have demonstrated the importance of examining patterns of inequalities *within* families. These may structure both attitudes and access to resources, many of which have implications for health-related behaviours (Kerr and Charles 1986; Charles and Kerr 1987).

In different ways the study of 'health' in 'families' is presently at a point where new conceptual and methodological orientations are necessary. It can be argued that the dominance of the biomedical model has resulted in many of the concepts of medical sociology being developed on the basis of study of negative health experiences to the neglect of positive health (Research Unit in Health and Behavioural Change 1988: ch. 3). The 'taken-for-granted' nature of health should also be further explored by examining how lay people themselves view health and illness, and their place generally in life. Equally, until the past decade, the legacy of structural functionalism had resulted in a family sociology, many of whose concepts were predicated on an idealized consensual nuclear family form. Both demographic changes, resulting in extremely diverse patterns of domestic groupings, and analyses of the many inequalities within these groupings have meant that researchers must now reassess their concepts and methodologies for understanding the processes of 'family' life.

STUDY DESIGN

An empirical study in progress in 1987 and 1988 was designed against the background of a critical appraisal of both medical and family sociology. Linked methodological and theoretical concerns influenced the study design. The need for an exploratory qualitative study was seen as paramount. A methodology was also required which aimed to understand respondents' own perceptions of health, illness, and health-related behaviours within the social context of everyday domestic life. A multi-interview study was therefore designed to explore these perceptions and behaviours in depth and over time. Also, the intention of using techniques of grounded analysis by a single interviewer/researcher meant that, inevitably, such work could only be carried out with a small sample of family groups.

These constraints, combined with an interest in understanding positive rather than negative health, led to the decision to concentrate on one well-defined type of household grouping with specific socio-economic characteristics. Twenty-eight couples, each with two children, were recruited from one group general practice serving a geographically well-contained area of Edinburgh. They were randomly selected from the total population of eligible families attending this practice. All of the couples are home-owners, and one or both spouses are in non-manual occupations. They are being interviewed in depth four times over an eighteen-month fieldwork period. In the first round men and women are interviewed separately, and two return visits involve joint interviews. The interviews all last one-and-a-half to two hours, and tape recordings are transcribed verbatim. Grounded analysis of these transcripts is an integral part of the fieldwork process, as themes and ideas from earlier interviews influence the content of the later sessions. This chapter is based on analysis of first-round interviews; it is informed also by pilot interviews and discussion groups with men, women, and couples.

The present study was developed in response to particular theoretical and conceptual issues and gaps in medical and family sociology. These are presented in this section as specific rationale for particular study interests.

1 Studying families as groups

It is essential to obtain detailed information about everyday caring and health-related behaviours in families, since this is the location for much primary health and illness care and maintenance. Many health policy decisions are based on assumptions about what is going on in families in these respects (Graham 1984; Court Report 1976). Despite this, a review of health care and the family concluded that 'empirical knowledge has remained relatively limited, plagued by methodological imprecision and minimal integration with family theory' (Litman and Venters 1979: 379).

Work on the psychosocial interior of the family has emphasized the value (and the complexities) of studying whole families (Handel 1968). Therefore, although in the present study the couple is taken as the main unit of analysis (Rapoport, Rapoport, and Thiessen 1974), attention is also being paid to the effects of children *on* family behaviours (Bell and Harper 1977), as well as parents' images of their children (Backett 1982), and their views on children's health and health-related behaviours.[2] Thus, couples are being studied in their interlocking roles of spouses *and* parents. Popay (1986) has drawn attention to the paucity of data on the health status of parents, and commented that this is remarkable 'given our society's concern with the welfare of children and the premium put on good parenting' (p. 5). However, when studying health in families it is always crucial to be aware of the moral imperatives attached to caring and parenthood, of how these are experienced differently by mothers and fathers, and of the particular expectations of mothers in these areas (Graham 1982). In addition, on a general level, the routine nature of much everyday family life gives scope for examining contextual and situational aspects of health-related behaviours (Alonzo 1979). If movement is to be made away from *biomedically* determined concepts of health, one fruitful area must be the examination of aspects of domestic life as they pertain to health. Graham (1984) has maintained that 'In reality, health attitudes are embedded in domestic activities, and these activities — shopping, cooking, washing, waiting — are moulded by the practical constraints of time, space and money' (p. 153).

Studying family groups also allows insight to be gained into particular interactive effects of members on one another's health-related behaviours. Family members have potential insight into one another's health in several ways. They have access to a rich fund of genetic, biographical, and contextual *knowledge* about one another's health. Also, there is particularly high *visibility* of the individual's health and illness, whether or not any 'problems' are deemed to be occurring. Thus, family members are directly affected by one another's health and ill health to a degree, and with an intensity usually not experienced in other social settings. This bears directly on issues of the moral aspects of health (as 'good') and illness (as 'bad'), since family members may both take and assume direct *responsibility* for one another's health and illness.

It is also important to incorporate a time dimension into studies of health in families. It can be argued that a multi-interview study is required if the researcher is to move from 'public', socially acceptable accounts of behaviour towards 'private' accounts, which may better reflect respondents' personal views (Cornwell 1984). On a theoretical level this approach is a response to work such as that of Herzlich (1973) and others which indicated that concepts of health and health behaviours may have static elements but may also fluctuate in response, for example, to other changes in people's lives. A further aspect of the dynamic nature of health may be the actual experience of illness, and experiences with health professions. In addition, health behaviours and attitudes of different *family* members may be subject to regular changes in ways perhaps incompatible with the needs of others in the group. For instance, child care alters with each stage of their growth. Also, the health of the adults may be affected by the current material and social context of their lives, not the least of which is parental status itself (Popay 1986).

2   Gender and health

A most significant gap in this area is the lack of information about men's health beliefs and behaviours as they relate to family life. Apart from large-scale survey work (such as Wadsworth, Butterfield, and Blaney 1971; Cartwright and Anderson 1981), and smaller-scale studies of men's attitudes towards pregancy (Richman 1982), birth (Brown 1982), and family planning (Simms and Smith 1982), little detailed investigation of men and family health has been carried out (Cornwell 1984). The present study focuses equally on men and women. Furthermore, the bulk of previous research into family health has relied only on interviews with women. Popay (1986) has pointed out that, in fact, quite different research questions have been formulated regarding men's and women's health. She said:

> On the one hand much research concerned with women's experience of health and illness flows from a concern with the gender related differences in *morbidity* reported in much research and explanations are sought in the private *social* world of the family. Women's parenting role has been an important element in much of this research. Work on men's health in contrast flows disproportionately from a concern with social class differences in mortality and explanations are sought in the public *material* world of the labour market.

> (Popay 1986: 5)

Research must also be related to the statistical associations between gender and health reported in Verbrugge's (1985) literature review. She concluded that gender differences in morbidity may be represented as an iceberg. The bulk of less life-threatening conditions constitute the iceberg's broad base and are predominantly female; whilst the tip of the iceberg, representing the more potentially fatal conditions, tends to be characteristic of males. Studies which demonstrate gender inequalities in health and differences in health behaviours point to the need to examine aspects of men's and women's everyday lives which might contribute to these differences (Gove and Hughes 1979; Arber *et al.* 1985). The present study addresses these issues qualitatively by examining the production and negotiation of meanings attached to health and illness by males and females within the family group.

3   Lay health beliefs

The qualitative approach taken in this study aims to explore health and health-related behaviours from the viewpoint of the respondents themselves: to take as data the issues in their everyday lives which *they* view as affecting health. Broadly, this area may be called 'lay health beliefs'. This is an area of increasing interest for health professionals and researchers (Anderson, Davies, Kickbusch, and McQueen 1988). Work in America (Harris and Guten 1979; Crawford 1984), France (Herzlich 1973; Pierret 1988), Britain (Pill and Stott 1985; Calnan and Johnson 1985; Cornwell 1984; Blaxter and Paterson 1982; Williams 1985; Cunningham-Burley 1984), and internationally (Currer and Stacey 1986) has examined relationships between lay health and illness beliefs, social class, age and generational factors, work situation, and environmental stresses.

Most of the British work to date has studied predominantly women and working-class groups; and there is, therefore, a need to examine gender-related behaviours and a greater variety of socio-economic groupings. Also, as with lifestyle research, some of the work may be criticized for taking 'health beliefs' out of the social contexts within which lay people translate them into meaningful behaviours. (In any case the relationship between beliefs and behaviours is, in itself, intensely problematical.) Also, most of the previous studies of lay health beliefs have begun with a biomedically defined problem which has, so to speak, set the research agenda (Research Unit in Health Behavioural Change 1988: ch. 3). The present study assumes that, in fact, many health-related behaviours may very well be carried out for reasons not directly connected with a concern for 'health' (Hunt and McLeod 1987). They may also be constrained by social and lifestyle factors in which domestic life itself plays an important part.

SOME METHODOLOGICAL PROBLEMS OF STUDYING HEALTH IN FAMILIES

It is often stated that qualitative methods will help to clarify the social processes, contexts, and meanings which underlie statistical associations at the population level — between, for example, living conditions and health. In the present study grounded analysis of interviews is intrinsic to the fieldwork process (Lofland 1976; Glaser and Strauss 1967). Themes arising from interviews are identified and assembled in the form of 'disciplined abstractions' (Lofland 1976). Influenced by the work of Schutz (1972), a major aim is to detect 'course of action' typologies, or, as Lofland has preferred to call them, 'strategies'. The methodology involves developing an 'intimate familiarity' (Lofland 1976) with respondents, and an immersion in the data best achieved by the researcher being both interviewer and analyst. The process of analysis is a constant reflexive process of checking concepts and hypotheses against data, invest-igating data which do not fit, and refining the initial concepts (Lofland 1971; Schatzman 1973). These are the main methodological tactics of this particular qualitative study. However, an important feature of any exploratory study is constantly to be aware of how such tactics work out in practice. The interrelationship of methods and data should be addressed in every piece of social science, and here some reflections are offered on issues which have arisen in the present study.

It is evident that in studying 'health' in 'families' people are being asked to talk about *two* major areas of their lives which tend to be taken for granted, and often not reflected upon until there are diffi-culties or things go wrong. Couples were visited and the study explained prior to their agreeing to participate. Everyone visited in this way in fact agreed to take part. However, a frequent response during this introductory visit was for respondents to say that they doubted there would be much to talk about since they never thought about health. This taken-for-grantedness is one explanation of why so much previous work on 'health' has ended up discussing 'illness'; and why so much family or primary group research in the past, at any rate prior to feminist, conflict, and radical critiques (Burr, Hill, Nye, and Reiss 1979; Barrett and McIntosh 1982) tended to be superficial, consensual, and to describe what may now be seen as 'public accounts'.

A basic tenet of qualitative research is to try to move beyond the taken-for-granted and uncover the varied and often contradictory meanings which people use to interpret the area of life under study. This is both an individual and a social process, as such interpretations are continuously tested out and reformulated in everyday inter-actions. In the present study, the main way these ideas are put into practice is by interviewing people several times; by trying to gain their confidence; and by encouraging respondents to raise issues themselves. Additionally, respondents themselves are involved in the analytic process by, at a later stage in the fieldwork, being invited to comment on the researcher's interpretation of their accounts. Cicourel (1973) called this 'controlled indefinite triangulation'.

However, both the method and the present subject matter impose their own constraints. A multi-interview in-depth study of a small sample is only really successful if respondents stay the course. A major study interest is in health as a dynamic concept, and therefore one aim is to see what factors respondents perceive as affecting their family and health behaviours over a period of time. In the early stages of the fieldwork it seems to be important therefore *not* to be too challenging or disruptive and to be very much a listener rather than an interrogator. In fact, the only query a few people have raised prior to taking part is whether or not the interviews will be very 'personal'; and the researcher always replied that people are free to raise those subjects that *they* wish to talk about. However, letting respondents make these decisions can restrict the range of topics raised. For example, in the first round of interviews, except for very occasional reference to gynaecological problems or AIDS, only one person raised the topic of sexual relations and good health.

The exploratory, qualitative researcher must therefore appreciate that giving up some control over the determination of which issues are important may in fact result in a lack of information about topics which the researcher herself may feel are of relevance. In addition, it must also be recognized that a topic may not be mentioned because the respondent does not think it relevant or does not bring it to mind during that particular interview. Thus, qualitative methods are themselves restricted by social conventions and methodological/ethical constraints. The first round of interviews have to be comfortable enough to keep people involved. However, a non-challenging interview is likely to generate a lot of 'public accounts' of health and family behaviours. Despite this, it was evident early in the fieldwork that many of the 'oughts' of health and family life are indeed highly problematical even for this supposedly motivated and economically cushioned group.

If the method itself affects the material obtained, the central topic of health-related behaviours provides other methodological problems. Qualitative methods must do more than simply ask people what they do about the various biomedically based health-related behaviours, such as diet, exercise, alcohol, and smoking; and then *assume* that *this* is what positive health is all about. But how? One alternative, as in the present study, is to ask people about their lives, here particularly domestic lives, and then make inferences about which aspects of their 'lifestyles' may have implications or just relevance for 'health'. Either way it seems that the researcher is still making judgements and setting the agenda. Of course, the many strands that respondents *themselves* view as being part of health and as affecting health will be carefully monitored and analysed. However, it is important always to be aware that *their* accounts do not exist in a sociological vacuum. Their accounts are being presented in the context of the fairly high media profile currently given to individually based preventive health practices, at the expense of social and political influences.

As several researchers have pointed out, this high media profile is not without moral and emotional pressures on its audience. In the USA, Crawford (1984) has nicely analysed, as a cultural theme, the aspects of control and release implicit in some of the currently fashionable, approved, health-related behaviours. As he has said:

> To be healthy is to demonstrate to self and others appropriate concern for the virtues of self control, self discipline, self denial and will power.
>
> (Crawford 1984: 78)

Whilst not going so far as to claim any causal links between worsening economic conditions and the increased interest in personal health, he suggested that:

> As we internalize the mandate for control and discipline, 'health' and 'fitness' are readily available means by which we literally embody that mandate. Our bodies, 'the ultimate metaphor', refract the general mood. We cut out the fat, tighten our belts, build resistance and extend our endurance. Subject to forces that lie beyond individual control, we attempt to control what is within grasp. Whatever practical reasons and concerns lead us to discipline our bodies in the name of health or fitness, the ritualized response to economic crisis finds in health and fitness a compatible symbolic field.
>
> (Crawford 1984: 80)

The methodological consequence of all this is that asking people about health may invoke complex responses of guilt or smugness, aggression or resignation, all of which affect what the respondent then decides to talk about. Also, just as respondents may find it personally threatening to have a researcher question their taken-for-granted modes of family behaviour, so also current emphasis on personal responsibility for health makes it a far from neutral topic for investigation.

EXPLORING FAMILY HEALTH: THE VALUE OF QUALITATIVE WORK IN CONCEPTUAL CLARIFICATION

An important contribution of qualitative work is to stimulate reflection about theories and concepts. These may have become so much part of research currency that they sometimes continue as underlying assumptions behind work perhaps beyond their meaningful academic shelf life! Research both in medical and family sociology seems at present to be at a stage where long-established concepts are increasingly open to challenge. These challenges may stem in part from general changes in society but also they derive from a growing dissatisfaction with the actual *heuristic* utility of some previous work. In these final sections some examples are given of how qualitative research can help to open up debate about the continuing empirical validity of some long-established concepts.

One such concept is that of 'family health culture'. In the present study, analyses of pilot discussion groups and interviews and the first round of fieldwork have led to a dissection of some components of this concept. It is part of the process of grounded analysis to develop and explore theories and concepts during the fieldwork phase. Some theories stand the test of reflexive analysis, whilst others prove harder to substantiate and may be revised or kept in reserve for future research.

Any brief introduction will inevitably do disservice to the highly complex concept of 'culture'. However, a working definition is that a culture involves items of social and material life which are shared within a group and may be passed on to the group's successors. In western society it is obviously more difficult to study cultures holistically. Therefore such *processes* tend to be assumed to be occurring and are not often studied as subject matter in their own right, although an exception to this has been the work on the culture of poverty (Askham 1975; Rutter and Madge 1976; Blaxter and Paterson 1982). Equally, ideas about 'family health' which may be used as the basis for policy decisions may be premised on perhaps empirically unfounded assumptions about what goes on in family groups (Graham 1984).

Furthermore, images of what constitutes a 'typical family' may be crudely out of date in the face of rapid demographic changes currently taking place in western society (Gittins 1985).

In the present study, therefore, a methodological imperative was to research a particular kind of family form: two-parent, with two dependent children, who were living in broadly similar conditions — that is, home-owners in a middle-class area of a large city. It was hoped that by putting such careful controls on the small sample a degree of consistency in explanatory theories could be achieved.

Socio-economic factors undoubtedly influence health outcomes in *individuals* and, indeed, this was one of the assumptions behind the study design. Also, many researchers have already documented inequalities in health *between* different domestic groupings or households in different sectors of the population (Whitehead 1987; Townsend and Davidson 1982). However, it is increasingly being questioned whether members of the same family or domestic group, whatever their circumstances, in fact share the same health-related constraints, opportunities, behaviours, and even outcomes. Methods of gathering official statistics can mask differences within family groups (Moser, Pugh, and Goldblatt 1987); as can reliance by social scientists on the reports of only one family member.

Against this background some components of 'family health culture' will now be discussed, and some findings from a preliminary analysis offered which suggest that these may in fact be empirically problematical.

SOME COMPONENTS OF THE CONCEPT OF 'FAMILY HEALTH CULTURE'

1 Generational 'effects' in families

As might have been anticipated, most of these middle-class respondents tended to view health as something which can be achieved rather than as something ascribed through heredity (Backett 1987). In fact most aspects of health, whether in terms of well-being, fitness, or even lack of disease, were presented in respondents' accounts as theoretically amenable to manipulation by the individual, primary groups, or the state. Few appeared to see genetic inheritance of illness as a major concern; it was seldom even mentioned.[3] In fact, the three men who *were* concerned about implications for themselves of their fathers' premature deaths did not appear to be translating this concern into any particular preventive health practices. All of these men saw their lifestyles as having become more structured, moderate, and sensible than in their younger years (a common theme); however, as one of them commented:

> I think having children makes you more aware of wanting to retain your health . . .
>
> KB: Does it?
>
> . . . to see your children mature really. My father died when I was sixteen, that wasn't through any non-healthy diet or anything, he just had a disease and died when he was fifty. Em, and I would hope that wouldn't happen to me, but I don't rush round the block every night worrying about it. Em, perhaps I should take more care of em being fit, er, sometimes I think I should. I bought an exercise bike and don't use it. Em, I think a lot of people do that.
>
> KB: Yes.
>
> . . . a lot of people think, 'Oh I must keep fit, give me another roll, what's on telly?'

Another man, whose father had died young of Alzheimer's disease, commented that he had not changed anything much regarding things that might affect his health, except having his blood pressure checked now and then, and said he was interested in watching programmes about Alzheimer's, but 'I was going to say "What's for you will not go past you" my mum used to say, so I don't worry about what's going to happen but I mean I try to make my life as healthy as possible.'

The last of these three, whose father had died of chest complaints, was vehemently anti-smoking but not particularly 'health-conscious' in any other respects.

Mostly, respondents saw their own lives and health-related behaviours as very different from those of their parents when they were children. However, whilst several respondents found specific matters to criticize about their parents' behaviour, such criticisms were often couched in an appreciation of the different social attitudes or economic circumstances prevailing at that time. In other words, respondents also explain health-related behaviours in terms of socio-cultural context! (For further discussion see Backett 1988.) For example, many said that their parents smoked because everyone did at the time and its harmfulness was not then recognized. Or, as another example, their parents ate, or gave children what might now be considered 'unhealthy' foods because *they* had little money, or because nutritional ideas were different, or because certain foods were scarce. Again, almost all of the respondents said that *their* parents took little or no physical exercise, and certainly such activities as swimming or sports were not 'family' activities in *their* childhood in the way that they might be these days.

Thus, generational 'effects' in families seemed to have little relevance for most respondents. Some of them in fact now felt *so* different from their parents in everyday health-related behaviours that visiting each other had its problems in terms of the kinds of food eaten, perceived over-indulgence of the grandchildren with sweets, and feelings of intolerance of their parents' smoking or physically inactive lifestyle.

These findings also accord with those from studies of other social groups. Blaxter and Paterson (1982) noted that although some of the young working-class mothers they interviewed in Aberdeen *did* think that their upbringing had influenced them and that they were behaving like their mothers, there were *in fact* few attitudes that could be identified as deriving directly from the older generation. My findings echo their conclusions; they said:

> It appeared that inter-generational changes — inextricably bound up with changes in lifestyle and circumstances, changes in the provision of services, and general changes in public attitudes — were more important than direct familial transmission.
>
> (Blaxter and Paterson 1982: 183)

Helman's (1987) work also indicated considerable intergenerational change in 'folk models' of illness causation. In particular he noted that, compared to his older patients, the younger generation were much more likely to blame various illnesses on germs or viruses. Reviewing these and other studies led Graham to conclude that 'the learning process is mediated not through the family's health culture but more directly through experience' (Graham 1984: 164).

2 The assumption of similarities between men and women in the same family group

An intriguing contradiction in health research is that, whilst statistical differences between the health experiences of men and women are consistently demonstrated, nevertheless, once they live together in the same family group it is assumed that their health-related beliefs and behaviours are similar. This assumption has been compounded by methods of data collection about 'family health'. To repeat, typically such data are obtained from only one family member, usually the woman. Arguably this has resulted in misleadingly homogeneous accounts of the 'health culture' of the group. Data collected in the present study suggest that an alternative approach may be more appropriate. This involves understanding the 'health culture' of a family as a complex social product representing the outcome of clashes and compromises amongst its members who, moreover, are of different ages, sexes, and may each be leading disparate lives.

In this study men and women who share the same domestic family situation are being interviewed. Amongst other things, the first- and second-round interviews have explored the interactions between work, paid and unpaid, domestic life, parenting, and the implications of these for health-related behaviours. Analysis indicates that these men and women are in fact leading quite different lives regarding their health; and it could be argued that these differences *may* have greater implications for health than does membership of the same family group. Bernard (1972) has written of 'his and her' marriage. It would seem also to be appropriate to consider 'his and her' family health. In this section some examples of these differences are outlined: these are related to the different socio-cultural contexts of men's and women's lives.

Respondents' accounts revealed many contrasts between the sexes in the general orientation to health matters. This was reflected in the quite different picture which emerged of the place of health in the everyday conversation of men compared with that of women. The majority of respondents felt that men were much less likely to talk about health matters amongst themselves than were women. By and large it was claimed that men would usually only talk about such things if someone was ill. In contrast, women were seen as having many opportunities to introduce a health-related topic into the conversation. For example, it was suggested that, for women,

71

discussion of children's ailments and upbringing, or conversation about food and cooking might lead easily to conversations about health in general. Also discussions about health might be triggered off by women's experiences of the menstrual cycle. Thus, the fact that men were viewed as seldom talking about health was related, in part, to respondents' perceptions of the content of their everyday conversation generally, as one woman explained of her husband:

'Well this is something that John's spoken about before. Er, I know that it seems to be the agreed thing that women talk more personally to their friends whereas men tend to speak about football, rugby or whatever. I mean John has one or two friends I think that he would speak to about personal things like, like health, you know. Perhaps not as much or as easily as I would to my friends, but then it's often easier for me perhaps with my friends when I'm speaking to them. We might be speaking about the kids anyway and it's not a very big jump then to say "Oh and I've not been feeling very well either" or "I've got a lump in my arm" or, you know, whatever. Whereas if you're speaking about rugby it's quite a big jump to say "Oh my stomach's been bothering me" [laughs] you know, other than "Oh I've got another bruise on my leg" kind of thing. So perhaps I think women probably do speak about it more.'

Thus interactional and situational constraints (Alonzo 1979) may be seen to affect men's and women's opportunities to have everyday conversations about health. Moreover, if such conversations *did* take place, most respondents felt that their content would differ. Women, it was suggested, would be more likely to discuss matters such as diet and nutrition, children's ailments and care, exercise and looking after their bodies, and women's health problems. Men, it was claimed, were more likely to compare sporting activities, fitness, training times, or sometimes weight gain. As one man said: 'I think we probably might talk about maybe small achievements in fitness rather than actually the foods that we eat.'

An interesting paradox was that almost all of the men who were involved in sports where fitness might be valued, such as rugby, football, squash, or golf, said that the topic of preventive health was either never mentioned or, if raised, it might be mocked or scorned. However, thinking more broadly another man commented:

'I think if, er, you know, somebody is growing a paunch at work, then I think, you know, that sort of thing would be brought up in conversation as a joke [laughs]. Och aye, couldn't let anybody away with that sort of thing. Em, I'm trying to think, you would not discuss health as a topic in general, well, not really. I don't think you would say, "Oh I had a lovely plate of beansprouts last night, it would do you a lot of good" [laughs]. I don't generally tell people about my vitamin eating habits. Although as soon as that proves to be a success I will broadcast it worldwide [laughs] and then they will think I'm a drag.'

Women's and men's attitudes towards food and feeding people

Although health surveys regularly document dietary behaviours, the social meanings attached to food, eating behaviours, and feeding people in western cultures are seldom addressed (Murcott 1983; Orbach 1978; Fieldhouse 1986). Following the work of Kerr and Charles (1986), the present study shows a similar degree of apparent control by most women over this area of domestic life; and also indicates that her decisions are made within the confines of pleasing the tastes of other family members. This kind of analysis is similar to the distinction made in the studies of the organization of domestic financial resources between the everyday 'management' of money and the actual overall control over decisions about its allocation (Henwood, Rimmer, and Wicks 1987; Brannen and Wilson 1987).

Analysis of respondents' accounts also suggests that the decisions of these middle-class women are further complicated by their awareness of so-called 'healthy eating practices'. Both men and women gave many examples of how they or their children ate 'unhealthy' foods. A regularly occurring example of how they coped with this gap between knowledge and behavioural practice was the use of the notion of balancing out the 'bad' with the 'good'. The following quotation usefully illustrates several of these points; one woman said:

> I suppose by the right kind, I'm thinking of foods that are as fresh as possible, fresh fruit, fresh vegetables, fresh meat, and I'd like to think, em, I'm aiming at giving my family as little processed food as possible, but that hasn't turned out the way I have wanted it either.

KB: Tell me what happens?

I mean I always vowed once my children came along, *my*

children would not have any of these sausages, beefburgers, all these processed foods. But, em, I'm afraid it was getting to the point where my children wouldn't eat very much [laughs], if I stuck to my rigid, em, opinions. Having said that, we don't really, I don't think we do eat an awful lot in the way of beef-burgers and sausages. I am very fortunate in that both of them like fruit. Em, my son is a lot more fussy, though, to feed than my daughter. She would eat more in the way of fresh vegetables and he is not very keen on fresh vegetables, neither is my husband [both laugh]. Which means that unless I was prepared to make two or three different meals every evening it would be very difficult.

The relationship to food of the majority of men in the sample was somewhat different. Their retrospective accounts of their lives suggested that, at all stages of the life-course, most of them were largely being 'fed' either in the domestic or public domain. It was the unusual man who had voluntarily regularly undertaken and enjoyed the role of cook for himself and others. By comparison, all of the women had gradually accumulated knowledge about food and usually taken ever increasing responsibility for their own and others' eating practices. Many of the men now said they were unable to cook. Never-theless a minority of men, it was claimed, *could* cook and were cast in the now well-analysed role of 'helper' if they were available. Even amongst this minority, however, there was a great deal of 'tokenism' regarding food preparation. For instance, their cooking ability was most likely to be demonstrated in the preparation of a special 'adult' meal or dish at a weekend when the usual constraints applying to feeding people — notably time, budgeting, and nutritional concerns — were suspended. An example of this was the following man, who said:

> I did about three different night school classes on the trot, em, in cooking. I found that quite interesting.
>
> KB: So you are quite proficient, are you?
>
> Well, yeah, I think I probably am. Em, I sometimes help out there, make a meal when we have visitors or something.

Different patterns of exercising throughout the life-course

As might be anticipated, more of the men than the women were actively involved in sports or exercise when they were younger.

However, over the years, several women who claimed not to be particularly interested in sport in their youth had become keen on doing some form of exercise to keep fit. Nevertheless, very different accounts were given of the place of exercise in men's and women's lives. Basically, the majority of men who take some exercise have kept this up regularly in some way throughout family, career, and residential changes.

A quite different picture emerges from the women's accounts, where family, work, and domestic commitments were much more likely to be given preference over personal exercise choices. Even for those women who are interested in taking exercise, it is taken up or dropped as is convenient with other work or family commitments. One woman, for example, explained that her involvement in volleyball, netball, and squash had 'fallen away' because she had lost partners through moving around geographically, sometimes to areas with few facilities. However, it was also because 'both of my children were quite clingy so they were not the type that went into creches very happily'. Nowadays, with children at school and nursery, although she works two evenings a week and takes courses on certain days, she has a little more time available for activities such as swimming. However, she tends to take her children along with her, and supervises her 3-year-old's activity rather than go alone herself to have a proper swim. By contrast childminding concerns do not impinge as much on her husband's sporting activities. He plays football on Saturday mornings with workmates and, as she explained:

'He really wasn't a sporty person at school I don't think but he always played golf and football. He jogs, maybe once or twice a week from the office generally at lunch time. Jogs and comes back and has a yoghurt or something for lunch, he does it from here sometimes, he'll take Simon [son] out for a jog along the old railway line to the golf course and back, Saturday morning or Sunday morning. And he'll play tennis if he can get anyone to play with him.'

Currently, therefore, for the majority of these families, men's exercise is given priority over women's in the timetabling of family commitments generally. The two exceptions to this in the sample, where women have had continuous and prioritized sporting or exercise activities, stand out as unusual. More usual is this woman's story, told in the context of her husband's *regular* weekday football and weekend rugby commitments. She said:

'I used to play hockey, I played basketball, netball and all these things . . . and em squash. We both used to play squash. But em, when the boys came along, between the boys I managed to get back to play hockey. I would get someone to come along and stand with the buggy at the side, you know, in fact it was a relation. But to ask someone to look after two boys was a bit unfair. And I did used to play mixed hockey on a Sunday and my husband would look after the boys, this was down south, but since we moved up to Edinburgh I haven't played any hockey. I do keep fit and I used to jog. Before I got my teaching job I would go out jogging, maybe three times a week. But the teaching job's made it impossible.'

Different interpretations of men's and women's stress

Analysis of first-round interviews indicated that the identification of causes of perceived stress, its evaluation, and its management varied considerably for men and women. Two-thirds of women in the sample are currently employed outside the home, and all lead very full and busy lives; but still the tendency was to focus on stress in the male. The woman's stress was actually underplayed unless it was perceived as causing domestic friction or had resulted in medical problems. In part, this must be seen as related to respondents' identification of the source of the stress. Invariably, men's stress was viewed as a direct result of job pressures, both in terms of the nature of their work and the long hours required of several respondents. Women's stress was usually presented as deriving from the organizational demands required of them to ensure the smooth running of the lives of all of the members of the family. One man saw the difference between his life and his wife's as follows. He said:

A lot of the responsibility for the children has fallen on to her, partially because she has got the car during the day and because her day is more flexible than mine, with her working shorter hours. She tends to do the leaving and uplifting of the children, go to the bank and such things like that. And she has got, because of that she's got more bits and pieces so her day consists of running back and forward more than mine. Whereas I have a more set routine, therefore it's probably the easier of the two really.

KB: How does she feel about what you have just described?

She doesn't like it [laughing].

KB: So what happens?

Em, blue smoke occasionally, she lets off steam, and er, sort of, we re-arrange the who does what for a while, then gradually it drifts again.

The women who were in paid employment were usually in part-time jobs, taken on to fit in with looking after their families. Both spouses frequently commented that in fact, the *woman*'s job was not, in itself, a source of stress. Paid employment for the woman was expected only to be a source of *reward*, both financial and personal. An extreme illustration of this came from a man who commented on his wife's evening job:

'She's not in a stressful job, em, I think if she was in a stressful job we would have to consider, you know, changing, because we can't afford for me to come in snappy, and her to come in at quarter to twelve snappy, and not be able to get to sleep. You know, it's up the stairs because I am up at twenty past seven.'

Men's stress, deriving from a source outside the family, was required not to overspill into domestic life. This ideal was frequently not achieved; but lapses were felt to be understandable and were usually legitimated as being caused by unavoidable pressures. However, it could be argued that the onus of providing a low stress atmosphere in the home fell predominantly on the woman, since she was primarily responsible for its day-to-day organization. A woman who, like the respondent mentioned above, works three nights a week from six-thirty to a quarter to midnight, in addition to carrying out almost all of the domestic chores and childminding, said that her husband was very busy at work with a lot of decisions to make, 'so I try to keep life running round as smoothly as possible in the house so that he doesn't have a lot of stress in here'.

Another woman felt guilty that her pre-menstrual and other hormonal difficulties often badly affected the domestic atmosphere. She explained that her husband knows her menstrual cycle:

'He just sees the change. It's very unfair actually, I know it's unfair. Sometimes I even get to the point that the minute I answer the door to him at night I am in an instant bad mood, and he's done nothing, he's said nothing. He's come home and, you know, instead of being greeted with a smiling face, he's em, he's kind of growled at.'

Both of these women, like the majority of those in the sample, suffered considerable stress each month with pre-menstrual tension. An interesting aspect of the interviews was that such a dominant aspect of their well-being was frequently not mentioned at all by women until the penultimate question: 'Do you have days when you feel healthy and days when you don't?' Some of the husbands never mentioned their wives' pre-menstrual tension at all. This normalization and accommodation of often quite severe symptoms, compared with the reactions to stress in the male, is one of the areas being further investigated in the study.

3   The assumption of similarities between adults and children in the same family

Another example of 'family' health is the assumption that adults and children share what might be termed the same health environment and culture. In the present study, however, respondents clearly differentiated between adults' health and illness, and children's health and illness. It was interesting that, despite expected and, in fact, frequent minor illnesses, children were usually seen as automatically and naturally having a healthy lifestyle; thus the frequent contradictory images of children as vulnerable but resilient. For example, several respondents commented that children were always running about and naturally taking exercise. Also, although many respondents worried about the 'unhealthy' nature of some of their children's dietary preferences, nevertheless they felt that poor eating habits were doing no serious harm. As one woman commented about the ingredients of good health: 'I know you should say things like good diet, but when I think of my son, who's the healthiest one in the family and has the worst diet imaginable, I sometimes wonder.'

In comparison, adults who were perhaps ill much less often were seen as having to work at or 'achieve' a healthy lifestyle (Backett 1987). The majority of respondents felt that their children took health totally for granted. Many claimed that it was precisely that *awareness* of health which changed as one became older; however, as has been discussed elsewhere, the greater awareness of 'healthy' and 'unhealthy practices' is by no means automatically reflected in

78

relevant behaviours (Backett 1988). Analysis of respondents' accounts indicated the value of further examination of socially based meanings and motivations for understanding health-related behaviours. They gave many examples of how these had altered for themselves over the years. For example, exercising in childhood and youth was often motivated by sociability and the pleasures of playing sports, with minimal concern for keeping fit. By the time of the interview the ordering of these motivations for an adult might be quite different.

Again, however, there were many contradictions in views about adult health and illness. Despite the emphasis on adults working at health, respondents often claimed to be, in fact, more neglectful of their own health than that of their children. They might, for example, try to insist on 'healthier' behaviours in their children than they required of themselves. As one man said:

> They're very unlucky because I'm far harder on them than I am on myself . . .
> *KB:* Oh I see.
> . . . in terms of what they eat. I mean we insist that they eat with us, and eat the food that we eat, and if they don't want it then they don't eat it and they don't get a pie instead. We try to regulate their sweeties to a certain extent, it doesn't always work.

Other respondents also confessed that they limited their children's intake of certain 'bad' foods but then indulged their own preference for sweets, junk foods, tobacco, and alcohol somewhat furtively so as not to set a 'bad example'. Sometimes these contradictions caught up with them, as a man explained in one of the pilot discussion groups, to the amusement of his fellow members. He said:

> 'Whilst we're cooking the supper and we talk about the day and get a glass of sherry or a glass of beer or something. And I enjoy it, positively enjoy it. [Noises of agreement from others in the group] The bad thing is I can't do it without eating crisps. [Laughter from the group] And of course Helen [his daughter], you see, is desperate to get into the crisps and, well, *you're* eating them.'

Another man in the group commented: 'That's right, where's your example now, then?'

Respondents' accounts also suggested a rather different approach to adult and children's illnesses. Children's illnesses were usually carefully attended to, and medical help readily sought if necessary. One woman saw the difference as follows. She said:

'Well they're so, children are so obviously well, you know, when they *are* well, that when they are ill it's sort of an immediate situation that has to be dealt with straight away. Em, because it deteriorates. Em, with my own health, or with adults, you tend to, if you're feeling tired or if you're sort of under stress, you just wonder whether it's a problem that's really needing dealt with. So that you tend to leave it a bit longer.'

Most of the adults claimed that they simply carried on as normal if they were ill. The men in particular were described by both spouses as tending not to seek medical help even if they *did* feel it to be necessary or were really worried about some aspect of their health.

4 Influences of 'family life' on health and health-related behaviour

There is, however, one area where, with reservations, the concept of 'family health culture' does appear to have considerable empirical validity. This is the micro area of immediate interactional effects on well-being and behaviour. Taking well-being first, the many *negative* effects on physical and emotional health of family life are increasingly well documented (Haavio-Mannila 1986). Again it is not so easy to dissect the positive effects — for instance, on well-being — although almost all of the respondents said that an important ingredient of good health was happiness, contentment, or, more specifically, a 'happy home life'. One reservation about this positive aspect of 'family' health is that the statistical and empirical evidence again suggests an uneven distribution within families. For example, although causal links are by no means certain or clear, it would appear that living in a family may have more positive effects on men's health than it does on that of women (Verbrugge 1985).

If, however, one examines the immediate interactional effects of family members on one another's health-related behaviours the examples are legion. Health-related behaviours constitute one of the many areas of family life which are open to conflicting demands, compromises, and negotiations. Moreover, health-related behaviours also involve negotiating some of the most basically routinized and deep-seated of individual needs and preferences such as eating, sleeping, sex, physical and emotional comfort, and hygiene. The intricacies of family life as described in the interviews will be analysed fully on completion of the fieldwork. However, an interesting point which emerged from the discussion groups was the clear indication that, whilst there might be broad agreement over the 'oughts' of health-related behaviours, there were *many* disagreements between family members over actual practices. Such disagreements became most evident when some behavioural change was desired of another family member. For example, two participants in the men's discussion group compared as follows their reactions to their wives' wishes to lose weight. The first man said:

> In my case, it's more just, not quite a frustration either but, you know, I'm going to diet or whatever, and the next minute see that the promise is thrown out of the window. There are times I find that difficult to understand when there's such a hellbent commitment, which probably is just discarded at the next breath.
>
> *KB:* So what do you say or do?
>
> Well it comes so frequently I don't say anything [laughter from the group], it's here again, it's the same old story.

The second man said:

> 'You're putting your finger on a problem that I certainly perceive in that I simply do not know how to encourage my wife on what she wishes to do when it comes to dieting. Every, em, so-called encouragement that I follow just doesn't get anywhere; goading or sweet talk or sheer outright disgust at the fact that she's yet again failed two days in, em, snide comments, there's no answer.'

In fact, analysis of the complexities of attitudes to food, and eating behaviours, in families provides a useful case study of interactive effects. Take, for instance, the issue of commensality. In the present study, the accomplishment of the 'family meal' provides illustration of the many interactive factors underlying the usual 'data' of those foods which respondents actually eat. Taking for granted the practical constraints on meal preparation of economics, cooking ability, and time availability, respondents' accounts show that the content of the 'family meal' is affected by the following factors: time schedules of different family members; attitudes towards appropriate socialization of children; biographical experience of the eating preferences of family members; the importance placed on commensality as a forum for communication between family members; pre- and post-prandial activities. Some of the everyday rationales behind the 'family meal' are described in the following quotation from a woman who said:

> 'I sometimes find I'm making maybe two different kinds of meals like em, well especially with me at the moment being on a diet I'm not watching, I'm not eating as much what the children are eating so much. And er I tend to buy convenience food for myself sometimes, and it's out of Marks and Spencer's, it tells you the calories on it. But not at weekends, I do that when I'm working. Well yesterday I had a prepacked meal from Marks and I bought fish for Jonathan [son] because you can't keep eating fish fingers, and then Caroline [daughter] doesn't like fish so she, the three of us had different meals. Jack [husband] doesn't have a meal because he was training, he has a sandwich when he comes in, so it can be a bit awkward at times.'

There are problems, however, with 'family health culture' as a meaningful concept on this interactional level. Of course family members *do* constitute an important social context in which health-related behaviours take place; and well- or ill-being is created. However, the overall effects of familial interactions on health status must be evaluated in the context of demographic trends, which mean that an individual can now expect to live in several different kinds of domestic household during the course of his or her life (Henwood, Rimmer, and Wicks 1987; Gittins 1985). Each of these may have quite different implications for health. Although the great majority of adults do still experience forming and living in their own nuclear families, increasingly this is only for a part of their life-course. The significance of its sustained effects on health must therefore be a matter for continuing empirically based debate.

CONCLUSION

Studying health in families is a complex task which raises many methodological and conceptual issues. This chapter has described some of the issues which have already emerged in a qualitative study under way in Edinburgh. However, it is important in a multi-interview study to be aware of the dynamic nature of the fieldwork and

analytical processes themselves. This has implications both for substantive changes and for the generation of different accounts by
respondents over time and in a variety of interview settings.

The material in this chapter is based on analysis of pilot work and
first-round individual interviews with spouses. The wide-ranging,
open-ended questions aimed to stimulate respondents to talk about
their views on health and illness; and how these related to their
particular domestic and working lives. In the second round of interviews couples are being interviewed jointly; and the focus is on their
detailed accounts of a recent weekday and weekend. The material
obtained is different in many ways from the first-round data. For
instance, particular behaviours often differ from the generalized
descriptions given in first-round accounts. Also, on the basis of
questioning related to immediate direct experience, respondents'
accounts suggest a lesser everyday adherence to those ideals of
'healthy living' often expressed in the previous interviews. Furthermore, while in the first round spouses usually claimed to have overall
agreement about ideals of 'healthy living', the practical accomplishment of such ideals on a daily basis appears to be much more problematical and subject to mutual criticism and disagreement. This also
emerged from the comparative analysis of couples' and single sex
discussion groups during pilot work (Backett 1987).

Thus each round of interviews may result in qualitatively different
material, not only because of substantive variations but also because
the form, content, and context of the interviews are themselves
altering. All of these accounts have value for understanding health,
but they must be analysed reflexively as social products. It seems
likely that first-round interviews tend to generate predominantly
'public' accounts which reflect respondents' perceptions of social
norms and morally approved codes of behaviour (Cornwell 1984). In-
depth interviews, such as those in the present study, may encourage
respondents, even on first meeting, to reveal personal behaviours in a
generalized way (for instance, 'this is what *usually* happens'), and
occasionally to explain views and behaviours in a manner characteristic of 'private' accounts (for example, by personal anecdote). It is
difficult, though, with a topic as broad and potentially sensitive as
'health in families' to progress much further than 'scene setting'.
(Arguably, this in fact constitutes the greater part of work accomplished by researchers and respondents in any first-round interview.)
Essentially such material allows analysis of structural effects, and

'usual' forms of social behaviour and their perceived constraints. This was the main aim of the present chapter. Fieldwork continues, however, which aims to provide a richer picture of how, within these broad structures, health-related behaviours are being developed in everyday interactions.

ACKNOWLEDGEMENTS

The author wishes to acknowledge the financial support of the Scottish Health Education Groups in the preparation of this work.

NOTES

1 Patterns of domestic life may vary considerably depending on the household structure involved. There are always problems in any discussion of 'families' because of the great diversity in household types in western society. In this chapter, therefore, it is important to be clear that the families being studied are composed of married couples with dependent children. These comprise approximately one-third of households in Britain in 1987 (HMSO 1987).
2 The children themselves have also been interviewed.
3 Prior to random selection of potential respondents, the total population of eligible families was screened, with the GP's assistance, to eliminate those currently coping with a member suffering severe mental or physical disorder. Seven families were eliminated at this stage. However, nothing was known in advance about the existence of any hereditary disorders; and therefore sample families cannot be regarded as pre-selected in this respect.

Chapter Four

MOTHERS' BELIEFS ABOUT AND PERCEPTIONS OF THEIR CHILDREN'S ILLNESSES

SARAH CUNNINGHAM-BURLEY .

This chapter reports on a study of mothers with young children which aimed to investigate their perceptions of their children's symptoms, to elucidate their norms of help-seeking behaviour, and to uncover their sense of normality with respect to health and illness.[1] After briefly outlining the study, and some of the problems involved in investigating mundane illness, this chapter will focus on the processes involved in the day-to-day monitoring of children's health and illness in the home. Changes in behaviour, particularly with reference to eating and sleeping patterns, will be discussed. The notions of normality underlying these processes will then be examined. And lastly, the mothers' beliefs about causality will be described.

INTRODUCTION

As Kleinman (1981) has argued: 'It is the lay, non-professional, non-specialist, popular culture arena in which illness is first defined and health care activities initiated' (p. 50). It is now well established that much illness, whether in adults or children, never comes to the attention of health professionals (Hannay 1979, 1980; Spencer 1984) and is dealt with in the home or community through various forms of self-care (Dunnell and Cartwright 1972; Cunningham-Burley and Maclean 1987a; Cunningham-Burley and Irvine 1987). Although medical sociology has made a significant contribution to our understanding of particular illnesses (for example, polio, Davis 1963; epilepsy, West 1976; leprosy, Waxler 1981); of specific medical settings and interactions (for instance, general practice, Bloor and Horobin 1975, Stimson and Webb 1975; paediatric clinics, Davis 1982, Silverman 1987), there is a need for medical sociologists to develop investigations of the everyday context of health and illness. 'Patients' must be perceived beyond the immediate setting of the consultation and examined in terms of their social and cultural experiences. A step in this direction is to study members of a given population, whether or not they are currently involved in any medical encounters, and to focus the investigation on the negotiation of health and illness within such settings as the family (Blaxter and Paterson 1982; Locker 1981; Mayall 1986), the work place (Bellaby 1984), the community (Cornwell 1984), or schools (Prout 1986).

Of course, most sociological research aims to fill gaps in existing knowledge, and much medical sociological research is oriented to even more specific tasks: the study reported here arose out of a perceived need to investigate the social and cultural context of childhood illness — not least because of the impact childhood illness has on general practitioners' work loads (RCGP/OPCS 1979). This need was identified by both researchers and health professionals. Those studies which have sought to describe how mothers cope with illness in their children have tended to focus on interaction with services (Biswas and Sands 1984; Campion and Gabriel 1984), or on their knowledge of and reaction to pre-defined symptoms (Pattison et al. 1982; Field et al. 1983), but have not got to grips with mothers' perceptions of illness nor the categorization of illness itself.

Although adequate grounds for researching health and illness in the family can be found by considering the theoretical and empirical lacunae in medical and family sociology (see Backett, this volume), I also felt much encouraged about the general direction of the research by the positive reactions of those participating in the study, directly as respondents, or indirectly as friends and colleagues acting as 'sounding boards'. As I noted in my research diary during the early stages of the project this seemed to provide 'grass-roots' justification in support of the study's empirical and theoretical concerns. I found that many people I spoke to, especially women who had experienced the bringing-up of children, felt the study to be important in that it sought to reflect the problems they had to face daily in recognizing and dealing with children's illnesses, using methodological techniques which seemed to be amenable to representing women's own experiences (Oakley 1981; Graham 1984; Finch 1984).

THE STUDY

The study was carried out in a new town in Scotland. It drew its sample from one health centre which mainly served its immediate locality. The town has a particularly young population; and for many people the move to the area brought an improvement in living conditions, although problems of unemployment, isolation, and limited resources persist. A brief period of observation in the locality's health centre, and other community facilities, and a sensitizing pilot study of six women were conducted initially. These women were interviewed informally, and asked to make a daily record of their children's 'health and illness' for a week. I then called to see them again for a brief talk about the week.

The main study involved a further fifty-four women with at least one child under 5, and was undertaken in 1983. These families were randomly selected from the general practitioners' lists. I made personal house calls to each woman selected, and explained the nature of the study to her, and what participation would involve. This initial encounter was obviously important in establishing rapport, and in encouraging the mothers to feel that I wanted to learn from their experiences. All but two agreed to participate in the study, and both of these declined because of ill-health.

Most of the sample lived in development corporation housing, and about half the mothers were in some kind of part-time employment: they all had primary responsibility for the care of their children. Most of the families were working class, and five of the husbands were unemployed (the sample members were not therefore as deprived as the families studied by Blaxter and Paterson 1982). The mean age of the women was 28 years, and one was unmarried. There were 113 children altogether, with seventy-four under 5 at the time of the study. The sample therefore contained a variety of family structures, and different family sizes and ages.

The study used two complementary data collection techniques: intensive interviewing and health diaries. In addition, I also noted down observations and informal chats I had with the women during the diary-keeping period. I visited the women three times during the month following the interview. The aim of the interviews, which were as unstructured as possible, was to talk around notions of illness and help-seeking behaviours, so that the most mundane activities would be considered worthy of attention. Whilst talking to the mothers I tried to ensure that I was not seen to be checking up on them, and distanced myself from the health centre with which they were registered, by stressing that I was not a health worker, and that I was interested in the everyday difficulties which mothers might have to face in dealing with all the ups and downs of caring for children.

By describing, in their own words, how they managed children and illness, I felt that the women I spoke to displayed their competences, inadequacies, and difficulties. However, as I outline in the next section, it was quite hard for the women to describe, in detail, the routine process by which they recognized and responded to everyday illnesses in their children: this was also clear from the pilot study. The interviews tended to focus on the mothers' accumulated experience and knowledge of her children, her views on health and illness, her interaction with services and friends, plus descriptions of current or memorable incidents. We also talked about other topics pertaining to family life, children, and health.

As Bloor has pointed out, 'retrospective interview data and selective recall may impart a spurious post-hoc finality to respondents' decision making, a finality that is less evident in observational data' (1985: 301). Participant observational data on families, although not impossible to obtain (Henry 1972), were not considered feasible in this investigation. As an attempt to look at specific incidences of decision making and interpretive procedures the mothers were asked to keep health diaries for a period of up to four weeks. These health diaries, which had been successful in the piloting, were intended to complement the interview data. As Comaroff has noted, perception of illness 'is only fully revealed when examined over time as a process of interaction' (1978: 251). Unlike many other studies which have used this technique (Alpert *et al.* 1967; Morrell and Wade 1976; Pattison *et al.* 1982), these diaries were unstructured (Robinson 1971); I simply asked the mothers to note whether they had noticed anything about their child(ren) that day; whether they had done anything for their child(ren); how they themselves had felt; and how the day had gone generally. This left the mother with the necessary interpretive and definitional work in deciding what to note down, although, of course, they knew that my interest was in routine, everyday health and illness, and its management. The women in the pilot study kept diaries for one week only. In the main study, forty-two of the fifty-four women completed the diaries, although with varying commitment. The mean number of days completed was twenty-two, and the total number of diary days was 927. The diaries enabled the extent of maternal monitoring of children to be examined, and this will be discussed later in the chapter. They also overcame the problem of *post-hoc* accounts of decision making. Many days, where something was noted down about a child, did not result in any action on the part of the mother, and often no episode developed.

SOME PROBLEMS INVOLVED IN STUDYING EVERYDAY ILLNESS

Although the study aimed to investigate people, not patients, it is difficult to move away entirely from preconceived or medically constructed notions of illness, symptoms, diagnosis, and treatment, while accepting that within these categories there continues to be debate about appropriate definitions (Locker 1981; Blaxter 1978; Currer and Stacey 1986). A concern for a 'lay perspective', which is itself a highly problematical term, should be concurrent with a concern to hold in abeyance such pre-defined categories.

Comaroff stresses the need to derive the primary focus of such study from emic definitions of relevance and writes that, 'although this might appear self-evident in the study of foreign cultures, it is often not considered an issue in sociological observations closer to home' (1978: 249). So, rather than retaining *a priori* definitions of what constitutes health and illness, these should be informed from the data, by the 'lay perspective'. Attempts at defining such concepts are numerous, yet flounder in trying to provide abstract formulations for what are essentially socially constructed and highly contextual terms (Eisenberg 1977; Field 1976; Parsons 1958; Erde 1979; Fabrega 1975).

Although at the level of theory and analysis it may be possible to 'regard our own cultural categories as problematic' (Comaroff 1978: 252), at the level of data collection, both researcher and respondent rely on a commonsense stock of knowledge which includes a medical vocabulary, and also many other terms which gloss over the meaning of health and illness. Shared meanings and commonsense knowledge form the basis for successful research interviews, irrespective of how oriented the interviewer is towards the perspective of the respondent (Cunningham-Burley 1985; Cicourel 1964; Brenner 1978). No matter how much as a researcher I wanted to avoid defining the topic for investigation, I had, at some level, to draw on common cultural understandings about children, families, health, illness, and medicine. As Frake noted, 'knowing the queries that can be appropriately posed about a given topic reveals the features of that topic that are relevant to the inquirer' (1964: 134).

To some extent I tried to use the respondents as co-researchers: I explained that this was an exploratory study. I tried out ideas by suggesting questions, asking whether this was something they had already thought about or had heard other people speak about. Certain ideas and practices emerged as important — for example, noting changes in eating and sleeping behaviour — and these could then be introduced in any subsequent interviews (Schwartz and Jacobs 1979). It seemed that the very processes involved in defining and coping with health and illness at a mundane level were carried out routinely, almost without thinking. The respondents, then, had to become investigators into their own actions and behaviour, and I found that they were able to be quite reflective about their management of health and illness. An investigation into everyday illness experiences was not itself always treated as relevant, and some mothers thought that I must be concerned with more significant illness episodes (hospitalization, accidents, convulsions), and apologized if they did not have much to talk about; for example:

> *R.13:* And apart from that [referring to a febrile convulsion] I haven't had much bother with them. No infectious things. Occasional cold, a bit of a cough, but nothing to speak about.

Since I wanted to study the very routine assumptions which the mothers made with respect to health and illness, it was important to be aware of the difficulties involved in researching what is ordinarily taken for granted, and try and make this a topic for discussion:

> *SB:* What sort of things do you normally look out for, then?
> *R6:* Well, in the case of these two, if they do start to cry a bit more than normal. Both of them are not cry-babies unless it's really something.

By encouraging the women to talk about what they felt to be important, the study developed analyses informed by this: a focus on behaviour; normality; normal illness; and the use of explanation.

Although all of the women interviewed could speak to varying degrees about their children's health at a general level, it seemed considerably easier for them to 'tell stories' about memorable episodes than to comment on the routine and thus taken-for-granted ways in which they recognized that something was perhaps wrong with their child. While such stories are important in understanding some aspects of illness experience (Stimson and Webb 1976), and also represent an amenable way of expressing ideas (Askham 1982; Graham 1984), they gloss over the very practices which must be involved in recognizing illness in the first place. When asking one woman about her child's health over the past few years she replied:

> *R.54:* I cannae remember to tell you the truth — the ear infection has always stuck in my mind.

Such phrases seem almost to curtail further discussion: specific episodes are not only memorable but can be accounted with hindsight. Talking about how one would usually react to ill-defined situations (I did not want to pre-determine what could be considered problematic to the mothers), posed greater problems to the people I spoke to, although the health diaries proved to be a useful source of data here.

The researcher's problem in investigating mundane illness is thus tied to the respondents' modes of expression. At one level the respondents seemed to rationalize their behaviour, by describing experiences after they had occurred. While this can be a problem for research aiming to uncover health related practices, it is the respondents' method of making sense of their experience, and of reflecting on the legitimacy of their actions. It is not a process merely used to cope with a sociological interview or a medical encounter; it is a way of making sense even to oneself of what has happened. Asking people to consider trivial illnesses, which are not necessarily memorable, and childhood illnesses (such as measles) which may not yet have happened, is to request abstract expressions which necessarily contain an element of uncertainty. Indeed, many potential illness episodes do not develop, and describing this may not be compatible with the presentation of rational or appropriate behaviour. Care had to be taken during the course of the fieldwork to encourage the feeling that I was interested in the mothers' doubts, in small details, and that what they said was interesting and appropriate, especially when they felt they had no major illness experience to discuss.

MONITORING CHILDREN'S HEALTH AND ILLNESS

The study sought to reflect the ways in which mothers recognize and deal with children's illnesses. This meant focusing on what might be seen in outward appearances to be the trivial and mundane, and analysing in detail the mothers' individual responses and general practices involved in making sense of the health and illness experience of their children. As Kleinman has pointed out, 'Since beliefs about illness are always closely linked to specific therapeutic interventions and thus are systems of knowledge and action, they cannot be understood apart from their use' (1981: 34). Health and illness then must be seen as process and practice, rather than abstract concepts. Blaxter (1981: 100) has noted that the notions of symptoms and illness may be totally different for children than, say, for a wage earner. The practical circumstances of family life surround the recognition and response to children's symptoms and illness: 'The weighty responsibility . . . which adults have for their children's health and illness, a responsibility not backed with years of training, but with recipe knowledge and practical everyday judgement' (Davis 1982: 24).

Through analysis of the interview transcripts and diaries, I attempted to elucidate the nature of these everyday judgements, and the knowledge on which they are based. In common with other studies (Blaxter and Paterson 1982; Locker 1981; Spencer 1984), the mothers in this study closely monitored their children's well-being (Cunningham-Burley and Irvine 1987): they, as primary carers, were routinely and constantly involved in managing and constructing health and illness. Concerns about health and illness were embedded in everyday activities, and intermingled with a range of other issues: competent mothering; daily routines; coping strategies; disturbances; experience and knowledge, both relating to individual children and 'common' knowledge.

The health diaries showed that the mothers were very watchful: on the 49 per cent of the days recorded they noticed something in their children: on 35 per cent of these days no action was taken at all. In the interviews, the women would often say that they would wait to see what happened if they had started to notice changes in their children. They also said that they would often just let an illness run its course anyway:

> R.47: I haven't found anything that is really good to shift it; a cold just runs its course, it just unsettles her.

The commonest 'symptoms' for which no action was taken were colds, runny noses, and changes in behaviour, especially irritability and tiredness.

The mothers were aware of subtle changes in their children, changes which may or may not be related to illness, but which form part of the active monitoring process.

> *R36:* Daniel complained of a headache quite a few times in the morning, so gave him Junior Disprin, and he seemed happy to go to bed. Two minutes later he was up saying he felt better and full of fun. Looks as if he was having me on.

A typical diary entry where a change in behaviour was noted, and an 'illness' developed was:

> *Day 1:* Susan a bit tired late afternoon. She wanted to lie on the sofa. Bit of a cold starting. No action.
> *Day 2:* Susan has a cough and a runny nose. Gave Susan Disprin and some cough bottle [*sic*].

The mother here noted a change in behaviour, and connected this with a cold starting — relying both on her knowledge of her child's likely illness behaviour, and her general knowledge about how colds start. No action took place until the cold started. There were many episodes in the diaries where something would be noticed, but the episode would end on the same day. Often potential precursors to illness would not develop into anything; for example:

> *Day 1:* Mark a bit grumpy today. Very tired and cross.
> *Day 2:* Mark OK today.

The interviews provided further elaboration of the interpretive processes involved in monitoring:

> *R.22:* Well, funnily enough he coughed this morning, and I thought 'a wee cough starting'. He hasn't coughed since. It was just when he got up, but I have had a cold sort of hanging about for days.

A clear symptom is noted, although it did not develop. However, the mother's knowledge of her own cold 'hanging about' made her wary. 'Hanging about' was a description often used to define the early stages of an illness episode, or the stage immediately prior to an illness 'coming out'.

RECOGNIZING THAT SOMETHING WAS WRONG

Much of the process involved in recognizing illness was grounded in behavioural change rather than just in specific physical symptoms such as a runny nose, stomach ache, and so on. In fact, behavioural changes were noted a total of 314 times in the diaries. Often more than one change, or a change plus physical symptom, were noted together. Changes in sleep patterns — either sleepy, tired, or wakeful — figured predominantly. Changes in eating behaviours were described much more in the interviews. These changes may be cues (Locker 1981), or triggers (Blaxter and Paterson 1982), but were not always related to underlying illness. The changes in themselves, however, were considered relevant by the mothers.

The mothers did not necessarily work with a framework of symptom, diagnosis, and treatment, and were not always concerned with underlying illness but rather with the management of a child whose day-to-day behaviour was giving cause for concern, or some kind of trouble; for example:

> *R.47:* I thought there must be something wrong with her, you know, she's no crying for nothing. . . . I would be walking the floor with her.

Not all recognized change was considered a symptom of illness. Not all acknowledged illness was acted upon. From the accounts which the mothers gave it would be impossible to say how often a whining child was interpreted as being ill, or sickening for something. The mothers themselves said that they did not find that process difficult, for instance:

> *R.35:* I don't do nothing 'til I see for myself that they are not well, and with him he goes round girnin' and moanin' and just can't be comforted by anybody . . . when he's no well he can't even be bothered with me so I know he's sickening for something.

The processes involved in recognizing illness are perhaps the same whether or not illness is then thought to have occurred. The recognizing process and subsequent illness are related in a *post-hoc* way, through the management of specific episodes, and the accumulated experience that brings.

Strikingly, the mothers who were interviewed seemed confident in their abilities to recognize when something was wrong with their children, although this was an intuitive process, for example:

R.68: I think it helps if you are with her all the time. You know what to look out for. That's my opinion anyway. I just feel you can sense when she's going to be ill.

As outlined above, this skill is tied to their special knowledge of what their child is normally like:

SB: Do you find that you can always tell if they are going to get something?

R.42: Uh huh . . . you get signs and all the kids are different. If *she* is not really very well she stops eating.

Since these processes are part of the routine caring of children on a daily basis, they are hardly worth mentioning:

R.2: You just think to yourself, 'What's wrong with you today' sort of thing.

Although there were individual differences in children, there was considerable similarity across the sample in terms of what the mothers would worry about. However, a mother would not use 'crying' as a means of recognizing illness if she knew that her child cried a lot anyway. Because some children routinely display aspects of behaviour which normally seem to be coupled with illness (crying, not eating, 'greeting'), a few of the mothers did look out for more physical signs of illness. One respondent described her daughter as not eating much anyway, and that 'it is not until she's as white as a ghost or too warm or that, you say oh there's something wrong with her'. Her son, however, went quiet and wanted cuddling, 'whereas he's away playing by himself' (R.62). Otherwise, just a few mothers spoke only of physical signs when speaking about recognizing illness, and only two said that it was difficult to tell if their children were sickening for something.

In suspecting illness, phrases such as 'sickening for something' or 'something hanging' were used. The same few words were used to describe a child's changed behaviour, or state, right across the sample. Words such as 'clingy' were used to describe a child who hung about when you were ill, wanting attention, yet also somewhat listless. 'Crabbit' or 'girnie' were used to describe a cross, irritable, moaning child. A 'greeting' child was one who cried all the time. Other phrases were used which glossed a whole host of behaviours — 'not her usual self' or 'feeling funny'. Their precise meaning may differ for each mother or each child, but a general sense of what mothers look out for in their children could be gleaned from their vocabulary. For example:

> *R.35:* I don't do nothing, till I see myself that they are not well, and with him he goes around girnin' and moanin' and just can't be comforted at all by anybody . . . when he's no well he can't even be bothered with me so I know he's sickening for something.

SLEEPING AND EATING AS PROBLEMATICAL CONCERNS

Although Blaxter and Paterson (1982) noted that there were no universal principles for the interpretation of specific symptoms, this study found that sleeping and eating were major concerns for the mothers when talking about their children's health and illness: they were also behaviours on which a normal assessment of the child was made. These were behaviours which nearly all the mothers mentioned in various ways: not-eating; not-feeding; not-sleeping; sleeping too much. Analysis of the mother's description of their concern over eating and sleeping behaviours shows a complicated relationship between behaviour, illness, and health. A mother may be concerned generally that her child is not eating or sleeping enough, and may therefore not develop healthily.

Healthy development

Eating, particularly, was related to a concern for healthy development, with implicit or explicit recognition of this being related to health as an ability to resist or cope with illness/disease:

> *R5:* He's no got the weight behind him, if he gets anything serious. That's what really bugs us, ken.

This illustrates a concern with a child's general health and well-being, and the idea of having to retain a certain amount of weight to protect against illness, or the consequences of illness. The mothers were concerned that their baby or child was not getting enough to eat, for example:

R.40: You see with me feeding him myself I was never sure if he was getting enough and he wouldnae take a bottle at all.

It seemed a natural response for the mothers to interpret their child's crying as hunger, and to be concerned about their food intake. Crying was hard for the mother to cope with and caused worry, especially in young babies. However, feeding problems did not stop there, and some mothers described difficult periods with their children right through weaning and subsequently as toddlers.

While few of the mothers were concerned that their child might be overweight, most were worried about a child losing weight and appearing skinny. One mother noted:

R.17: I used to get bothered that he would lose a lot of weight, and they would think I'm no feeding him.

This example highlights a concern which many of the mothers had: they did not want to appear incompetent in the eyes of others. Having a thin child could be treated in that way. It is perhaps not surprising that these issues should be considered important by the mothers, given the emphasis which society puts on the nurturing role of the mother, and on the adequate physical and emotional development of an infant.

However, eating and sleeping behaviours were also more directly related to actual illness in various ways. Problems experienced with a child's eating or sleeping may suggest that illness is or soon will be present: they may be treated as symptoms. They may also actually constitute 'illness' in a mother's eyes, and be a direct reason for seeking professional advice or treating the child at home. Such problems may also be a result of illness, and turn out to be more troublesome than the illness itself. They may be the cause of disruption, which is itself problematic and worthy of intervention from friends, relatives, or health workers. Lastly, they may just be displays of bad behaviour, or changes in behaviour which come to nothing. They may be all of these things at different times, or some of these things at the same time. Thus in monitoring their children and noting changes, the mothers are not always concerned with potential symptoms of illness; it may be the disturbed behaviour that is the problem. These categories will be considered in turn, as they shed light on the interpretive procedures the mothers use in monitoring their children.

Eating/sleeping as a symptom or precursor to illness

Changes in behaviour were often seen as potential precursors to illness. The diary example given on page 93 suggests that tiredness was connected with a cold starting. Such changes, then, could often be the first sign that something was wrong. For example:

> *R.11:* Carl used to go off his food for a whole week, and, well, as I say, he was bad with eating, but he went right off it if he was going to be ill.

Changes in eating and sleeping behaviour may be a sign of ill-defined disturbance, possibly an illness as yet unknown. For example:

> *R.19:* He was a baby that never cried during the night. He slept and then when he did waken up during the night I first started panicking. There was one night I don't know what was wrong with him.

Eating/sleeping as the result/concomitant of illness

Changes in sleeping and eating were often cited as accompanying an illness, and thus making the episode more worrying or more troublesome. For example, the following respondent describes the differences between her two sons:

> *R.2:* Kim, he's no a person that sleeps off his illnesses. He would rather moan. The few times that he has been ill he gets really moaning and just wants to sit on your knee all the time. I mean whereas Robert he'll lie up there and go to sleep. He always slept through his illnesses all the time which suited me. This wee yin, he sits and moans round your neck the whole time.

The following example shows the way not sleeping can be seen as a result of illness which clearly concerned the mother:

> *R.59:* He had, it was like a stomach bug or something he had, a while back now, and he wasnae getting a chance to sleep with it.

Changes in eating and sleeping could also be used as a yardstick by which to gauge whether or not an illness needed professional attention, or was anything to worry about. The following two examples show such a yardstick operating in different ways:

R.12: He certainly wasn't ill with it [German measles]. He wasn't off his food or feverish or nothing.

R.68: If Nicole was really ill, like if she was off her food and that I would go to the doctor, but at the moment she's got wee spots on her face, so I was thinking of going to see the health visitor tomorrow to see if she had any idea of what was causing it, but the way I feel, as long as she is eating and that, and she is running about quite happy, so there's nothing to worry about.

Eating or sleeping as the problem itself

The mothers often described the problems of coping with a child whose eating patterns or, more often, sleeplessness were giving cause for concern. Given that these behaviours may be used as a yardstick by which to assess the extent that an illness may be a worry, it is not surprising that the mothers may also be more concerned with the result of the illness (the not sleeping, for example), rather than the illness itself. In the following example, the mother describes her wakeful, crying child:

R.47: I thought there must be something wrong with her, you know, she's no crying for nothing, and I would go to the doctor and the doctor would say . . . 'she's just crying, there's nothing wrong with her'.

Such behaviour can be very disruptive, influencing the well-being of the whole family, and thus constituting a very real problem, for example:

R.17: It got to the stage that my husband was coming out of work at tea time and I was going to bed until he was ready for bed because it was the only way I was getting a sleep. She just doesn't need sleep.

Eating and sleeping as behaviours that come to nothing, or bad behaviours

As mentioned, the monitoring process can in many ways be related to illness in a *post-hoc* way. Many changes in behaviour are noted but develop into nothing:

R.10: You just have to wait and see what's going to develop. It might be just a cold or they might just be off for a few days. . . . Sometimes they are just sort of off their food or that for a couple of days, a bit girnie, and then they just seem to start eating again. It has not really come to anything at all.

Young children may also just play up, and even babies were occasionally described as being just bad:

R.59: Paul beginning to play up at bedtime for some reason. Screaming for me the whole time.

R.44: He was a good baby right enough, I must admit . . . a good sleeper, and fed no problems [sic]. It is just from about a year and a half, two, that he's turned into a bit of a horror, not sleeping, and picky, you know.

Analysis of eating and sleeping behaviours demonstrates the relationship between noting such changes and illness. The four categories discussed above unpack the interpretive process involved in monitoring children, and show the importance of recognizing the different ways in which such changes can be interpreted. It is also clear from the above that mothers draw on a stock of knowledge of what is normal in order to make their judgements about their children's changed states.

NORMALITY

The mothers' negotiation of their children's behaviour and illnesss was embedded in commonsense assumptions and individual experiences about what was normal and acceptable in a child. They used a notion for what was normal for their child or children as a method of interpreting that child's action or demeanour, while also recognizing that the notion of normality itself derived from that child's behaviour and the mother's own accumulated knowledge. The concept was reflexive, in both serving to elucidate what was normal for the child itself, and being informed by the mother's experience of that child. For an episode or change to be worthy of attention it had to deviate from the normal, although this was not a static notion. What could be taken as normal changed over time as a child developed from a baby to a toddler. Thus, for example, a baby not eating was a worrying deviation from the normal, and a cause for concern. A toddler not eating might simply be part of a normal 'fad', and not anything to worry about. The mothers also learned from experience, and changed their definitions of normality accordingly. For example, many mothers said that they accepted less as normal in their first child, and tended to worry about every little thing, but with subsequent children, more knowledge and experience their category of what was normal broadened, for example:

> R.2: The second one's a lot different; you know a lot, you feel as though you know a lot. You have had one to bring up, so when the second one comes along it's easier. But when the first one comes along you tend to worry 'Oh what is it?'.

However, the mother's view of 'the normal' was also closely related to her child's individual behaviour, and to her unique knowledge of her child or children. It is somewhat contradictory to a general notion of normality that each child was also perceived as unique, for instance:

> S.B. Does it make a lot of difference if you've had a lot of experience before?
>
> R.50: I don't know, half of it is trial and error. I mean every child is different, although you could have a dozen children and there wouldn't be one of them the same.

and

> R.11: She gets kind of cross if she is getting anything. Chris used to go off his food. . . . Lynne gets fretty if she is under the weather, you can tell.

The mothers, then, built up a unique stock of knowledge relating to their own particular child or children. In the diaries the mothers often noted when their children deviated from the normal:

> R.18: Don was more cranky than usual, he was rather hot and flushed at bedtime.

Sometimes remaining normal was in itself noted, showing the extent to which normality underpins the mothers' interpretation of their children's behaviours and other 'symptoms':

> R.10: He has been his usual self.

The mothers were also able to recognize when a child was back to normal, and episodes in the diaries, which may or may not have developed into anything, often ended with the phrase 'back to normal', for example:

> *R.9:* Slightly sore bottom not eating much (he often goes off food for a day or two then gets back to normal).

and

> *R.20:* He was a lot better today, back to his normal self.

NORMAL ILLNESS

A healthy child is not necessarily one who is never ill, and a range of minor illnesses were considered normal and somewhat separate from health (Blaxter and Paterson 1982; Locker 1981; Spencer 1984; Cornwell 1984). Normal illness had to be made a relevant topic in the interviews, because it tended not to be treated as noteworthy, for example:

> *R.38:* But as I say we've never had much experience of anything. They've never had anything to really worry about other than normal childhood illnesses.

and

> *R.58:* Well they quite often just get the runny nose, but as I say they are quite healthy children.

The notion that some illness is normal, or interestingly even healthy, is reflected in the following comment:

> *S.B.* How have the children been then, sort of healthwise?
> *R.31:* Just healthy colds, and things, you know, nothing that stops her.

The child here was obviously able to carry on as normal, so was considered healthy: in other words, the child was displaying none of the behavioural disturbances which are usually associated with illness or which are routinely used to recognize illness.

In addition to some 'illness' being considered normal, others were normalized (Locker 1981), for example:

> *R.58:* I have been very lucky with both of them as regards their health. If you looked up their medical records you would see there is very few entries for them. They both had chickenpox,

and just after that Sally took a fit, but it was just a one-off thing, you know, she was in Sick Children's and she has got a wee touch of eczema just now but that's about all. They get coughs and colds and but they are very healthy.

In the following example Mark's croup becomes normalized, and the mother's overall assessment or her child's health as good is left intact.

S.B. And how have the children been sort of healthwise?

R.2: Oh they've been great. They catch colds like every other child. Mark's bothered with croup, but apart from that, that's all.

Normality, then, can be interpreted as a yardstick that operated in a variety of ways, as a measure of whether or not the child was 'ill' with the condition (such as a cough), whether the child is sickening for something, is experiencing normal illness, or is experiencing illness normally.

BELIEFS ABOUT CAUSES OF ILLNESS

Having considered how the mothers monitored their children, how they interpreted changes and the notions of normality underpinning this process, I shall now lastly consider some of their beliefs and theories about the causes of illness. It is important to note though, that moving on from this focus on practice to beliefs does not indicate that beliefs exist as a coherent logic outside of the everyday action in which they are manifested. As Blumhagen has noted, 'It is an unusual individual (or indeed practitioner) who has worked out all the interconnections of his belief system so that it has become an integrated whole' (1980: 200). While many studies have focused on cause (Pill and Stott 1982; Cornwell 1984; Locker 1981; Blaxter 1983), I found, like Pill and Stott (1982), that most people do not think about the topic of cause in general terms, but only in relation to particular episodes. The women did not elaborate complex theories of illness causation. Unlike previous studies, I did not ask the women specifically about their ideas on illness causation. Consequently, cause emerged as part of their method of interpreting and explaining illnesses (often just coughs and colds).

First, I shall draw on the diary data to look at the way the mothers used cause to explain disorder. it should be noted, however, that the mothers did not always impute cause: often a description of disruption, abnormality, change in behaviour was offered but no concern for cause was expressed. Symptoms can be treated as explanations in themselves with no need for further elaboration, for example:

R.9: Slightly sore bottom, not eating much. [Diary entry]

Or illness itself was an explanation for what was going on (Kleinman 1981):

R.19: Yes — he has took the cold again but this time it is quite bad, it seems to be more in his chest, but I will leave him and see how he is tomorrow.

Two categories of cause were identified in the health diaries. I shall discuss each of these in turn.

Cause as professional diagnosis

Advice from doctors was put down explicitly, and the doctor's terminology used afterwards. People used 'cough', 'cold', 'tummy upset' on their own, but 'infection' was usually used after going to the doctor. The mothers went to the doctor if they thought that the symptoms were not clearing up as quickly as they had anticipated, or if the chest was involved. But they went for many reasons: to get relief for symptoms; to check that all was well; to make sure that nothing worse was going on; and to see if the mother was providing the right treatment. Diagnosis may be simply reassurance. The following two examples show cause as professional diagnosis:

R.20: The doctor checked Margaret and said both of her ears had an infection.

R.8: Diane went off her solids and was very crabbit. I went to the doctor with Diane, she said that Diane has a virus but she wasn't ill, that she just wasn't herself (no prescription, just give her Calpol to settle her, and if feverish to sponge her down with cold water).

Cause as lay diagnosis

Making sense of everyday experience sometimes gave rise to lay diagnosis: finding a reason for a symptom, whether a physical sign or behavioural change, or simply stating the fact of illness as explanation. Sometimes these causes were not illness-related at all. Behavioural disturbances may be caused by visits to grandparents, going swimming, father being away — any number of things, as the following example illustrates:

> *R.6:* Mark very irritable today, up too early. Both fed up being stuck in all day.

Lay diagnosis was often tentative, suggestive of cause:

> *R.24:* Susan covered in spots, I think it could be measles.

Teething was an oft used explanation (Mayall 1986):

> *R.54:* Peter was crying in the afternoon due to a sore bottom. This was caused by him teething, I think.

Or germs and viruses:

> *R.48:* Steven contacted virus.
> *R.42:* Jane's cough worse again. I think she got some of Simon's germs.

From the interview data certain categories of causation were indentified, although often more than one would be imputed in any one explanation of a particular event or illness. As I have noted, these did not form part of a coherent set of beliefs, but were rather an ill-articulated set of practices based on experience, knowledge, and everyday concerns.

External causes

Germs/viruses, expressed as 'bugs', 'the cold', were known to be in the environment: they were often 'going about', or a child could catch something from a particular person. I was once cited as the person who had brought the germ into the house, and I certainly caught a few too during the fieldwork period! For example,

> *R.40:* But I think it's my cold he has got the now.

and

> *R.53:* I think it was just a twenty-four-hour bug he had.

Other external factors were also cited as important; the weather, for example, could be seen as a reason for certain illnesses:

> *R.28:* It's just the kids seem to have had one thing after the other. Cold, coughs, and things like that. I suppose it's the weather. Everybody's the same.

Or very specific external factors were mentioned, often to explain specific episodes: hot milk; house plants; different water; different air; central heating.

In addition, getting cold or chilled were also described. These were associated with coughs, colds and chills, although the mothers said that they tried to wrap their children up to prevent the effects of the cold:

> *R.56:* I always make sure she's well wrapped up you know, hat, scarf, and that sort of thing.

> *R.17:* He gets quite a few sore throats now and again, but I think it is just with him outside. He runs about all the time and I mean you cover him up but he is always taking his socks and shoes off and taking his jacket off.

Child's characteristics/hereditary factors

The child's own characteristics were sometimes cited as reasons why they got certain illnesses; being prone to an illness was something intrinsic to the child:

> *R.32:* She's bad for sore throats.

Or else the proneness or condition ran in the family:

> *R.5:* It is worrying especially when you know that it runs in families, chest illnesses.

> *R.17:* Well it was mostly his eczema. He didn't have it when he was born. He was about six months when he got it, but it's in both families, so it was only natural he would get that.

Luck/fatalism

Many everyday illnesses, like coughs and colds, and childhood illnesses were often considered as matters of luck:

R.50: But I think these childhood things, I mean, if they are going to get it, there's not an awful lot you can do apart from keeping them in the house and wrapping them in cotton wool, sort of thing.

And whatever you may do as a carer does not influence the outcome:

R.10: And she's been kind of touty all this winter, you know, with one thing and another. Dear knows why because she is getting first class treatment but there you are. I suppose the neglected ones don't take anything.

The above shows that a variety of causes were identified in the interview transcripts and used by the mothers to explain illness in their children, either generally or in relation to specific episodes. However, they did not have a strong model of causality. As Herzlich and Pierret have noted (1986: 73): 'Our understanding of illness is not based on the distinction between cause and effect; in some cases, the effect may have the same theoretical status as cause.' They cite Foucault, and note that ' "proximate cause" of illness is often difficult to distinguish from the symptom it is supposed to explain; it is simply, according to Foucault a sort of "causal actualization of its qualities" ' (Foucault 1961: 262, cited in Herzlich and Pierret 1986: 74).

Since the study focused on childhood illness, including much that is routine and common — coughs and colds, for example — it is not surprising that the mothers did not have elaborate theories of cause. They did not have to explain long-standing chronic illness (Williams 1985), but rather make sense of many self-limiting episodes. As Blaxter and Paterson (1982) have noted: 'It has, of course, frequently been pointed out before that it is normal and natural for the individual to strive to provide explanations for bodily states, using whatever evidence is available to him' (p. 35). The changes in behaviours and bodily states which the mothers had to deal with were ephemeral: they brought a slightly raised level of awareness that something might be happening, probably only a normal illness, possibly something more serious. The mothers then drew on their stock of knowledge about likely explanations — teething, a bug going around — with which to explain the change. Mundane illness, itself, especially since it is often defined as normal, needs no explanation or complex theory of causality.

107

CONCLUSION

In this chapter an attempt has been made to hold in abeyance professional notions of health, illness, and symptoms. While recognizing that many medical terms have lay currency, lay and medical meanings may vary. The methods which the mothers used to recognize illness did not necessarily involve an appraisal of traditional, medically defined symptoms. Their concern with changes in behaviour focused mainly on eating and sleeping problems. These were related to illness in a complex way but also constituted concerns in their own right. The categories of health, illness, and symptoms may indeed not be very relevant at all. To this end the focus has been on behaviour rather than illness, and the relationship between the two phenomena. The advantages of analysing the mothers' accounts using general behavioural categories is that a better understanding can be achieved of their concerns and worries. The same problem, such as 'not sleeping', can have different meanings and implications, both to the mothers and to health professionals. For example, if not sleeping is accompanied by a 'recognized' illness, and results in a consultation, the mother's primary concern (the child's sleeping behaviour) may not be attended to if the general practitioner focuses on diagnosing and treating a physical condition. Similarly, many of the mothers said that they felt that their doctors or health visitors did not deal appropriately in consultations about sleeping or eating problems (Cunningham-Burley and Maclean 1987b). Some had been told to leave a child to cry, which did not help the mothers cope with or solve the problem. Advice about feeding was also considered inappropriate by the mothers, who often said that they started solid feeding earlier than recommended, as a way of coping with a wakeful, crying baby. The problem of conflict between lay and medical concerns are highlighted through this analysis of the mothers' concern with behavioural changes in their children.

Notions of normality were explored, and they were shown to underpin the processes by which mothers recognized illness or trouble in their children. Normality was not a static notion, but changed over time, remaining quite individual. Illnesses, both trivial and more serious, were to some extent normalized, especially in *post-hoc* accounts, if the children were otherwise considered fit and healthy. It is only through understanding the features of their concept of normality that deviation in their children's behaviour or state took on any meaning. Interpreting what the women said in this way helps to provide some understanding of how they construct illness, other than simply recognizing pre-defined or commonly known conditions.

Since the management of health and illness in the home is mostly routine, the women did not seem to have to elaborate complex causal explanations for what was going on. The types of cause they did cite reflected the common categories found in other work (for example, Blaxter 1983), yet importantly, this study located cause and explanation within the interpretive process involved in identifying deviations from the normal which might be associated with illness.

ACKNOWLEDGEMENTS

I would like to acknowledge all the women who took part in the study. I also thank Una Maclean, Sandy Irvine, and John Davies for their help during the course of the study, and Neil McKeganey for helpful comments on the chapter.

NOTES

1 This study was funded by the Scottish Home and Health Department, Health Services Research Committee, 1983–85, at the Department of Community Medicine, University of Edinburgh.

Part Three

THE SOCIAL CONTEXT OF DRUG AND ALCOHOL ABUSE

Chapter Five

DRUG ABUSE IN THE COMMUNITY: NEEDLE-SHARING AND THE RISKS OF HIV INFECTION

NEIL McKEGANEY

INTRODUCTION

Throughout the 1960s and 1970s sociologists were often rather chary of being seen to adopt a social problems perspective — that is, a perspective in which they are called upon to explore particular social problems in the expectation that they will produce information relevant to the control or reduction of the problem at hand. At least part of the reason for this unwillingness was a feeling that it was somehow inappropriate for an evolving discipline to have its topical concerns defined by others; and that if this were to occur on a regular basis, then sociology might become no more than the handmaiden to other, more established, professional groups (McKeganey 1989). Nowhere was this feeling expressed more succinctly than in Straus's (1957) differentiation between those sociologists studying medicine from the outside ('sociologists of medicine') and those who were operating from within medicine itself ('sociologists in medicine'). The latter, he cautioned, risked losing the ability to think and write sociologically as a result of working closely with medical practitioners and allowing them to set out the topical agenda of sociological analysis.

The reluctance of sociologists to adopt a social problems perspective was further underlined by the recognition that the power to define social problems was itself unevenly distributed in society. By exploring particular social problems sociologists were always in danger of providing a further legitimation for the imposition of definitional power by one group over another. This is not, of course, to suggest that there were no sociologists arguing for the discipline to represent the interests of particular groups. Howard Becker (1967), for example, posed the polemical question of 'Who's side are we on?' to encourage sociologists to display their own political commitments. However, it is probably fair to say that the majority of sociologists, although possibly embracing Becker's polemical questioning in theory, remained rather agnostic on the issue of taking sides in practice.

It is particularly striking in the light of this that in the mid- to late-1980s there should have occurred a dramatic upswing in interest in a social problems perspective with sociologists of all varieties keen to demonstrate that a sociological contribution can amount to more than a contribution to sociology. One area where this has occurred particularly forcefully is in the burgeoning field of AIDS-related research studies (Aggleton and Homans 1988). Clearly, there is not the space to examine the basis for this shift. Nevertheless, it does appear that the sheer magnitude of the crisis which AIDS represents has been sufficient for researchers perhaps to downplay the importance of their own disciplinary concerns in favour of the possibility of identifying information which may be of some practical value.

In this chapter I would like to describe one research study which has arisen out of a social problems perspective; in particular, the growing recognition that injecting drug use represents one of the main risk activities for contracting and spreading HIV (AIDS) infection. The research I will describe here is attempting to gain some understanding of current levels of risk amongst a sample of injecting drug users.

Initially I will provide a short review of some of the epidemiological information on the relationship between injecting drug use and HIV infection. This will be followed by a section which looks specifically at the methodology of my own research. I shall then concentrate upon (1) the level of drug use within the study area in which research is being undertaken, and (2) the extent and nature of needle-sharing amongst injecting drug users. In a final section I will briefly consider some of the policy implications following on from this research, as well as the implications for medical sociology of adopting the kind of social problems perspective outlined in this chapter.

INJECTING DRUG USE AND HIV INFECTION

In 1986 blood samples taken from 164 injecting drug users attending an Edinburgh general practice surgery produced what at the time seemed an unbelievable result. Tests carried out for the presence of antibodies to the Human Immunodeficiency Virus indicated that 51 per cent of the tested individuals had become infected with the virus. Retests confirmed the original results, and demonstrated beyond doubt that the city's injecting drug-using population were experiencing an epidemic of HIV infection (Robertson *et al.* 1986). The extent of that epidemic was, at the time, matched only by a comparable epidemic amongst injecting drug users in New York City (Cohen *et al.* 1985).

In the period since these studies were published it has become apparent that there are at least two models of epidemic spread amongst injecting drug users. On the one hand, there is the very rapid increase in infection characterized by the two cities already mentioned as well as northern Italy (Conte *et al.* 1987), Spain (Camprubi 1987), and more recently Bangkok (1989 — personal communication World Health Organization Global Programme on AIDS). On the other hand, there is the much more gradual increase characterized by such cities as Copenhagen (Worm 1986) and Glasgow (Follet *et al.* 1986).

It is a striking feature of the epidemiology of HIV infection amongst injecting drug users that these two models of infective spread can occur in areas that are geographically very close. Although the reasons for this are ill understood, it is possible that differences in the cultural context in which the drug use is occurring may in part explain such differences (Robertson, Bucknall, and Wiggins 1986). It has been suggested, for example, that the rapid rise in infection in Edinburgh was driven in part by the practice of local police officers of confiscating needles and syringes once these were found in the possession of individuals suspected of abusing drugs. Such a move led to a decrease in the numbers of needles and syringes in circulation and an increase in the levels of sharing amongst drug users (SHHD 1986; Mulleady 1987). However, such explanations amount to little more than informed speculation, since we know very little about either the behaviour generally of people injecting drugs or about those specific aspects of their behaviour which may be related to the spread of HIV infection.

According to Moss (1987), the epidemic of HIV infection amongst injecting drug users comprises what he calls the 'real heterosexual epidemic'. Similarly, Des Jarlais and Friedman (1987) have recently cautioned that:

Once HIV becomes established among IV drug users in a local area, drug use becomes a primary source of heterosexual and in-utero transmission. In New York city IV drug users are the apparent source of the virus in 87 per cent of the cases in which heterosexual activity is believed to be the mode of transmission, and in 80 per cent of the cases of maternally transmitted AIDS. . . . Control of the AIDS epidemic in the United States and Europe will thus require control of HIV infection among intra-venous drug users.

(Des Jarlais and Friedman 1987: 676)

Efforts aimed at limiting the spread of infection amongst injecting drug users have been hampered in the same way as attempts at explaining variations in the epidemiology of infection — namely, by how little is known about the whole area of injecting drug use; we have little information on how common such drug use is within different communities, what the patterns of such drug use are, whether injecting drug users tend to associate with other drug users or non-users, whether there are specific rituals associated with drug preparation which may have a bearing on HIV infection, whether individuals clean their injecting equipment and, if so, how and in what situations, whether they tend to lend their injecting equipment to others and, if so, why and to how many others. These are just some of the questions which are likely to have an important bearing on the spread of HIV infection amongst injecting drug users and others, but to which we have very few answers at present. Despite our lack of information on these important topics it is apparent that injecting drug use in Britain is being increasingly taken up by new social groups — among them being working-class adolescents in some of Britain's poorest inner city areas (Parker et al. 1987; Pearson 1987).

In the research that I shall describe in this chapter, an attempt has been made to make contact with a range of injecting drug users in order to identify the nature and extent of their current risk activities. This has involved contacting individuals who are themselves in contact with services as well as those who are not in contact with treatment services. It will be worth describing some of the methods used in this research.

THE STUDY[1]

The aim of this study is to collect detailed information on current levels of risk behaviour; for example, needle-sharing amongst individual drug injectors. In addition to concentrating upon young people who are currently injecting, this study also focuses upon individuals who, although they are not injecting at present, are nevertheless at risk of contracting HIV infection either through beginning to inject themselves or through establishing sexual contact with such drug injectors.

The study is taking place in an area of Glasgow that has been identified on the basis of local knowledge as a centre of drug injecting activity. It is also an area where HIV amongst the injecting drug-using population has been estimated as running currently at around 15 to 18 per cent (Goldberg 1987). The area is characterized by wide-ranging social deprivation; the social class mix is entirely working class: 54.3 per cent of the 16–19-year-old age group are unemployed, as are 53.2 per cent of 20–24-year-old age group; 93.1 per cent of households are without a car and 33.6 per cent of the households have been classified as overcrowded (McKeganey and Barnard 1988).

Methodologically this research involves a combination of different approaches: direct observation and informal interviewing of drug users at a range of naturalistic locations — for instance, on the streets, in cafés, bars, and community centres; semi-structured interviewing of drug injectors attending a range of treatment facilities — for example, needle-exchange clinic, residential detoxification and rehabilitation units, and HIV clinics; structured interviewing of individuals purchasing injecting equipment at a retail pharmacy. This combination of qualitative approaches was felt to be appropriate for a number of reasons. Given the sensitivity of the sorts of topics on which data needed to be collected — drug use, risks for HIV, needle-sharing, and sexual contacts between drug injectors and others — a necessary first step to collecting such data was to establish relationships of trusts with the various individuals concerned. Clearly, it is extremely difficult to establish such trust whilst employing a standardized instrument like a questionnaire. In addition, since the focus of this research was to explore the social meaning of activities like needle-sharing to the drug users themselves it was clearly important to adopt an approach which would allow them to convey that meaning in their own terms. It will be worth providing some illustrative examples of the use of qualitative techniques in this study.

The first fieldnote here was written following one evening's observation in a community centre:[2]

Community Centre — 22/9/88, 7.30 p.m. — 10.30 p.m.
For much of the early part of this evening I sat watching television with Kevin and Michael, both in their early twenties, neither of whom, as far as I can tell, are drug users. Once the programme we were watching finished, Kevin said that he would take me for a walk around the inner areas of the housing estate — for the most part I have stuck to the main streets. As we walked around the street, virtually empty of cars and with whole blocks boarded up, I felt as though I were in another country. For me the place had an almost eerie quality. From time to time I would look at what I thought was a derelict block and then see in the darkness the vague outlines of someone sitting at one of the windows, their faces seemingly camouflaged, noticeable only when they moved. We walked on through the estate and came to a public house which I have heard is one of the main dealing points. It is also a pub which almost everyone has warned me about entering. Still, when Kevin suggested going in I felt it would be okay since he seems really well known locally. As we entered, various people shouted a greeting to Kevin over the sound of the juke-box. We walked through to a cubicle in the back and Kevin introduced me to a group of young men saying to them that I was writing a book about this part of the city. One of the group leaned forward and indicated a spare stool. I sat down and the others introduced themselves saying that I could come in at any time and chat with them — 'Whatever you want to know we'll tell you.' Throughout all this two joints were made up and passed openly around. Two members of the group were clearly out of their minds on heroin or Temgesic and another leaned forward as if to speak but then let a long dribble of brown spittle fall to the floor in front of him. Without any doubt this is the roughest pub that I have ever been in.

On this occasion my access to one of the main drug-dealing centres was achieved on the basis of having established a personal relationship with Kevin; without that relationship there would have been no way in which I would have entered that particular setting. It is also worth pointing out here that by spending an extended period of time with the various individuals in this study, it has often been possible not only to observe their behaviour directly but also to carry out informal open-ended interviews with them on such topics as their drug use and their sharing of injecting equipment. Of course, there have been occasions when the nature of the observed activities has precluded such interviews. This was certainly apparent on the following occasion:

Community Centre (undated)
There was an edgy atmosphere in the centre tonight with a lot of toing and froing and of people huddled together watching who's arriving and who's leaving. There are people I've never seen in the centre who are older. One guy in particular, tall, maybe 40, dressed in black bomber jacket and jeans is wandering about, occasionally talking to one of the young people. Amongst the staff there is a sense that something is going on. 'Are you hanging about later?' one staff member asks of another. 'You're joking' he answers, 'not tonight.' A car pulls up outside and the driver, suited, gets out. Though there did not appear to be a mass exodus, I notice that virtually all of the young people who were in the room at that time have drifted out. Throughout all this I am sat at one table with a couple of staff and one young lad. To me it seems a bit like something out of a film and I joke that I'll go out and interview some of the kids. 'I wouldn't do that if I were you,' one of the staff says and I can tell he's not joking. As the kids drift back in the staff watch closely what is happening until the young lad at our table says simply, 'You're clocking too much.' It is apparent, even to me, that some kind of major drugs transaction has just occurred. The tall guy is no longer around and the car has departed.

Plainly it would have been very unwise, and potentially dangerous, to have attempted anything more than a very detached observational monitoring of these events.

Although it has been possible to use the more unstructured techniques of observation and informal interviewing within such settings as the community centres, bars, and so on, within the retail pharmacy it has been necessary to adopt a more structured approach to data collection. Broadly, there are two reasons for this: (1) the fact that many individuals only purchase injecting equipment once they have already purchased the drugs to be used and therefore are unlikely to want to spend an extended period of time talking informally with a researcher, and (2) the importance of reducing to a

119

minimum any disruption to the existing routines of the pharmacy posed by, for example, having groups of drug injectors spending time standing around within the pharmacy.

As an alternative method, data were collected in the pharmacy by using a short, structured questionnaire that was delivered verbally to the various individuals purchasing injecting equipment; their answers were transferred on to a standardized sheet once the interviews had been completed. This questionnaire covered information on the following list of topics: the nature and extent of their drug use; the age at which they had begun injecting; whether they would consider switching their drug use from injecting to non-injecting; whether they were worried about AIDS, knew anyone with AIDS; whether they felt they would be able to avoid contracting the virus; whether they cleaned their equipment and, if so, how; whether they shared their equipment with others; whether they were worried about contracting AIDS sexually and took precautions to minimize that risk. Interviews using this questionnaire have been conducted with sixty-five drug injectors. One of the benefits of having used a short questionnaire in this way has been the capacity to collect information on the same topics from a range of different individuals. In addition, it has also been possible to compile fieldnotes on each interview.

It had been agreed within this setting that the pharmacist and his shop assistants would ask individuals purchasing equipment if they would mind having a confidential chat with a researcher, which would take place in a small part of the shop shielded from the main area. The following extract from my fieldnote diary illustrates the use of this approach within the pharmacy setting:

Chemist Shop 27/8/88
This young man (18 years old) said that there was still a lot of sharing in the part of Glasgow he was living in: 'I've had people come up to me and ask for ma works and when I tell them I have the virus they still ask'. At one point in the conversation I asked him if he used his needle until it was too blunt to use any more or whether he resharpened it — he then reached into a breast pocket of his windcheater and produced a dirty, rolled-up piece of tissue paper within which he kept his needle. I noticed that my anxiety level at this point peaked and I became uncomfortably aware of how confined a space I was interviewing him in. At this point he dropped the needle to the floor and I think I must have involuntarily moved

to pick it up because he said, 'Don't do that. I'll pick it up', and indeed he reached forward, collected it up, re-wrapped it in the tissue paper and returned it to his pocket. I am certain that the reason he did this was in the knowledge that the needle may well have had the virus in it. I was both impressed by his reaction and shocked at my own.

On this occasion it was the awareness of potential danger associated with the proximity of a possibly infected needle which gave rise to my anxiety. In the main, however, interviews conducted within this setting have been quite unproblematic. As a result of the close and trusting relationship which the pharmacist has been able to establish with the drug-injecting individuals purchasing equipment it has been possible to get them to accept the presence of a researcher within that setting.

Having outlined the approaches taken in the study, I would now like to focus on the extent of drug use within the study area generally and the sharing of unsterile injecting equipment in particular.

DRUG USE IN THE COMMUNITY

I have already noted that the study area was identified on the basis of local knowledge of its being a centre of drug-injecting activity. From contacts established with a wide range of young people at a street level it was clear that many of them had experience of having used various drugs:

Community Centre (undated)
Eddy, one of the boys I had explained my research interests to, beckoned me over to a group of eight or nine lads whose ages ranged from fifteen to eighteen.

'They want to know what you're interested in,' he explained. I described the project as simply as I could and the group began to talk about drugs. 'They're everywhere,' one of them said, and the others nodded in agreement. I asked if they themselves used any drugs and this produced a quite astonishing list: DFs (DF118), Dope, Jellies (Temazepam), Sulph (amphetamine sulphate). I asked if any of them had used heroin and none of them said they did. 'That's a mug's game,' one of them commented. Later a couple of the lads I had been talking to approached and said that they had used heroin but only occasionally.

121

What was often most striking about such occasions, apart from the bewildering array of drugs that would be mentioned, was the matter-of-fact way in which drugs were spoken about. Even amongst those people who said that they personally had never used drugs, there seemed to be a widespread acceptance that drugs were a part of their world:

Community Centre (undated)
Mark: 'I could take you to a café only a few minutes walk from here and by the time you had reached the counter ten people would have asked you what you wanted.'

Although such drugs as DF118, Temazepam, and Temgesic were spoken of in a way which signalled their acceptance within the young people's culture, heroin was spoken of as something that was qualitatively different. In his study of the hippy culture in Sunderland, Willis (1977) noted the way in which heroin was regarded with awe by individuals who freely admitted using a range of other drugs. Heroin, for Willis' respondents, was spoken of as something which signalled a fundamental break with straight society:

To get to heroin was not just to pass through the symbolic barrier dividing the straight from the hip, it was the unanswerable closure of relations with the straight world. . . . On H you had not only made the passage to that extreme degree, you had burnt your boats and could not return.

(Willis 1977: 117)

Although heroin was not spoken about in quite the same way as many of the other drugs the young people had tried, it was not spoken of in the dramatic terms of Willis' respondents; rather, it appeared to be becoming an increasingly accepted part of life within the area. Many of the young people commented how freely available heroin now was:

Community Centre (undated)
Mike: 'It [heroin] is all over the area now. I know one fourteen-year-old who's using. When I started you had to look for it. Now you have to work to avoid it. I could take you to a place just down the road and get some stuff. It's good, not great, but good.'

Others explained that the quality of the heroin that was available was so poor and that it had been 'cut with such rubbish', that they preferred injecting Temgesic tablets or the contents of Temazepam capsules, the pharmacological purity of which they could be assured.

This impression of how widely available injectable drugs were within the study area was further underlined by interviews carried out with a range of service providers (McKeganey and Boddy 1988). One general practitioner, for example, recounted with dismay a recent consultation with a young man who had consulted saying that he wished to give up heroin (McKeganey 1988). The doctor esti- mated his chances of success as poor, and explained the reasons for his pessimism:

> We estimated that within a small area round his flat there were seventy dealing points. There were two on his floor and at least another six on the floor below. He could hardly go out of his flat without half a dozen people offering him smack.

This impression of the extent of drug misuse within the area has been underlined by more statistically oriented research in Glasgow. Haw (1985) reviewed referrals to formal drug clinics in the city, and identi- fied what she described as 'a rapid and linear increase' between 1980 and 1983. Somewhat earlier Ditton and Speirits (1981) had identified an increase of almost 400 per cent in referrals to the two main drug clinics in Glasgow for the first half of 1981.

There seems little question that over the last few years Glasgow has been experiencing an epidemic of injecting drug use. Certainly the extent of this epidemic was very evident in the study area where injecting drug use for many young people had become almost a commonplace activity (McKeganey 1987).

THE SHARING OF INJECTING EQUIPMENT

Although there remains a good deal of uncertainty as to the relative proportions of the HIV epidemic which are due to needle-sharing and sexual transmission, it is now widely accepted that the sharing of unsterile injecting equipment represents one of the highest-risk activities for contracting and spreading HIV infection. In both Britain and other European countries measures have been under- taken aimed at reducing the levels of equipment sharing amongst injecting drug users. Principally, these methods have involved a combination of (1) education as to the risks of sharing, and/or (2) the provision of clean injecting equipment — the 'needle exchange schemes' (Stimson *et al.* 1988). In the United States, where the provision of clean injecting equipment has been deemed politically unacceptable, in some cities a good deal of emphasis has been placed on providing drug injectors with the means for sterilizing their equipment.

Efforts aimed at limiting the sharing of injecting equipment, however, have been hampered by how little is known about current levels of sharing, about the social context within which sharing occurs, and about the social meaning of such sharing to the individuals themselves. Clearly, if one is going to design intervention strategies that are to have anything more than an incidental chance of success, then it is very important to collect information on each of these topics. The data collected from the pharmacy interviews (N = 65) has proved very helpful in exploring the extent of equipment sharing, its social meaning to drug injectors, and the social contexts in which it is occurring. Before looking in detail at these topics it will be helpful to outline certain features of the pharmacy sample.

The age and sex differentiation of this sample is shown in Table 5.1. As can be seen from this, there is a male to female ratio of approximately 3:1, with the average age of females purchasing equipment being 22.2 years and males 24.1 years; 23.5 per cent of the females and 22.9 per cent of the males interviewed were under 20 years of age. The fact that males outweigh females in this sample may indicate a number of things. It may indicate that more males than females are involved in injecting drugs. Certainly, a good deal of research has suggested a similar sex differentiation in patterns of injecting drug use (Des Jarlais *et al.* 1988; Haw 1985). This ratio may also indicate, however, that female drug injectors find it more difficult than males to purchase sterile injecting equipment. Once again, research has shown that injecting drug use carries with it a greater negative sanction for females than amongst males, particularly where the females involved are mothers (Rosenbaum 1981). In the light of such research it would be entirely understandable if many women found the experience of purchasing such equipment — thereby effectively declaring the fact of their drug use to others — prohibitively embarrassing. This sex ratio may also indicate a division of labour amongst drug-using couples such that the purchasing of the drug to be used and the injecting equipment is seen as a male rather than a female responsibility. Finally, of course, this ratio of 3:1 may well represent a combination of all of these factors.

Table 5.1 Age and sex differentiation of pharmacy sample of drug injectors

Age	17	18	19	20	21	22	23	24	25	26	27	28	29	30	31	32	33	34	35
Female	—	1	3	2	2	4	—	2	—	1	—	1	—	—	1	—	—	—	—
Male	2	4	5	4	3	5	2	2	2	2	3	3	2	5	1	—	1	1	1

In Table 5.2 it is possible to examine the length of time injecting of those individuals purchasing equipment. These figures need to be regarded with some caution, however, since they are based on the individuals' own estimate of when they began injecting rather than a detailed and rigorous examination of their drug-using career. It should not be assumed, either, that the figures reported here refer to periods of continuous drug injecting since some individuals reported periods when they had ceased injecting.

Table 5.2 Length of time injecting*

Time	2 mth	6 mth	1 yr	1.5 yr	2 yr	3 yr	4 yr	5 yr	6 yr	7 yr	8 yr	9 yr	10 yr	11 yr	12 yr	13 yr	14 yr	15 yr
Females	1	—	1	2	1	—	3	1	—	1	3	—	—	—	—	—	—	—
Males	—	2	2	1	—	6	8	3	9	2	2	1	5	1	2	—	—	1

*Length of time injecting was not obtained for 4 females and 3 males.

As can be seen here, there is a wide variation in the length of injecting career, from 2 months to 15 years, with an average for females of 4.17 years and for males of 5.83 years. Once again this may be signigicant in indicating a reluctance on the part of younger and more recently initiated drug injectors to begin purchasing clean equipment.

In Table 5.3, I look specifically at the question of sharing unsterile injecting equipment, and divide this between (1) being asked to lend used needles and syringes, (2) being prepared to make use of injecting equipment that had been used by others, (3) being prepared to make one's own injecting equipment available to others, and (4) being prepared neither to borrow nor lend used equipment.[3]

The data here certainly indicate that a culture of sharing, of asking to borrow used equipment, and of making used equipment available for others' use, remains. There is also a marked discrepancy here between the preparedness to lend and the preparedness to borrow.

Table 5.3 Lending and borrowing behaviour amongst a sample of injecting drug users

	Males (N = 48)	Females (N = 17)	Total (N = 65)
Report being asked to lend used needles and syringes	35(73%)	10(59%)	45(69%)
Report having recently borrowed or being prepared to borrow other's used injecting equipment	16(33%)	4(24%)	20(31%)
Report having recently lent or being prepared to lend own injecting equipment	30(62%)	8(47%)	38(58%)
Report that are neither prepared to borrow or lend	10(21%)	2(12%)	12(18%)

Although less than a third of those asked were prepared to engage in the personally risky activity of borrowing, well over half were still prepared to lend equipment. Lending injecting equipment in this way carries little personal risk provided that the lender sterilizes the returned equipment or refuses to accept its return, something which many of the interviewed individuals reported. However, such lending is likely to spread HIV infection. It is particularly important to note that only a small proportion of the total sample (18 per cent) reported being neither prepared to lend nor borrow used injecting equipment.

In the remainder of this section I would like to draw upon the ethnographic data collected in this study to look at some of the contexts within which the sharing of injecting equipment was reported to have occurred. Broadly, these were: (1) situations of a general lack of availability of clean equipment; (2) situations of specific unavailability; (3) situations where individuals were anxious or embarrassed about acquiring clean equipment; (4) situations where individuals were unconcerned by the risks involved in sharing; (5) situations where the sharing of equipment had a symbolic meaning in signalling family or friendship ties; and (6) situations where individuals were concerned to help one another out. Although it is certainly possible to differentiate between these situations, it will become apparent that there may be a good deal of overlap between them within any particular episode of sharing.

1 Situations of a general lack of availability[4]

It might seem rather curious that one can speak of a general lack of availability of clean injecting equipment within an area where, at least as far as the pharmacy was concerned, something in the region of 3,000 to 4,000 needles and syringes were being sold on a monthly basis. Nevertheless, the fact that the area was so well served in terms of the provision of clean injecting equipment did not mean that there were no situations of a general shortage of supply. Perhaps the clearest example of this occurring was once the pharmacy had closed for the night at 6.00 p.m. At such time the general lack of availability of injecting equipment within the area became clearly apparent:

Grieg Street/Ashburn Street Junction 23/8/88
This evening from 7.30 to 10.30 p.m. I spent the time hanging around the main drug dealing area. As on previous occasions I noticed various small groups of young men hanging around Grieg Street which is a well-known centre for drug dealing. Despite recognizing a few faces, however, I was conscious of not wanting to be seen observing their behaviour, so for the most part I simply leant up against the railings eating some fish and chips. I noticed the groups walking hurriedly from one locale to another in a way which I now recognize as part of the search for drugs. One group walked hurriedly past me on up the hill either having scored themselves or been provided with an address as to who is holding drugs tonight. It occurred to me that if this group are successful in their search then unless they have already purchased equipment then they will have to share. I don't think I have ever had such an acute sense of how separate the mechanisms for providing needles and drugs are — not only physically but also in terms of time. The buying and selling of drugs is in full flow here and the only place where needles can be bought closed down three hours ago.

Although this fieldnote does not report upon an actual instance of sharing, nevertheless it does illustrate very well something of the general context within which such sharing may occur.

2 Situation-specific gaps in availability

In situations of this kind the sharing of unsterile equipment occurred as a result of sterile equipment not being available within the immediate situation in which the drugs were being used. Perhaps the clearest example of this was provided by one male drug injector who was interviewed within a residential detoxification facility. He described his most recent experience of having shared equipment with others in the following way:

Parkhead Detoxification Unit 11/6/88
Stephen (early twenties) described himself as starting on drugs (glue) when he was twelve and then gradually progressing through hash, amphetamine sulphates, LSD to injecting heroin and Temgesic. I asked him to describe the last time that he had shared needles with others: 'There was three of us and we had gone over to the pub in . . . to buy some Tems [Temgesic]. It was about 12.00 in the afternoon and we'd picked up a bottle of water to hit it up. Walking back over the golf course we hit the Tems up using the one set of works.' Stephen then added that following this he had become quite anxious that he might have contracted AIDS. I asked him if the other two were good friends of his. 'Well, no good friends like but they were people I had grown up with, I knew them to say "hello" to but they weren't people I hung about with.'

Although clean injecting equipment was available at this time of day from the pharmacist near to where the drugs were purchased it was not available within the specific situation in which the drugs were being injected. What was also striking about the situation as described here was the fact that, far from being an impromptu outing, the search for drugs involved a degree of planning which, while it extended to the acquisition of water to dissolve the drugs, did not include the acquisition of clean injecting equipment. This particular episode of equipment sharing occurred then as a direct result of sterile equipment not being available in the immediate situation within which the drugs were being used, nor of its purchase being part of the planned preparation process. The fact that that setting was a golf course gives some indication of the magnitude of the task of ensuring that clean injecting equipment should be available in the range of settings in which drugs are used.

It is worth stressing here that the question of availability, both generally and in specific situations, does not simply refer to any injecting equipment but rather to particular types of equipment. This was apparent, for example, on the following occasion:

Chemist Shop — 9/8/88
Interview with twenty-year-old male drug injector
'Last night I let this lassie use ma works. I had some smack which I gave her — she only uses Tems in a 1 mm spike (needle) so the smack needed a 2 mm spike. She asked if she could use ma orange but I gave her ma blue instead. But if I hadnae had the blue I would have given her ma orange. I've been in prison and I've used lots of different people's tools really manky [dirty] sets of works. I think that most people would tell you that if they had smack and no tools they would use what was around.'

The sharing described in this extract arose out of a combination of the drug being used (heroin) and the type of needle required.

3 Anxiety at purchasing equipment

As I have noted, in any situation where drug use carries with it a negative social sanction it is highly likely that some individuals will find the purchasing of equipment, or the attendance at needle-exchange clinics, prohibitively embarrassing. It is in the nature of negative evidence, however, that it is extremely hard to illustrate this occurring in practice. In the extract below, though, it is possible to gain some idea of this process:

Chemist Shop — 27/5/88
Interview with 19-year-old female drug injector
This girl described herself as having been injecting for one year. I asked her about AIDS and she said that she was worried about it and that she flushed her own needles out with bleach. She added that although she has been asked for a loan of her works she always says 'No, I don't even share with my boyfriend.' This girl then said that she was in a hurry because she had a girlfriend waiting outside — 'This other set is for her, she's really embarrassed about coming in and buying them so I do it for her.'

It is at least conceivable that if the girl waiting outside of the pharmacy had not been able to identify a friend who could purchase equipment for her then she might have been more inclined to use another individual's injecting equipment.

4 Lack of concern

Each of the situations so far described suggests that the sharing of injecting equipment has been conceived as something which would not have occurred had clean injecting equipment been more widely and readily available. However, there certainly were occasions when the sharing of equipment arose out of the fact that the individuals involved were unconcerned or insufficiently concerned about the risks involved. For some of the individuals observed and interviewed in this study, the risks of contracting HIV infection simply represent one more risk in a lifestyle characterized by risk — for example, the risk of overdosing, of contracting Hepatitis B, of suffering abscesses, of being arrested, of being ripped off whilst purchasing drugs, or of failing to generate sufficient funds to buy drugs.

For some individuals there seemed to be an almost fatalistic attitude that the risks involved in their lifestyle were so wide-ranging that failure in some respect seemed almost inevitable. For others there seemed a belief in the pre-determination of certain events:

> *Briony Place. Residential Detoxification Unit 29/4/88*
> *Discussion with Mickey and Greg (late twenties)*
> Both of them described a long history of injecting drugs. I asked about AIDS and HIV, to which Mickey responded, 'If it's for you it'll no go past you', adding that he wasn't worried about AIDS at all. A bit surprised by his answer I asked if that meant he had not changed his drug use since AIDS and HIV became known about. 'No', he replied. Asked directly about sharing he said, 'If you want a hit and it's there and you've no yer own works you'll use somebody else's.' Asked if he meant that he, himself, would share he agreed that yes, he would and he had.

One can see here that if AIDS/HIV infection is seen as something about which very little can be done to minimize one's chances of becoming infected, then the whole question of reducing the numbers of people with whom one is sharing equipment becomes rather meaningless. It is hardly surprising if those individuals maintaining such a view persist in high-risk activities of one kind or another.

5   The symbolic significances of sharing

In *The Gift*, Mauss (1954)[5] has examined the centrality of the gift-giving relationship within North American Indian and Melanesian societies. In particular, Mauss was able to show how the various rights and obligations associated with the process of giving and receiving gifts served to construct the social reality of relationships within these societies:

> It follows clearly from what we have seen that in the system of ideas one gives away what is in reality a part of one's nature and substance, while to receive something is to receive a part of someone's spiritual essence. . . . Whatever it is — food, possessions, women, children or ritual, it retains a magical and religious hold over the recipient. The thing given is not inert. It is alive and often personified, and strives to bring to its original clan and homeland some equivalent to take its place.
>
> (Mauss 1954: 10)

Although it would be inappropriate to draw too close an analogy between the giving and receiving of gifts within these societies and the lending and borrowing of injecting equipment within our society, nevertheless it is apparent that on certain occasions the sharing of equipment may itself be pregnant with meaning, in signalling the depth of a relationship between friends and family members. Some indication of this can be seen in the extracts below:

Chemist Shop — 2/9/88
This afternoon a group of four young men (all in their 20s) entered the shop and purchased one set of works (injecting equipment). I chatted to them in the main area of the shop and asked first if they ever shared works. 'No', one of them answered, 'we only use each other's, we're a team. We get asked for a shot of our works but we dinna bother.' I asked if they were not worried about contracting AIDS/HIV and one of them answered that he 'was just out of gaol and they tested ma blood there so if I had the virus they would have told me so I know that I'm in the clear'.

Chemist Shop — 10/3/88
This afternoon I interviewed two male drug users. We talked in the side area of the shop. I sat on one of the chairs and the younger of the two (late teens) sat on the knees of the older (early twenties) on

the one remaining chair. I asked them about sharing other people's equipment and the older one added, 'I use his works' (pointing to the younger one). I asked if he was not worried about contracting AIDS. 'No', he laughed, 'anyway, he's ma brother so if he wis gonna die then I'd want to die too.'

In the first extract it is striking that the group did not regard use of each other's equipment as sharing. 'Sharing' involved either using the equipment of people outside their group, or making their own equipment available to such others; it specifically did not refer to making their equipment available to each other. Their use of each other's equipment was justifiable to them in terms of their identity 'as a team'. One can see here that the perception that anybody might infect anybody else with the virus actually runs quite counter to the notions of group solidarity underlying such social relationships. Similarly, the fact that one is dealing here with a virus can lead to a terminal illness, far from undermining such sharing, in fact makes it all the more impressive as a way of signalling friendship or familial solidarity.

6   Helping somebody out

In the previous section I looked at the way in which the sharing of injecting equipment could signal the depth of a relationship between friends or family members. In addition to this it was also apparent that some sharing occurred between individuals who otherwise had very little contact with each other and for whom there was clearly no equivalent need to display the depth of their relationship. This can be seen, for example, in the following extract:

Chemist Shop — 4/10/88
Gary (mid-twenties) came into the shop today asking the chemist for a set of syringes and showing him his badly swollen ankles. 'I went to ma doctor with these but he just said don't bother pulling your trouser legs up. He did'na want tae know.' Gary then chatted to me about how he had been out the previous night at the junction of two streets (a known dealing point) when a group of people whose faces he recognized but whom he did not know very well asked him if he had a set of works (syringe and needle). Gary — 'I said that if they wanted ma used set it was up to them but I did'na want them back.'

In seeking to understand the sharing of injecting equipment between relative strangers, certain characteristics of the wider culture amongst people generally in the study area, and the specific culture amongst the drug injectors, are relevant. Perhaps the first point to note here is that amongst people generally within the study area there was a highly developed sense of mutual support; individuals could be seen sharing virtually every facet of their everyday lives — cigarettes, alcohol, food, sweets, soft drinks, and so on. The arrangements for looking after young children can be taken as an illustration of such widespread sharing:

Community Centre (undated)
The community centre tonight was busier than on previous occasions with quite a few groups of young women (early twenties) sitting chatting and drinking coffee. I sat with another group of younger girls (mid-teens), one of whom was writing out 'lines' that she had been given that day at school. There were also quite a few children running round who did not seem to me to be associated with particular adults. Rather it was as if all of the adults, including the teenagers, were keeping an eye on the children, correcting them and calling out to them, sitting them down next to them at different times. I later realized that the children were with their mothers though it had been impossible for me to identify family ties — rather it was as if the children were communal property. I was reminded in this of a conversation I had had earlier with a junkie who, on learning that I was from London, commented that it was a violent place where kids were in danger on the streets at night. 'It's different here', he explained, 'they could be on the street till 11.00 at night and everyone would keep an eye on them.'

It is important to stress that, when considered in the context of this deep-seatedly social culture, the sharing of injecting equipment can be seen not so much as a deviant and irrational activity, but rather as part and parcel of the dominant culture of sharing and mutual support.

With respect to the specific drug-using culture, it is worth pointing out that the illicit nature of the drug economy makes it very dependent for its survival upon a level of mutual support and sharing amongst drug users. This can be seen most clearly in relation to the pooling of local knowledge as to the availability of different drugs:

Ashgrove Detoxification Unit — 23/3/88
Interview with James, twenty-one-year-old injecting drug user
James described how he had been injecting Temgesic for the last 9 months. I asked if he was worried about AIDS: 'Not at the time but ah've thought a lot about it since.' I then asked him where he got his needles and syringes and he said at the chemist. He then added that a group of friends would buy a set and share it amongst themselves. James then explained how easy it was to buy drugs locally — 'I can go out on to the street, go up to anybody and ask who's got what and they'll tell me and you just follow that up.'

The sharing of injecting equipment can be seen as a further feature of the interdependence between drug injectors exemplified in the pooling of local knowledge. Certainly there were very few individuals who did not feel an obligation to help out others who found themselves in the position of having drugs to inject but no equipment to inject with. Significantly, this obligation remained even amongst those individuals who commented that they would not themselves re-use equipment which they had lent in this way. Such lending behaviour, however, is unlikely to be of a purely altruistic nature since individuals making their injecting equipment available to others will be doing so at least in part in the knowledge that, should they find themselves in a position of need, then they too could ask others for a loan of their equipment.

SOCIAL POLICY AND SOCIOLOGICAL IMPLICATIONS

I began this chapter by noting the upswing in interest in a social problems perspective that had occurred in sociology over the last few years. I noted that this shift was very apparent in the area of AIDS-related research projects where there was a definite concern on the part of medical sociologists in particular to demonstrate that a sociological contribution could amount to more than a contribution to sociology. It is appropriate to end this chapter now by considering the social policy implications of the research described in this chapter and the implications for medical sociology of adopting a social problems perspective.

The social policy implications of this research have largely to do with the sharing of unsterile injecting equipment. By adopting an ethnographic perspective it has been possible not only to elucidate the social meaning of needle-sharing to drug injectors themselves but also to locate that sharing within the social context in which it occurs. Within these terms such sharing has been shown as a complex phenomenon with a multiplicity of causes and social meanings. Whereas some of these causes are undoubtedly tied to the question of the availability of clean injecting equipment, others relate to notions of risk, risk avoidance, and individual and group relationships between drug injectors. In the face of this complexity it will be necessary to combine a range of approaches in the design of intervention strategies aimed at reducing the levels of sharing amongst injecting drug users. Whilst the provision of clean injecting equipment may reduce the situations of general shortage, nevertheless situations of specific unavailability are likely to remain so long as the systems for providing drugs and for providing clean equipment are not brought into closer alignment. One way in which this might be achieved would be through contacting drug dealers and encouraging them to distribute clean equipment, or alternatively through attempting to set up points for the distribution of clean injecting equipment within or adjacent to centres of known drug dealing. Detailed ethnographic knowledge of the local drug culture within given geographic areas would obviously be of enormous benefit in identifying locations for such distribution points.

It is also apparent that, although the wider provision of clean equipment might remove situations of general or specific unavailability, it is less likely to influence sharing which arises from a lack of concern as to the risks involved or from the signalling of family or friendship ties. In addition to the provision of such equipment, there is also a need for allied educational interventions aimed at informing drug injectors of the risks involved. In designing such interventions some attempt will have to be made not only to stress the risks involved as these are conceived from within a medical perspective, but also to address the meaning and significance of such sharing to the individuals involved. It also seems likely that campaigns aimed to prevent the sharing of injecting equipment will need to focus not only on encouraging individuals to acquire clean equipment but on the safe disposal of that equipment or its effective sterilization in situations where it is to be used by others. In addition, drug injectors need to be encouraged to recognize that, although the lending of injecting equipment carries with it a low personal risk to them in the short term (so long as they do not re-use that equipment or sterilize it before re-use), nevertheless such lending can further the spread of HIV over time and thereby increase their own risk of infection either sexually or otherwise in the long term.

Finally, in considering the implications for sociology of adopting a social problems perspective, I noted earlier that one of the reasons why sociologists had been reluctant to adopt such a perspective was a feeling that by allowing other, often more established, professional groups to define one's topical concerns, one might lose the capacity to think sociologically. Obviously one can only convincingly argue this case by defining what thinking sociologically means — which there is not the space to do here. Nevertheless, I would argue that an element of what thinking sociologically involves is the capacity to conceptualize a given topic in terms other than how that topic may be typically addressed.

Part of the danger facing sociologists adopting a social problems perspective in the field of AIDS-related research, where the demand for information that can be of immediate practical value is so great, is that of foreclosing upon any line of enquiry which either calls into question the dominant biomedical definition of the phenomenon or which seems unlikely to produce information of immediate practical value.[6] Within such a perspective the space left for the more speculative and academic consideration of social phenomena can become very small indeed. One of the challenges then facing sociologists adopting such a perspective may be one of providing information which is of practical value whilst also contributing to the body of sociological work.

In the study that I have described here an attempt is being made to produce an ethnography of risk-taking behaviour which, in its focus upon such topics as needle-sharing, is of relevance to AIDS policy but, by examining such a topic within the local culture in which it surfaces is also of relevance to the wider discipline of sociology itself.

ACKNOWLEDGEMENTS

For comments on an earlier version of this chapter I am grateful to Marina Barnard and Sarah Cunningham-Burley. The research reported in this chapter is being funded by a grant from the Economic and Social Research Council as part of their AIDS initiative. I am grateful to Margaret Dobbs for providing secretarial support on this project.

NOTES

1 Data for this study are being collected by myself working as a medical sociologist and Marina Barnard working as a social anthropologist.
2 Where names are used in this chapter they have been changed in order to protect the anonymity of respondents.
3 These activities are not of course mutually exclusive.
4 Within any individual episode of equipment-sharing more than one of these contexts may be present.
5 I am grateful to Marina Barnard for bringing Mauss's essay on the topic of gift-giving and receiving to my attention.
6 It is worth pointing out that the AIDS field itself provides ample evidence of the importance of sustaining lines of enquiry that appear to be of little practical value. Certainly in the period prior to the identification of HIV research into retroviruses was itself regarded as an area that was unlikely to produce findings of much practical human import. It would be difficult to find a more relevant area of research now, however (Schilts 1987).

Chapter Six

DRINK IS ALL RIGHT IN MODERATION: ACCOUNTS OF ALCOHOL USE AND ABUSE FROM MALE GLASWEGIANS

KENNETH MULLEN

INTRODUCTION

The concept of ambivalence is pervasive in the literature on attitudes towards alcohol use (Dight 1976; Rix and Buyer 1976; Mulford and Miller 1960; Heather and Robertson 1985; Marlatt and Nathan 1978; Pittman and Snyder 1962). In a study of Scottish drinking habits, Dight (1976) found that subjects tended to agree both with 'pro' and 'anti' drinking statements, showing that positive and negative attitudes towards drinking coexisted within the same person. A greater degree of ambivalence, however, was discovered among men. Similarly, in a comprehensive review of the alcohol literature, Marlatt and Nathan (1978) found that all national surveys and a large proportion of smaller-scale studies documented conflict within individuals and between groups about drinking. Such ambivalence was found in various areas: with regard to alcoholism, the beneficial or harmful effects of alcohol, and how to deal with alcohol problems.

One of the major attempts to state the idea of ambivalence in theoretical form is that provided by Pittman (1967). In his book *Alcoholism*, Pittman discusses the nature of the ambivalent cultures to be found in America and most other western nations. He describes such cultures as those in which there is 'a conflict between co-existing value structures' (Pittman 1967: 8). Pittman first describes the two opposing poles of value structure, the pro-drinking and abstinent sentiments, to be found within American society. Pro-drinking groups view drinking as hospitable and sociable; abstinent groups view drinking as sinful and hedonistic. These extremes of value orientation are then seen to lead to conflict within the attitudes of the majority, of drinkers within a society.

Pittman also discusses a different form of attitudinal ambivalence, one in which individuals hold different attitudes towards different aspects of alcohol use: 'Another type of ambivalence noted by Krauweel in the Netherlands is that some societies, such as the Dutch, accept drinking but reject the drinker who becomes an alcoholic' (Pittman 1967: 8). This type of ambivalence has been identified by other researchers (Stivers 1976; Dight 1976; Heather and Robertson 1985; Crawford 1987).

Attitudinal literature (Crawford 1987; Dight 1976) generally tends to concentrate on whether people are for or against drinking, drunkenness, and alcoholics, rather than asking people what drinking, drunkenness, and alcoholism mean for them. However, it is clear that a group of people could differ as to whether they endorsed drinking, but still be more or less in agreement that alcohol is a particular substance which affects consciousness and behaviour in particular ways. The first such component of attitudes relates to individuals' endorsement, and judgement, as to whether drinking practices are good or bad. The second component of attitudes and beliefs relates to the content of drinking practices, the 'what happens' when people drink.

It may be the case that much discussion of ambivalent cultures relates more to ambivalence over the approval or disapproval of drinking, drunkenness, and alcoholism, rather than to inconsistency of attitudinal content with regard to the effects of alcohol consumption. Of course differences in such attitudinal content have been found; for example, differences between Protestant and Catholic cultures (Mulford and Miller 1960; Mullen, Blaxter, and Dyer 1986; Skolnick 1958; Nusbaumer 1981; Schlegel and Sandborn 1979). However, it is still important to separate out judgemental statements from content statements of belief. And, of course, in general the two aspects may often be compounded in the same statement. For example, in the work of Pittman it is difficult to know if the two statements, 'drink makes people sociable' or 'drink makes people hedonistic', are two different beliefs about the effects of alcohol or, rather, approval and disapproval of the same effect of alcohol from the differing perspectives of the drinker and the abstainer.

Some of this confusion can be cleared up if we consider what have often been called the components of attitudes. In theoretical formulations attitudes are often analysed with reference to three components: (1) the cognitive (what an individual believes about an issue); (2) the affective (how an individual feels about the issue); and (3) the behavioural (how an individual is likely to react towards the issue) (Summers 1977). Ambivalence can therefore be present with regard to all or a subset of these components.

The focus of most alcohol research has tended to be on ambivalences at the affective level of attitudes towards alcohol use: how individuals feel about alcohol use rather than the meanings they attribute to alcohol use.

In this chapter I will explore aspects of ambivalence and the complexity of statements made about the effects of alcohol, through an analysis of interview material collected in a recent study on the alcohol beliefs of a group of men aged 30 to 50 living in the City of Glasgow. The study was a qualitative sociological study and so it will be helpful to highlight certain differences between the positivist and interpretive traditions within sociology and social psychology in their conceptualization of attitudes (Schwartz and Jacobs 1979; Benson and Hughes 1983).

Attitudes have been defined by Thurstone (in Summers 1977) as 'the sum total of a man's inclinations and feelings, prejudices and bias, preconceived notions, ideas, fears, threats and convictions about any specific topic' (Summers 1977: 2). For the positivist, such attitudes are deep within the individual's mind and cannot be measured directly. We can, however, get a hint of these underlying attitudes from the opinions a person has about a topic. Attitudes are therefore measured indirectly, utilizing opinions. In the course of an interview it is the respondent's opinions which are elicited by structured questioning, and these opinions are regarded as indicative of the underlying attitudes which the person may hold.

For the qualitative sociologist, however, utilizing an interpretive framework, the aim is not to get the respondent to proffer rigid opinions which can be measured and then taken as indicative of deeper, hidden attitudes, but rather to have the respondent express their ideas and feelings about a topic as fully as possible. The person is encouraged to give as many ideas on the topic as possible until s/he has exhausted what s/he has to say on the issue. Such statements are taken as accounts, given by the respondent to the interviewer about a specific topic (Schwartz and Jacobs 1979; Cicourel 1964; Scott and Lyman 1968). An account is any manner in which a respondent 'describes, analyses, questions, criticizes, believes, doubts, idealizes, or schematizes' a subject (Bittner 1973: 115). Such accounts are tied to the social settings within which they are expressed, in this case the interview. Similar accounts may be given by other members of society, some accounts by everyone, others primarily by certain social or cultural groups. Accounts may be true or false, on the level of commonsense or scientific knowledge, or may reflect stereotypes. What is important is to obtain as full a range of accounts on a particular issue as possible. Such accounts map out the common stock of knowledge held by individuals in society on a particular topic. It is with such accounts that this chapter is concerned.

The chapter covers three major themes corresponding to the three major areas of questioning about alcohol use covered in the interviews: normal drinking, drunkenness, and alcoholism. These are of course the major topics analysed in most research in this field (Crawford 1987).

Before presenting the data, however, I will give some details of the research method.

METHOD AND SAMPLE

The interview material on which the present discussion is based was collected during a recent qualitative ethnographic research study aimed at assessing the respective importance of class and religion on the health attitudes of a group of men in mid-life living in Glasgow.

The means by which the interview sample was collected has been described by Glaser and Strauss (1970) as theoretical sampling: 'The initial decisions for theoretical collection of data are based only on a general sociological perspective and on a general subject or problem area' (ibid.: 105). Since I wished to consider both social class and religious differences in beliefs between respondents, it was necessary to identify a sample of respondents which spanned these categories.

Because the sampling frame incorporated two social class categories (manual and non-manual workers) and three religious categories (Protestant, Catholic, and non-religious), it was necessary to identify respondents who would fill all six combinations of these categories. From statistical analysis of population data on Glasgow, it was clear that to obtain an adequate sample by the methods of door-knocking or random mail-shot would prove extremely costly and time-consuming. As an alternative it was possible to use a computerized list developed by the Medical Research Council's Hearing Research Unit in Glasgow. This list, which provided a random sample stratified by age and social class, fulfilled all of my research criteria apart from the determination of religious denomination. A short screening questionnaire was therefore sent to potential respondents to ascertain their religious adherence and to obtain a few details of their health status and smoking and drinking habits.

In all, 352 screening questionnaires were sent out, of which 183 were returned completed, giving a response rate of 52 per cent. Of these 183 returns, 70 were eventually interviewed (with only 4 people refusing to take part in the study). The interviews lasted from one to two hours, and were conducted either in the respondent's own home or in my office. Issues covered in the interviews included the respondents' health status, smoking and drinking behaviour, and their general attitudes towards health, tobacco, and alcohol use.

In the ethnographic interview method (Schwartz and Jacobs 1979) a strict order of questioning is not followed. If a respondent starts to talk spontaneously about one of the topics which occur later in the interview schedule, then that topic will be investigated at that time. This technique allows for a more natural, relaxed flow to the interview conversation, with the result that more in-depth answers are obtained. This method also allows issues to be probed and explored in depth, until the respondent's answers and elaborations on a topic are fully exhausted. This process can also be followed across interviews. As an area is explored in one interview a respondent may suggest new ideas on a topic which can be explored with other respondents in later interviews. All the interviews were tape recorded and transcribed verbatim.

Whenever possible respondents were interviewed on their own: either spouses or relatives left the main room, or the respondent and I moved to another room in the house. On the few occasions when spouses did remain in the main room, in general because of the impracticality of going anywhere else, it was not my impression that the respondents were significantly modifying their views. On the rare occasions when spouses did comment, this often had the effect of encouraging respondents to clarify rather than to change their own views. For example, when I asked one respondent what they would do if someone started smoking in a non-smoking area, the interview went as follows:

Husband: If I was, it would depend.
Wife: I think you would, I think.

Husband: If there was a lot of people there, I think, and nobody said anything, em, I think I would be inclined to approach them and just tell them that it is a non-smoking area and to move out, move out of it. . . . If there was nobody else there I would be less inclined, and he wasn't too close, or she wasn't too close to me, yes it wouldn't bother me. (R.652)

I will now briefly detail some of the characteristics of the respondents. The majority (60 per cent) were from manual occupational backgrounds, although at the time of this study seven were unemployed and five were permanently sick or disabled. In terms of religious backgrounds there were almost even numbers of Protestants and Catholics in my sample (28 as opposed to 29), although Catholics were more likely to describe themselves as going to church once a month or more. Thirteen in my sample described themselves as being non-religious. Most were married (73 per cent), with only one being separated and three divorced. Most had been born in Glasgow (78 per cent.)

The drinking characteristics of these respondents were as follows: 32 per cent described themselves as moderate drinkers, the most chosen self-categorization. Ten described themselves as hardly drinking, sixteen as drinking a little, thirteen as drinking a lot, and four as drinking heavily. One respondent had never drunk.

I shall now turn to the analysis of the accounts of alcohol use and abuse given by these respondents during the course of the ethnographic interviews. I will be particularly concerned to elucidate the meaning of any ambivalence expressed in the respondents' accounts, and to relate my findings to those of other researchers. I will begin by focusing on the general, most prevalent, ideas held by respondents, then turn my attention to a consideration of social class and religious differences.

ATTITUDES TOWARDS ALCOHOL USE

Among respondents there was a general approval of drinking. Even among those who hardly drank themselves there appeared to be no strong anti-drink feelings. Their pro-drink attitudes, however, were generally qualified; drinking was seen to be all right in moderation. In terms of what the respondents meant by 'moderation', it was clear that many had assimilated information from various health sources. As one respondent stated.

'I have read that it is better to drink a few glasses of wine a week or have a couple of drinks a week than it is to have nothing to drink at all.' (R.21)

In moderation, alcohol was either seen to be beneficial to health or — another common response — not too damaging. When asked how it was beneficial to health, respondents generally gave the reply that it reduced stress. When questioned as to whether some drinks were healthier than others they often said that there were no differences between drinks. Some, however, believed that spirits were more damaging. As one respondent said:

'spirits, it's more pure alcohol . . . at the end of the day you've got to drink a lot of beer to get it to do what maybe a couple of whiskies can do, or a couple of gins, so I would think spirits are more unhealthy than lagers.' (R.6)

Although most respondents had no objections to women drinking, general disapproval was expressed at the idea of seeing women drunk. Such responses were often linked to the idea of women's relationship to home and family. A typical response was:

'It does not look right to see women drinking to excess. It does not seem right to see a woman drunk in the street or anything like that.' (R.170)

Adolescent or teenage drinking was something about which many respondents spoke even more negatively. In particular this related to under-age drinking and mainly to the style of drinking behaviour to be found among young people: drinking by groups in public spaces (parks, waste grounds, around housing estates) or unsupervised drinking in bars, discothèques, and hotels. Solutions were often suggested for the problem of youth drinking: for example, some respondents felt the need for more health education in schools and others thought that children should be introduced to alcohol in the home.

In general, drinking in moderation was seen to be a good thing. But why did people drink? Overwhelmingly, respondents said that they drank to be sociable. As one stated:

'as I say . . . in my group it's sociable you know, I don't think there's any other reason I drink you know.' (R.3)

Social reasons for drinking were endorsed even among those who were faced with having to give up drink for medical reasons:

'as I say, it's just the company I go for. If I had to I'd just go on to orange juice.' (R.28)

and by total abstainers:

'and the social reasons why the pub is there. It is a meeting place, that's why they drink.' (R.21)

Sociability in the home was also mentioned. Respondents often kept drink in their homes, but would only drink if friends came to visit.

Social drinking was seen to be linked to a person's occupation. The importance of 'liquid lunches' for arranging business deals in certain jobs was stressed, as was the obligation for lunchtime drinking in others. Occupations which required respondents to work away from home for extended periods of time were again seen to entail 'social drinking'.

A symbiotic link between sociability and alcohol use was constantly referred to in the interviews. The pub was the main, if not the only, place to meet people, and most people do drink alcohol at these times. Did drinking add to their enjoyment? And if so, how?

In general, respondents saw alcohol as acting as 'a social lubricant'. It made people 'more voluble', more 'friendly from a conversation point of view'. It was seen to be able to 'bring people out', to make people 'more outgoing'. As expressed in one interview:

'people become friendly, happy-go-lucky, as I say they seem to sort of, their troubles and cares seem to disappear for that period of time.' (R.3)

These effects were often seen to be brought about by alterations in an individual's character or personality. As one respondent put it:

'they become less of a frontage, everybody seems to have their own frontage and it drops as alcohol affects them.' (R.3)

And another explanation:

'I suppose it may react within character, except what they do is rather more pronounced . . . things tend to be heightened, the way people act.' (R.5)

Such moderate changes in people's personality allowed them to become more relaxed, and to ease their tensions.

In general, respondents were in favour of drinking in moderation, and saw people as drinking for social reasons. Alcohol was seen to produce changes in people's behaviour or personality which enhanced the social pleasures to be found in drinking. Alcohol was seen to produce an easy sociability. Without alcohol, outside the contexts in which it is obtained, in the workaday world, people often believed that the social, more relaxed, sides of their natures were suppressed. However, not all drinking is moderate. I will now turn to my respondents' attitudes towards drunkenness and alcoholism.

Just as most respondents were in favour of the 'moderate social drinker', most were against 'drunks'. 'I cannae stand them', was a common reply. Or to be more precise, they could not stand them if they were pestered by them. People could not stand drunks leaning over them, or being annoying, or aggressive. To be drunk was to stagger, to be unable to co-ordinate physical bodily movement, but also, and perhaps more importantly, to be unable to communicate appropriately. As one respondent stated of his own periods of drunkenness:

> 'I probably talk a lot, . . . talk a lot of rubbish, and I feel a kind of false bonhomie.' (R.6)

And from another respondent:

> 'somebody being drunk is somebody who cannot articulate properly . . . maybe become confused, not know what they are talking about.' (R.5)

And again:

> 'some people may repeat themselves when they've just already told you something.' (R.9)

Although most respondents mentioned slurred speech, they also mentioned inappropriate speech. There is a definite boundary with regard to speech within which alcohol increases the possibility of sociable conversation, but beyond this boundary sociable communication starts to break down.

Again, although alcohol was, in moderation, seen to produce slight alterations in mood and character leading to greater informality and sociability, any intensification of such changes were viewed in a negative light, leading respondents to re-define the drinker as being drunk. Respondents were, however, divided as to whether they

146

believed that alcohol changed an individual's personality or merely emphasized what was already there. For example, one respondent stated:

> 'if someone's a happy drunk, well then he's a nice person, but if someone's kind of a violent drunk, he's no' a nice person.' (R.6)

This seemed to be a case of bringing out the person's latent character, while typical of the other kind of response was:

> 'Well, they have changed from the person you know, you can see a difference in them and you can detect a difference in their attitude.' (R.31)

Another respondent spoke about changes in personality in this way:

> 'A false confidence, I think they've got a false confidence, a false personality.' (R.6)

It seems as if the effects of alcohol which in moderation could allow for an easy sociability could, in over-indulgence, quickly lead to types of exaggerated volubility and character change which proved unacceptable to respondents.

The unacceptability of drunks and drunken behaviour influenced respondents' reported management of situations involving drunkenness. Avoidance was a major response:

> 'I usually try and steer clear of them, avoid them like the plague if possible.' (R.3)

And again:

> 'You tend to look down on that person, if you see a drunk person. It's got a, it's a kind of social stigma, I would say that drunkenness has.' (R.9)

With regard to their own episodes of drunkenness, respondents often commented that they 'knew their limit', and when this was reached would cease their alcohol intake and disengage from the situation. This often meant going home and going to bed.

Earlier the centrality of the social functions of drinking were discussed. Again, in terms of over-indulgence, when social drinking became problem drinking, social factors were mentioned; in the context of changes in, and restraints on, their own drinking behaviour. For example, marriage and settling down were often seen to have reduced respondents' intake of alcohol. As one respondent said:

> 'No, I used to be a heavy drinker . . . but my life is settled through meeting Ann (his wife).' (R.419)

The influence of responsibilities, and the economic cost of a family, mortgage, and car, were all mentioned as setting limits to drinking patterns. Changes in occupation — for example, a move from being a self-employed businessman to being an employee in a larger firm, changing from a job which demanded stays away from home to one that did not, or a move to a job that required a clean driving licence — were again seen to safeguard the individual from problem drinking. By contrast, the lack of such restraints was seen to open the doors to problem drinking. The small businessman who kept irregular hours and always carried cash, the single man with no responsibilities, and the unemployed person who had too much time on his hands and nowhere to go apart from the public house, were all seen to be in danger.

Leading on from respondents' attitudes towards drunkenness, two ideas about alcoholism surfaced repeatedly in the interviews. Alcoholism was often seen to be closely related to heavy drinking. The slide from social drinking into alcoholism was either conceptualized as pertaining to the individual (weak character, people with problems or worries) or to categories of individuals (the unemployed, or the excessively rich or poor).

Whatever disagreements respondents had about the causes of alcoholism, however, there seemed to be almost total agreement as to the central feature of alcoholism: the notion of dependency. As one respondent said:

> 'They take every opportunity of every situation to include alcohol.' (R.8)

and again:

> 'Well, alcoholic obviously suggests some dependency on alcohol, and em, that would tend to suggest someone who, again depending on the state of alcoholism, will have a drink at breakfast time and have drinks throughout the day, throughout the evening and at first up in the morning and have another drink.' (R.4)

Although it might be a relatively simple matter to judge dependency in other people, it might not be so easy for a person to realize this of himself. This was echoed in the interviews in two forms. First was the fear that the respondent himself might be dependent on alcohol and thus potentially an alcoholic. As one stated:

'I think I must have been as near as you can get to one without knowing it.' (R.23)

And from another interview:

'You know I could be in the early stages of it myself just now and kidding myself on, but I am the only one that will really know that. I like to think that I can monitor myself to the extent that I can say well I had three drinks for my lunch yesterday, that's me for the week.' (R.31)

As the last quotation illustrates, possible dependency was checked from from time to time: often by individuals staying off alcohol for a certain period, or again, by being able to have bottles of alcohol in the house without feeling the necessity to finish them.

Second, it was recognized that other individuals may not be aware of their own dependency. As one respondent stated:

'The way things are now . . . I think people can maybe become a wee bit more dependent on it than they actually realize.' (R.9)

However, a recognition of an individual's own dependence on alcohol was seen as crucial for the possibility of help. As one interviewee said:

'But first and foremost they have to realize that they need to help themselves, they are the persons that have got to admit it to themselves that they do have a problem and they do need help.' (R.3)

SOCIAL CLASS AND RELIGION

So far in the chapter I have outlined some of the respondents' general ideas about alcohol use and abuse. I would now like to consider some of the ways in which social class and religion relate to these topics. First, was there any variation in beliefs or systematic differences between respondents from different religious and social class backgrounds? And second, since I asked respondents to give their own opinions of the effects of social class and religion on their beliefs about alcohol use, how did these opinions vary?

When analysing the interview transcripts, the clearest difference between these two groups was that respondents from manual occupations mentioned the influence which social circumstances, and the urban environment, had on drinking. For example, one respondent, a maintenance electrical welder, when asked about the problem of alcoholism said:

'I think the serious thing in Britain is lack of work. To my mind it is all back to the government. If there are people on the brew give them a job . . . so what people are doing is going for a couple of pints.' (R.419)

A general labourer also mentioned the fact that 'social pressure' led people to drink. He believed that people in some parts of the country drank more than in others:

'I think cities tend to be more. It always comes down to the stress factor.' (R.39)

Although respondents from the non-manual group did mention social factors, these were related to particular occupations: travelling salesmen, business people, and so on. Comments were related to individual types rather than being directed to general social forces.

Turning to differences between the religious groups, it was apparent that although each group displayed a range of responses from the more to the less tolerant, the balance was different for each. Differing trends could also be noted between the groups.

The non-religious and the Catholic groups had similar beliefs, although there was a greater tendency to condemn drunkenness among Catholics. Protestants tended to be more proscriptive in approach, condemning the person more than the drink.

One way of conceptualizing these differences is to place these three groups on a continuum, from the non-religious, the least proscriptive, to the Catholics in the middle, to the Protestants, the most proscriptive.

For the church-attending Catholics, drunks were 'foolish' and it was seen as 'humiliating' for a person to have lost control through drink. The non-religious often said that drunks were 'okay', as long as they did not bother them. However, a few also said they were 'daft', or that drunks were 'sad'.

Although both Protestant and Catholic respondents condemned drunkenness, there was a slight tendency for Protestant respondents to be more negative in their comments about the drunk individual;

particularly with regard to being a nuisance and lacking will-power. As one regularly attending member of the Church of Scotland said:

'There is a distinction between a heavy drinker and an alcoholic. The alcoholic must be less strong willed. A strong-willed person might know what they were leading themselves on to if they continued to drink excessively a lot of the time.' (R.158)

And another respondent who attended church once a week replied:

'I suppose there was a puritan attitude towards drink . . . the attitude drinking is bad for you and you don't drink. . . . That type of attitude is in the mind from childhood. My father is teetotal because of family circumstances, because his father at one time was a very heavy drinker. So I think this attitude has stuck with me to a certain extent.' (R.306)

Catholic respondents, by way of contrast, tended to emphasize the damage to the body:

'Well, I don't see any sense in punishing your body . . . too much alcohol is bad for you, it obviously leads to dehydration.' (R.4)

And again one respondent said the following when talking about young people drinking:

'I don't think it is a good idea to start drinking too young. . . . They have not fully developed and I would think they would really need to develop fully into adulthood before they start drinking on a regular basis. I think they could stand it better and it would give their body time to develop properly. Later on there would be less chance of them being alcoholics.' (R.156)

I will now consider respondents' own ideas about the influence of social class and religion on attitudes towards alcohol use. A large proportion of interviewees believed that problems of drunkenness and alcoholism could be found at any level of society. The majority also believed that a person's own social class had little effect on their attitudes towards alcohol.

Those who did believe social class to be important mentioned the following. A few believed that drink was more acceptable among the working classes, that it was part of working-class culture. Reasons given for its importance were seen to be the lack of any other opportunities open to the working classes. A common style of response was given by one clerk of works in the study:

'I think there are people who drink a lot because they don't see any hope in their situation.' (R.125)

However, not all comments were about working-class drinking. Some respondents said that the middle classes tended to hide their drinking:

'I think there is a danger that you tend rather sanctimoniously to say, you know, "we", meaning the middle classes, are somehow or other insulated from all this, and of course the reality is that we are not. There is a tendency to try and disguise these problems amongst middle-class people, whereas you know that they (the working class) are more open.' (R.302)

Others mentioned how the pressures of life in the 'upper' classes could lead to excessive drinking.

Although unemployment was seen as a factor leading people to drink from despair, respondents also stated their belief that the unemployed were likely to drink less than those in work due to lack of money. The effect of unemployment on drinking came across in the interviews as a separate issue, related to, but not synonymous with, ideas of class.

When questioned about the influence of social class on attitudes towards alcohol, respondents often answered by saying that they considered family background to be the most important influence in moulding their own beliefs. As one respondent noted when asked about the influence class had on his beliefs:

'No. I feel my family background has. But not my class background . . . everything in moderation really. All my family are anti-smoking, they disapproved of smoking but they did not disapprove of drinking. So I probably went along the same road.' (R.158)

We have considered respondents' ideas about the influence of class upon alcohol consumption. What did they have to say about the influence of religion on attitudes towards alcohol use? For church attenders the concept of moderation was frequently expressed. Protestants were, again, more prohibitive in their attitudes towards the use of alcohol than Catholics. Catholics mentioned other faiths' proscription of alcohol, but occasionally saw their own religious beliefs as not having a dramatic effect on their own attitudes. However, although Protestants believed their religion to be proscriptive, they themselves did not always put these ideas into practice. One Church of Scotland member who attended once a week and was also involved in church activities stated:

> 'In the last few years we have more an evangelical type of ministry within the Church, which tends to be rather puritan, ''thou shalt not'' drink, smoke or whatever. I think more so in the last few years. But so saying I am one of the rebels in the group . . . if I want a drink I will have a drink no matter what you say.' (R.306)

Only two respondents, who no longer attended church, still thought that their present attitudes had been moulded by their earlier religious upbringing. For most of the non-religious (many of whom had been raised in either the Protestant or Catholic faiths) their religious backgrounds were seldom seen to affect their present attitudes towards alcohol use. They did, however, believe that people who were religious would probably be influenced by their religion in their attitudes towards alcohol. That some churches were against drink and that some encouraged moderation was frequently mentioned. Respondents also occasionally gave the example of priests who drank to put the counter idea that religion need not have a strong effect on a person's beliefs about alcohol use.

AMBIVALENT ATTITUDES

I have described respondents' beliefs about the use of alcohol, and although concepts of ambivalence have been encountered these have not been discussed systematically. In this section I will draw together the major themes regarding ambivalence.

One aspect of ambivalence towards alcohol use revolves round the concept of moderate drinking. For nearly all respondents moderate drinking was acceptable but non-moderate drinking was not. The question also arises as to where the dividing line between moderate and non-moderate drinking should be placed. Different respondents gave different limits in answer to this question. Thus, although nearly all respondents voiced the same affective feelings towards moderate and non-moderate drinking, their feelings about individuals who consumed certain quantities of alcohol were diverse depending on where they placed this limit. In other words, moderate drinking is a relative, not an absolute, concept.

Ambivalence is also apparent in people's attitudes towards drunkenness. Respondents said that if they were drunk in the company of others who were drunk, drunkenness could be condoned. However, if they were sober they were less likely to accept drunken behaviour. It was less the case that they were totally against drunkenness than that they did not want to be disturbed by it. Again we can note the relational aspect in connection with attitudes towards alcohol use. The social contexts of the drinker and the non-drinker differ, and so too will the attitudes of people, depending on which context they are in at the time and whether they are viewing others' behaviour across context boundaries.

The ambivalence in respondents' attitudes towards women also came through clearly in the course of the interviews. Although most respondents said that they had nothing against women drinking and that women had as much right to drink as men, under the surface most respondents also voiced more traditional views about the dislike they had in seeing a drunk woman and how this was related to their ideas about women's place in the home and family.

Respondents were also ambivalent about young people drinking. Respondents believed that young people should be educated how to drink but were often unsure as to how this could be accomplished. Problems were seen to be how to maintain control once young people had started to drink with their peer group in public houses. Education into drinking could be done in the home or through the schools (or by parents taking their children into hotels), but once they got into the public house then there was difficulty in seeing moderate drinking continue. Most accepted that young people drank, although not all were happy about it.

Nowhere, however, was the concept of ambivalence given clearer expression than when respondents described how alcohol affected behaviour. It would seem to be the case that at times of sobriety certain aspects of an individual's personality cannot be displayed. Alcohol is needed for an easy sociability, typified by freer conversation, a relaxed manner, often accompanied by humour. It is as if in normal, sober situations such a style of interaction is disallowed, curtailed — although as was also shown, the consumption of alcohol is not entirely necessary; being part of 'an occasion where alcohol is consumed' may be sufficient.

154

Alcohol, therefore, allows for different behaviour and for a different presentation of the attributes of an individual's personality. However, different respondents varied as to what they thought occurred and also in their stance towards such changes. Three categories of response were uncovered:

1 Some believed that in everyday life the person was not as truthful, or in some respects, not the 'real person'. Alcohol allowed for this 'real person' to be viewed. Of course the 'real person' might, or might not, have been to the respondent's liking. If people were intrinsically good or bad these facts were suppressed when people were sober.
2 Others believed that the self of everyday life was the real or complete person, and alcohol only deprived the individual of self-control, allowing lower qualities to become manifest.
3 Between these views were respondents who believed that alcohol exaggerated personality traits, and produced changes which could either be for the good or the bad. What existed in a muted form in everyday life could be brought out in a more extreme form after drinking.

Interviewees were ambivalent about the above issues, but when asked about more extreme forms of alcohol intoxication respondents came closer in their views by condemning drunkenness and expressing statements of annoyance and disgust about drunks. They also produced similar statements as to the attributes of drunkenness.

Finally, there was a general agreement among respondents as to the central features of alcoholism: that of dependence, and the lack of control over drinking behaviour. Interestingly, however, what was seen to protect an individual from such loss of control were the steadying social attributes of family and employment.

What seems clear with regard to ambivalence is that these respondents seem to be in agreement at the extremes in their ideas as to moderate drinking and in their attitudes towards alcoholics and alcoholism. It is in the middle range that people were seen to have conflicting views.

CONCLUSION

As well as having looked at respondents' accounts of alcohol use I have also attempted to demonstrate here the importance of the in-depth interview method for looking at beliefs about alcohol use. Due to the flexibility of its approach it can uncover the subtleties of people's ideas on a topic. It can also highlight any seeming contradictions in an individual's set of beliefs and attempt, by further questioning, to resolve them. If contradictions remain, then we can be certain that such inconsistencies between beliefs are genuine, and not due to a misunderstanding on the part of the interviewer.

This interview method is also of value in highlighting the importance of the way in which questions are framed. If one asks general questions about drinking nearly everyone will be in favour of moderate drinking, but if one asks specific questions about quantities then people will express different ideas. Again, if one asks questions about the effect that alcohol has on respondents, they are likely to give a different answer from their perceived effects of alcohol on other people. This is not a new finding but it does highlight the need for researchers to be aware of these relational shifts in the attitudes of their respondents. Again, the ethnographic method, by allowing the interviewer to ask similar but varied questions on a specific issue, safeguards the researcher against such problems.

Finally, the method has drawn out the complexity of interviewees' ideas of ambivalence. Ambivalence has been found in interviewees' beliefs about women drinking, drunkenness, and the nature of personality change produced by the consumption of alcohol. Lack of ambivalence has, however, also been discovered, particularly with regard to conceptualizations of alcoholism. Ambivalence has been defined as 'the co-existence in one person of the emotional attitudes of love and hate towards the same object' (Sykes 1982). This chapter has attempted to show the complexity of such a relationship with regard to alcohol.

ACKNOWLEDGEMENTS

I would like to thank Margaret Reid, Sally Macintyre, and Rory Williams for their supervision and encouragement during the research. I am also most grateful to Stuart Gatehouse for providing a suitable sampling frame; and to Edna McIntyre who carried out the bulk of the interview transcriptions. Finally, I wish to thank Sarah Cunningham-Burley and Neil McKeganey for their comments on earlier drafts of the chapter.

Part Four

THE PROFESSIONAL–CLIENT INTERFACE

SURVEILLANCE AND CONCEALMENT: A COMPARISON OF TECHNIQUES OF CLIENT RESISTANCE IN THERAPEUTIC COMMUNITIES AND HEALTH VISITING

MICHAEL BLOOR AND JAMES McINTOSH

INTRODUCTION

This chapter approaches the issue of power in therapeutic relationships from a Foucaudian viewpoint. Our main task will be the provision of a typology of client resistance to domination, drawing on our studies of therapeutic communities and health visiting. We hope to show that the most common form of client resistance is concealment.

Prior to Foucault's work, the central importance of surveillance as a technique of power was hardly appreciated; it may be that the role of the obverse of surveillance — concealment — has been similarly unappreciated as a technique of resistance.

The chapter begins with a summary statement of Foucault's approach to power and his analysis of surveillance. We go on to describe briefly the studies of therapeutic communities and of health visiting from which our data are drawn. This is followed by an analysis of the forms that surveillance took in the professional–client relationships which we studied, and by an analysis of the forms of resistance that such surveillance called forth. We conclude with the implications of our analyses for the sociological understanding of professional–client relationships.

POWER AND RESISTANCE

Foucault's writings offer a conceptualization of power quite distinct from the ways in which power is viewed in Weber and Marx. Foucault does not think of power as a commodity that can be possessed by an individual or group ('sovereign' power), a facility for exclusion or interdiction. Rather, power is conceived as having a local rather than a substantive existence: power is found solely in its *exercise*, a body of practical techniques to which knowledge is linked and which are exercised in social relationships ('disciplinary' power). In Foucault's view, the correct (indeed, the only) locus for the study of power/ knowledge is that of local techniques of power, and the exemplar for such an approach to the study of power is Foucault's study of the technique of surveillance incorporated in the philosopher Jeremy Bentham's design for a model prison, the 'Panopticon' (Foucault 1977, 1980).

Bentham aimed to control and reform a prison population with a minimal staff of warders by the architectural device of arranging cells centrifugally around a central observatory; the wardens would be hidden from the prisoners behind a system of shutters so that the prisoners could never know when they were under observation and must therefore act as if surveillance was constant. The prisoner's openness to surveillance was thought to lead to dissuasion, which led in turn to reform.

Foucault linked the exemplary Panopticon with his earlier analysis of the new 'language of seeing' that, according to Foucault (but not according to some other commentators — see, for example, Atkinson 1981), had its birth in the Paris clinics of the late eighteenth century, a new language that described and constructed the body as an invariate biological reality and laid the foundations for modern medical knowledge (Foucault 1973; Armstrong 1983). In these pioneer clinics a new strategic relationship was evident between an individualized body and a disembodied gaze — that is, the 'clinical gaze'. According to Foucault, the exercise of surveillance in the clinical gaze ('the eye that knows and decides, the eye that governs' — Foucault 1973: 89) constituted a power relationship within the therapeutic encounter.

In his later work Foucault argued that Benthamite observational surveillance had been extended by appeals to patients and clients to monitor their own behaviour and to confess their activities to responsible professionals. Foucault suggested that the ecclesiastical concept of pastoral care was the most appropriate scheme for the analysis of power relations in such circumstances (Foucault 1981; Cousins and Hussain 1984).

Power, Foucault remarked, provokes resistance. But while his academic writings discussed power, the topic of resistance was left to his political writings: his analysis of power in prisons — for example,

Discipline and Punish (Foucault 1977) — was complemented by his work for the Information Group on Prisons (GIP) and the Prisoners' Action Commitee (CAP), groups which sought to assist the prisoners' movement campaigning against the French prisons system in the early seventies (cf. Major-Poetzl 1983: 46–54). Resistance was conceived by Foucault as the crux of his concept of freedom: power is pervasive and so freedom cannot consist in its absence, but rather as the possibility of practical revolt in reaction to it. However, the absence of an analytical approach to resistance in Foucault should not be taken to indicate that the enterprise is unachievable. Indeed, in his discussion in 'The Eye of Power' Foucault is explicit that resistance can be analysed in 'tactical and strategic terms' (Foucault 1980: 163) in a similar fashion to his analysis of power. This is our object in the latter part of the chapter.

METHODS

Foucault's project was to be a historian of the present, and most researchers who have adopted his approach also followed him in studying documentary materials. In contrast, we shall employ field-work data. The data concerned are drawn from two sources: on the one hand, data are presented from a semi-structured interview study of eighty working-class Glasgow mothers; on the other hand, data are presented from participant observation studies of four therapeutic communities: namely, a communally organized house for disturbed and mentally handicapped adolescents, a psychiatric day hospital for personality-disordered and neurotic patients, and two contrasting halfway houses for disturbed adolescents. Readers are referred elsewhere (McIntosh 1986; Bloor, McKeganey, and Fonkert 1988) for reports of findings from the various studies and for detailed descriptions of such matters as the interview study sampling frame and the observational settings.

Of course, the health visiting and therapeutic communities studies were not undertaken in order to compare professional–client relationships in different types of service-provision, nor were they undertaken to elaborate a Foucaudian approach to client resistance. The possibility of writing this chapter only occurred to us *post hoc*, when we realized that we both had data bearing upon issues of power and contest which showed both similarities and dissimilarities in techniques of client resistance. Had we intended from the outset to produce a typology of client resistance we would have designed different studies, employing more readily comparable methods of data collection and possibly focusing on different research settings. Nevertheless, we feel that the analysis of client resistance produced here, albeit a mere by-product of *post hoc* comparisons of independent studies, may have some value, both in terms of its applicability to some other forms of professional–client relationship, and in terms of its uniqueness as a typology of client resistance.

We would add, parenthetically, that we have not missed the irony that our own research methods entailed the surveillance of our research subjects.

SURVEILLANCE

We will begin by showing how surveillance is a necessary precondition for the conduct of both health visiting and therapeutic community practice. Health visiting is essentially a preventive service concerned with monitoring the physical and emotional well-being of infants and young children and with encouraging healthy lifestyles and 'appropriate' practices of child care. Surveillance, we would argue, is an essential component of these preventive activities. This can be seen most clearly, perhaps, in the case of the monitoring of abuse and neglect and the assessment of children's current state of health and development. Obviously, the accomplishment of these tasks requires direct evidence of the child's well-being and of the adequacy of his or her environment. This information can only be obtained by means of surveillance.

However, surveillance would also appear to be central to the educative function of health visiting, although health visitors themselves, both individually and through their professional bodies, would claim to espouse a non-judgemental and non-directive approach to health education. That is, instead of issuing instructions of mothers, they profess to offer merely suggestions and information that will enable the mother to make her own informed decisions. Clearly, if this were the case, there would be no need for the educative function of health visiting to be accompanied by surveillance. The health visitor's interest in the family would begin and end with the imparting of information and advice with which the mother could do as she wished. But of course it is not so simple. Health education is not neutral or value free (Abbott 1987). Accordingly, it embodies a

162

range of values and attitudes that may not be shared by its recipients. Moreover, health visitors operate on the basis of an episteme or model which includes definitions of acceptable standards of child development, 'good' and 'bad' parenting, healthy and unhealthy life-styles, and appropriate and inappropriate child-care practice. The ultimate aim of the service is, of course, to attempt to implement these ideas by persuading families — or, more particularly, mothers — to conform to these standards.

Professional knowledge — like all knowledge — is never dis-interested: immanent in the discourse of health visiting are relations of power; power and knowledge are always intermingled (Foucault 1979). Non-directive professional advice is thus a chimera, or perhaps a strategy of influence in itself. Certainly, many mothers perceived health visitors' 'advice' as instructional — for example:

'I don't like the health visitors. I mean, it's no' like help or advice — they *tell* you. It wisnae, "Maybe you should do this," it was, "You *should* do this". Y'know, "You're doin' it all wrong".'

'She keeps tellin' me, "Do this, do that." It makes ye feel like a moron, that yer no' capable o' lookin' after yer baby. It under-mines yer confidence. Ah always feel guilty after she's been as if ah've been doin' everything all wrong. It makes me mad. Ah don't say anything at the time, ah just mutter a few oaths when she's gone.'

In this sense, then, health visiting could fairly be said to be about monitoring families for the purpose of promoting and sustaining behavioural change. A corollary of this, of course, is the need to know what is happening in families because it is only with such knowledge that the effectiveness of health education and the need for such inter-vention can be adequately assessed. The information required in order to satisfy these objectives can, in turn, only be achieved through some form of surveillance. Evidence that such surveillance actually occurs is provided by the number and range of questions which mothers report being asked about their practices of infant care. Clearly, a non-directive approach would have no need for such information.

This discussion also touches on one of the central ambiguities of health visiting. On the one hand, health visitors are expected to estab-lish a caring and supportive relationship with families, while,

163

on the other, they are charged with the responsibility of monitoring the occurrence of abuse, neglect, and inadequate parenting. It has been argued elsewhere (McIntosh 1986) that this contradiction greatly reduces the health visitor's acceptability and effectiveness, particularly where working-class mothers are concerned.

Surveillance is intrinsic to therapeutic work within therapeutic communities, just as it is intrinsic to health visiting. Therapeutic community work can be conceived of as an act of cognition which transforms any mundane event in the social life of the community by redefining that event by reference to some therapeutic paradigm. An event may be redefined as, amongst other things, showing responsibility, or seeking out a new and less pathogenic way of relating to others, with the precise nature of the redefinition (and of the paradigm on which it is based) varying from community to community. To redefine any everyday event as an occasion or a topic for therapy sets it apart and transforms it, much as the profane is transformed into the sacred by religious belief and ceremony. A simple act like cleaning the toilets or mending a leaking tap is invested with new meaning and held up as relevant to the cleaner's recovery or rehabilitation. Any and every event and activity in the therapeutic community is potentially open to such redefinitions; there is no nook or cranny of resident life that is not open to scrutiny and potentially redefinable in therapeutic terms.

Surveillance is a precursor and an essential component of this redefining process; there is a therapeutic gaze which parallels Foucault's 'clinical gaze', a gaze which observes and interprets residents' behaviour and constitutes residents as psycho-social beings with 'needs', 'motives', and 'problems' (Silverman and Bloor forthcoming). The role of surveillance is seen most clearly in those therapeutic communities where the staff observation of resident behaviour is divorced in time from the staff expression of their redefinitions of resident behaviour to the residents concerned. Thus, at Ashley halfway house staff did not supervise the cleaning work of residents during the morning work group — they mutely monitored poor work and confronted residents about it in the subsequent 'coffee group'. A fieldnote extract on a coffee group discussion runs:

Staff work at their own work-group tasks and incidentally observe the behaviour of the residents and the quality of their work in the process, say, of filling a mop-bucket or emptying a bin. Thus,

164

today Una remarked that Dickie had asked what was to be done outside [the house] and she set him to cleaning the drains of leaves and tidying the garage, but when Una went into the garage some time later (to return a mop) she found Dickie just standing there and the garage was in the state as before.

Whilst surveillance is essential both to the work of therapeutic communities and of health visitors, surveillance may take different forms, and different forms may be associated with different settings. We can distinguish three different techniques of surveillance: covert or naturalistic surveillance, supervisory surveillance, and surveillance by proxy or by the encouragement of self-reporting.

The distinction between naturalistic and supervisory techniques of surveillance parallels a distinction between different approaches to therapeutic work in therapeutic communities. One approach we will designate, following Morrice (1979), 'reality confrontation': that is, the repetitive portrayal of the subject's conduct as unacceptable coupled with the presentation of the community as a locale where new and non-pathogenic patterns of behaviour can be tried out. Communities emphasizing a 'reality confrontation' approach are generally permissive environments where residents are allowed to 'act out', reproducing in their activities and relationships in the community those inappropriate patterns of behaviour that led to their admission, thus providing the rest of the community with occasions and topics for therapeutic work. The other approach we will designate 'instrumentalism'. This entails the careful manipulation and control of the subject's social environment together with the planning, supervision, and didactic instruction of the subject's activities up to the point where new, non-pathogenic patterns of behaviour are learned and adopted. Communities emphasizing an 'instrumental' approach are normally hierarchical institutions with elaborate programmes of activities and high standards of task performance where behaviour change is not volitional but, instead, the unremarked consequence of the gradual accretion of experience. Covert or naturalistic surveillance was the dominant technique in reality-confronting communities. Surveillance in these communities had to be naturalistic because acting out might be inhibited by the subject's consciousness of being subject to scrutiny. As a consequence, surveillance in these settings is normally subsumed under other naturally occurring activities — cleaning the house, washing the dishes, watching TV —

and is often silent, the associated work of confrontation often being postponed (as we saw in the instance of Una and Dickie) until one of the daily or weekly formal group therapy sessions. Thus a member of staff in one community always brought his dirty washing with him when on the nightshift so that he would have a natural occasion for going repeatedly back and forth through the community's public rooms to check on the progress of the washing machine *and* to monitor residents' behaviour.

Supervisory surveillance was the main technique employed in what we have called instrumental communities. At one such community, Beeches, in contrast to the silent monitoring of the Ashley work group, the Beeches staff oversaw and directed the residents' cleaning work. Late-comers were clocked and had equivalent make-up time allocated for the weekends; there was a list of daily and weekly cleaning tasks posted up in each room; one staff member was expected to work alongside residents in one of the rooms whilst a second had a general responsibility to ensure the smooth running of the work group throughout the house; high standards of work were expected and a staff member and the current chairperson of the residents would go on a tour of inspection at the end of the work group. Bloor's fieldnotes on the Beeches work group reflect the staff preoccupation with residents' task performances; for example:

> Workgroup. I . . . worked with Neil [resident] in the lounge, patio and resource room. The practice with Neil is to under-react to his conversational gambits and tantrums and concentrate on getting him to work. I let him do the smaller jobs in the lounge (cleaning the mats, re-arranging the furniture). But in the resource room I got him to mop the floor while I washed down the walls.

Planning facilitates supervisory surveillance in that it not only pre-scribes the content of resident activities, but it may also prescribe the kind of intervention required to procure compliance. In Beeches there was a staff 'Operations Manual' which meticulously stipulated staff tasks in various components of the community's programme of activities, and there was also an 'Interventions Book' which laid down the approved methods of intervening successfully with each individual resident.

The task of the overseer is one that has grim connotations that may be misleading. In fact, supervised work groups in therapeutic com-munities may be peppered with the same humour found in many work settings. Here is an example from a work group in another instrumental community, Parkneuk:

> In the afternoon, Nick, Robert [both staff] and myself work in the kitchen garden. Sally [resident] is directed to cut the lawn nearby. She does this lifelessly and ineptly — meandering in zigzags, wandering onto the gravel, stopping and staring into space. Nick at first attempts to direct her . . . 'Cut it in straight lines Sally — start at the edge and then do a line next to the line you've cut.' As the afternoon proceeds Nick is more sarcastic: 'The mower is running quietly, Sally — I haven't heard it for ages' and 'The gravel doesn't need cutting just now, Sally — I should concentrate on the grass'. This sarcasm doesn't seem cruel but a manifestation of the joking relationships that are very prominent in the community. . . . Nick talks about Sally: 'She used to have a lot of highs and lows. Now she's more stable. She's developed this stupidity as a way of protecting herself. It's her strategy.' In this light Nick's sarcasm seems very effective insofar as Sally's ineptness is drawn attention to but is not reinforced.

Supervisory surveillance, as practised in instrumental therapeutic communities, is clearly not feasible in health visiting since the latter lacks both the authority and the opportunity necessary for such supervision. Clearly, too, opportunities for naturalistic surveillance are limited in health visiting, being largely confined to chance occurrences such as the mother having to feed the baby during a visit. There are, however, exceptions to this as the following quotation illustrates:

> 'They find ways o' lookin round yer house. Ah get annoyed. Ah've got nothing tae hide. . . . They go on the prowl. They'll say, "Can I wash my hands?" That's the excuse to go into the bathroom. "Do you think I could have a glass of water?" And you go, "Right I'll just get it for you." She says, "No, it's alright, I'll do it myself." That's to go intae your kitchen. And they'll have a wee look around here (lounge) and, if they want to look at your stitches or anything, they insist you go intae the bedroom wi' them. Another excuse. If you're in the house yourself, they could easily do it here. Now ah leave all the doors open so that, when she comes in, she can see that the house is clean.'

Where the opportunities for naturalistic and supervisory surveillance are limited, then professionals are forced to rely on supervision by

167

proxy or by self-report. These are the modern techniques of surveillance which Foucault saw as contrasting with the 'archaic' techniques of surveillance embodied in the Panopticon: the subject is incited to confess (Foucault 1979, 1981), and others may be enlisted as proxies to urge the subject to confess or to report on the subject's behaviour if he or she remains silent. Health visitors lean heavily on the first of these modern techniques: in effect, they encourage their clients to furnish them with the information they require to monitor child care. Of course, health visitors may also obtain information on clients from fellow professionals, such as family practitioners, but rarely from the client's peers — friends, neighbours, and relatives. To the extent that professionals exchange information about a client, then that client may feel subjected to a disembodied, collective gaze — 'Them'.

Non-residential therapeutic communities (such as the psychiatric day hospital that Bloor studied) also have only limited opportunities for naturalistic and supervisory surveillance, and so encourage self-reporting. They also encourage proxy supervision, particularly by the subject's peers in the community. The pressures on subjects from their peers may be almost irresistible, since subjects may fear their peers reporting the matter in their stead if they remain silent:

Tina [patient] began the big group by saying that last night a group of patients had gone out for a social and there'd been a lot of loving and a lot of caring. . . . Edith [staff] returned to the topic at the end of the afternoon group: she attributed the lack of progress in the big group to the fact that things were happening at the Socials which were not being brought to the formal group. . . . Nick [patient] followed Edith by saying he was angry at people who had spoken at the Socials and been silent in the big group. He'd been put in a very difficult position — someone had cried in his arms and made him promise not to tell the big group. Still silence. He named three people and one of them, Mary, immediately began to speak.

And:

Nigel [patient] kicked off by saying he was going to break a confidence: Duncan had confided to him in the afternoon that he intended to commit suicide. Duncan did not attack him in the group for breaking this confidence, but Nigel did feel it was necessary to justify his betrayal to the group at some length.

Although this incitement and proxy surveillance by peers is most important in communities where opportunities for naturalistic and supervisory surveillance are more limited, in fact incitement and proxy surveillance are found in all communities. Writing of the American communities for ex-addicts, Sugarman described them in a felicitous phrase as 'boarding schools run by the prefects' (Sugarman 1975: 144).

Our discussion of surveillance in health visiting and therapeutic communities suggests that surveillance in professional – client relationships varies in extent as well as in type. We can posit a continuum, with surveillance being most extensive in certain settings, such as residential therapeutic communities, and decreasing in non-residential communities and in the domiciliary health-visiting service. Surveillance may be least extensive of all in those professional – client encounters that occur in bureaucratic service delivery systems, such as hospital out-patient departments.

RESISTANCE

Our project is to describe the local techniques of client resistance in health visiting and therapeutic communities. Since power provokes resistance, we may expect techniques of resistance to be diverse in form since they will be local reactions to local (and diverse) forms of power. Techniques of resistance must be understood in the context of our earlier discussion of techniques of power.

Among McIntosh's working-class mothers, resistance was a reaction to the perceived social control function of health visiting. When asked what they thought were the main aims of health visitors, the majority of the sample (69 per cent) mentioned some aspect of social control as one of their main functions. Indeed, more than half of the respondents (56 per cent) described the role of the health visitor exclusively in terms of social control. Control in this context included the policing of child abuse and neglect, the monitoring of maternal competence, the provision of support for the inexperienced or inadequate, and the assessment of the suitability of the home environment. For example, one mother described the purpose of health visiting as follows:

> 'Ah think it's tae see if yer doin' everything right. They're just checking up to see the house is no' dirty and he's no' got any black eyes or anything.'

These perceptions of health visiting are, it would appear, to some extent perpetuated and accentuated by health visitors themselves through their own words and actions. For example, five of our mothers reported being told by their health visitor that they only undertook home visits when there were problems of some sort. Others described what were, to them, rather clumsy attempts on the part of the health visitor to inspect their home surreptitiously:

> 'They come and look around. They think ye cannae see them, but ye can. They look about the house — ye can see their eyes though they try tae hide it — and the least bit o' dirt they put it in the book.'

In addition, many mothers saw the unannounced nature of the home visit as being part of a deliberate strategy to catch them unawares:

> 'They don't let ye know they're coming. They try tae catch you out.'

These perceptions of the service and its role resulted in a strong sense of resentment and antipathy towards the health visitor on the part of many of our sample:

> 'I'd rather they didn't come 'cause I think they're just nosey. They just come to check up that you're looking after the baby and treating her right. Ah'm a good mother and ah resent it.'

or:

> 'They're just pests. You see them looking about and checking tae see that he's clean and has no bruises. Ah hate bein' checked up on. It makes ye feel like a criminal.'

This resentment was also tinged with anxiety that the health visitor's observations might be used against them in some way. As an example of this one mother expressed the fear that the health visitor would have her baby removed if she discovered that her kitchen sink was temporarily out of commission. Given the perceptions which we have just described, it is not surprising that the monitoring and information-gathering activities of the health visitor encountered resistance in our sample of working-class mothers.

Similar resentments were aired in the therapeutic communities Bloor studied. In the day hospital, staff concern about a drunken patient's evening outing led to patients darkly quoting Burns to the

170

effect that 'There's chiels amang us takin' notes'. Resentment of 'prying' could be overlaid in residential communities by resentment at the threat of withdrawal of resident 'privileges' for non-cooperation. A fieldnote from Beeches halfway house reports:

> After lunch and before 'Education' at 2 o'clock, Kevin [resident] was in and out of the staff room. He kept saying it was too nice a day to stay indoors and do 'Education'. He'd like to go for a walk for half the time and come back and do a project on his walk for the second half of Education. . . . I asked Kim [staff] if we should let Kevin do his project. He said 'No', because Kevin would interpret it as staff surrendering to his 'pestering'. When Kevin returned to the office . . . he began to say that he wasn't going to do Education indoors. He was confronted by Jean [staff] who told him that if he refused to do Education then that was his decision but he must recognize that there would be certain consequences; he must also consider his position as a senior resident. . . . If he could not be trusted to behave as a senior resident should, then his senior resident status might have to be taken away. Kevin stormed out of the office. Five minutes later he stormed into Education in a terrible temper. Terry [resident] said to Kevin that the next thing 'they' would be doing would be threatening to take away his 'senior resident' status. Kevin said they'd already threatened that. Terry laughed bitterly and knowingly.

In the two services which we studied, resistance could take a variety of forms and included collective ideological dissent, individual ideological dissent, non-cooperation, escape or avoidance, and concealment. We will now consider each of these in turn.

1 Collective ideological dissent

In therapeutic communities collective ideological dissent consisted of an articulated counter-culture opposed in principle and practice to the aims of the staff and determined to capture the community as a locale for its own purposes. By definition, such ideological dissent is highly visible, and only one possible instance of such resistance was observed in the four communities Bloor studied. A more certain example of ideological dissent is provided by Sharp in his study of a halfway house community (Sharp 1975). Sharp noted the presence of a dissident clique of residents within the house who would persistently attempt to turn the group discussions into attacks on staff, the rules, 'the system', and so on, and who wished to turn the house away from its rehabilitative role and convert the community into an intentional commune which would allow more self-actualization for residents than 'outside' society (Sharp 1975: 88–97).

No such collective ideological dissent was evident among the working-class mothers. Of course, a random sampling technique is less well placed to identify such a phenomenon than, say, a snowball sample. But any widespread collective movement among the mothers seems intuitively implausible.

2 Individual ideological dissent

The near-absence of collective ideological dissent in therapeutic communities and health visiting may reflect the general judgement that resistance is normally localized and specific and only rarely has a unique focal point (Cousins and Hussain 1984: 243). Individual ideological dissent was more common. In health visiting such individual dissent was covert, whereas in therapeutic communities both covert and overt individual ideological dissent was encountered.

Many of the mothers challenged the legitimacy of health-visiting discourse. The mothers considered mothering, or infant care, to be essentially a lay skill developed in the course of practical experience with infants, usually under the guidance of women who were themselves experienced mothers. Consistent with this view, the great majority of our sample regarded personal experience of infants to be greatly superior to the theoretical or book knowledge which, they assumed, formed the basis of health-visiting expertise. Accordingly, experienced lay advisers were more highly valued than professional sources of advice:

'Half of the people who try tae tell ye aboot weans [children] have no' got weans o' their own. Ah mean, they're just readin' off books an' that. Ah prefer tae go tae people that's got experience. Ah mean, they just laugh at them up there [clinic]. A health visitor wi' nae kids trying tae tell a woman that's got five whit tae dae?'

Associated with this view was the belief, expressed by three-quarters of our sample, that health visitors should themselves be mothers. Since our mothers believed that personal experience of infant care was central to mothering skills, it followed that one could not possibly be competent to offer guidance on the subject without having had first-hand experience of motherhood oneself. Health visitors without such experience simply lacked credibility:

> 'I liked the second health visitor I had. She was an older woman, married with a family of her own and she knew things. The first one was just hopeless — a young, unmarried girl. It was just text-book stuff. They don't really understand. I don't think anyone can unless they've had a baby themselves.'

Covert ideological dissent could be heard being voiced in therapeutic communities when no staff were present. Bloor was particularly aware of such criticisms in the day hospital where he began his participant observation work as a member of the patient group, only subsequently switching to spend more of his time with staff members. The content of such dissent varied considerably. One patient who was undergoing his third stint as patient compared the current treatment regime unfavourably with his past experiences, which he had found invaluable. Another patient decried what he perceived as an unwonted staff emphasis on 'yer child days'. However, it was not evident that the content of covert dissent varied very much from that of overt dissent. In reality confronting the redefinitions of communities staff were a common focus of individual dissent. In the following fieldnote extract, the same patient who had covertly complained about the emphasis on 'child days' also overtly complained about staff harping on child–parent relationships:

> In the small group Tim was talking about a role play that took place last week between Edith [staff] and Hamish about Hamish's relationship with his mother. He said he'd watched spell-bound, totally unaware of his surroundings. He then said that just recently he'd been having difficulties with his own mother — he was avoiding her and unable to look her in the eye. Edith then said he hadn't been looking her in the eye either. This rankled Tim. At lunchtime he proclaimed . . . that he was going to bring it up in the Big Group; he swore a lot and some of his . . . fellow-patients treated it as a joke. In the Big Group Tim kicked with this issue: 'There's aye a lot talkin aboot mothers in here. . . . Edith reckons she's my mother. Well she isna my effin' mother. I've only got one effin' mother and when she's gone I dinna want anither.' The group countered by saying it was always him that brought up the

subject of mothers. Tim admitted that it was him who had broached the subject in the small group but doggedly stuck to his guns — he didn't regard Edith as his mother.

The mothers in the health visiting study did not report any *open* disagreements with their health visitors, although it is known from other research (for example, Blaxter and Paterson 1982) that such confrontations do occasionally occur.

3   Non-cooperation

Non-cooperation was a common form of resistance in both types of therapeutic community, usually expressing itself in the form of silence in the groups (or, more rarely, absence from them), in the reality confronting communities, and in the form of non-participation in some of the activities in the instrumental communities.

Non-cooperation was normally a matter of individual resistance, but on two occasions at an instrumental community Bloor observed instances of collective non-cooperation where some (but not all) of the residents boycotted the weekly community meeting and, two days later, a smaller group refused to take part in the morning work group.

Whereas in the therapeutic communities non-cooperation was overt, in health visiting non-cooperation consisted of covert non-compliance with the health visitor's advice. There was no direct confrontation: what usually happened was that the health visitor was appeased. In other words, when offered advice with which they disagreed, mothers listened politely, indicated compliance and promptly proceeded to ignore it and follow their own counsel. As one mother said:

'Ye just agree wi' her [health visitor] and do yer own things 'cause she's no' here every day to check.'

In this context, it is interesting to note, as an example of non-compliance, that 40 per cent of the babies in our sample were weaned by 6 weeks and three-quarters were on solid food by 12 weeks. This, of course, was very much against the explicit advice of the health visitors not to introduce solids before 4 months.

4 Escape or avoidance

None of the therapeutic communities studied was a secure institution with physical barriers to inhibit resistance in the form of premature departure. Nevertheless, departure without the aid and agreement of staff was no easy matter. Three of the communities had resident populations of adolescents often with long backgrounds of institutionalized dependence; they were frequently far from home, with only hazy notions of local geography, and without funds. Yet in two of those three communities successful or attempted resident escapes averaged around one per month during the fieldwork period. Considerable ingenuity was required and displayed. One resident hung about outside the house to intercept the postman and secure his giro before catching an inter-city bus. Another resident, although an elective mute, managed to find his way across the city to the railway station and sneak aboard the correct train only to be caught some miles down the line without a ticket.

In the psychiatric day hospital unauthorized departure might be considered a less difficult task: the patient might merely stay at home and refrain from attending the hospital again the next day. However, to anticipate our argument slightly, resistance provokes counteraction, and would-be defaulting patients would find themselves on the receiving end of a delegation of fellow patients who would attempt to persuade them to return. Few defaulters were proof against such persuasion, and so those determined to depart either had to state their determination to depart and their reasons in the day hospital's formal groups, or else they had to resort to subterfuge. One defaulting patient who had already been persuaded to return on a previous occasion was thought to be in his house but not answering the door when the patient delegation called, whilst another defaulting patient secretly left the country.

Escape from the therapeutic community by departing from it has a counterpart in health visiting in the avoidance of the service by mothers. This could take one of two forms: the health visitor could be avoided by not attending the clinic, or she could be avoided at home simply by not answering the door and pretending to be out when she called. Escape, as thus defined, was a much more common form of resistance in relation to health visiting than it was in therapeutic communities, partly because it was easy to execute and partly because no penalties were involved. Eight mothers reported stopping clinic visits

175

as an avoidance strategy, while seven admitted to avoiding contact with her at home. Since these accounts were volunteered spontaneously, they are, if anything, likely to represent an underestimate of the extent of use of these tactics.

5   Concealment

The most common form of resistance in both studies was concealment. The advantage of concealment as a technique is that it neutralizes the potential for the exercise of power without explicitly challenging it in ways that would lead to penalties. In short, concealment provides a way of avoiding control without confrontation. It was certainly an extremely common form of resistance in relation to health visiting. As we described earlier, mothers would often conceal practices — such as early weaning — of which they anticipated the health visitor might be critical. In addition, though, the process of concealment would also involve attempts to manipulate the information available to the health visitor by giving inaccurate accounts of what the mother was doing. One mother described this as follows:

> 'Ah tell them what they want tae know. Ah mean, she widnae be very pleased if she kenned we had him on solids when he was two weeks old. But ye don't tell her that. She'd do her nut. Ye say, "Oh no, he's just having his milk." '

This strategy was also widespread in the therapeutic communities studied and took various forms. Most obviously one could note straightforward attempts by residents to remove themselves from the gaze of the staff. A related resident strategy was that of contesting staff surveillance. On one occasion (and only one occasion) Bloor observed a collective, rather than an individual, assertion of the right to be free of surveillance. The occasion in the question was a community 'Think Day' in which the residents were encouraged to think of things about the house that they would like to discuss and suggest changes. A suggestion that generated considerable resident enthusiasm and interest was a 'residents' private room' to which staff would have no automatic right of access and where staff would have to knock and request admittance, mirroring the procedure that residents had to go through in order to gain admittance to the staff office. In the subsequent staff meeting the warden said he was very unhappy about the idea because it smacked of exclusion. It was not adopted.

A very common form of concealment was a kind of deviant conformity. This consisted of the adoption of forms of behaviour and speech which, on the one hand, displayed conformity with staff expectations at minimum cost to the resident but, on the other, might serve as a cover for private and non-conformist aspirations and gratifications. Such forms of institutionalized adaptation have, of course, been widely reported — for example, Goffman's analysis of the 'secondary adjustment' of psychiatric hospital patients (Goffman 1968). An illustration is as follows:

'I said I would work with Terry today in the workgroup (I was group member) because of the events of yesterday's morning meeting when Lisa (staff) confronted him about his poor performance working outside. I noticed that when I worked alongside him (sweeping the drive) he worked very hard, but when we divided the tasks he did the bare minimum. Also the work that he did do gave the maximum cosmetic effect for the resident chairman's inspection.'

Relatedly, in reality confronting communities it is sometimes possible to hear staff describe some residents as merely going through the motions of group therapy — that is, having a practised grasp of the conventions and the argot of group work but using this familiarity as a resource to avoid expressing their 'real' feelings and problems.

A further technique which may inhibit the penetration of the staff gaze is for residents to stress the secret character of shared knowledge:

'Sitting at table waiting for tea to be served with five residents. One of them began to talk about some incident that had occurred the other night. She was cut short by another who said, "There's only four people sitting around this table who know about that." Tom said, "I didn't know anything about it." "No, and you're not going to either." I was the fifth. During tea, Tom, sitting on my right, turned to whisper something to Pete, sitting on his right. He asked if Pete could hear him. "No." "Okay, I'll tell you later".'

A 'no grassing' convention, to be effective, does not depend on recurrent assertion and enforcement. Residents in interaction with one another become unwitting parties to the shared knowledge of the in-group. Much of this in-group knowledge is tacit and taken for granted (for example, who is sexually attracted to whom?) and never attains the form of an explicit statement which might carry a 'secret'

177

tag and a concomitant ban on its broadcasting elsewhere. Bloor was made uncomfortably aware of this when, in the course of the day hospital study, he made his afore-mentioned switch from associating largely with the patients (eating his meals with them, socializing with them in the evenings) to associating largely with the staff. Bloor then became aware that much of his unwittingly absorbed knowledge of the doings of the patients was quite hidden from staff.

COUNTERACTION

Strategies of resistance in therapeutic communities were transitory in their appearance: collective ideological dissent evident during pilot work, for example, was no longer evident in the main sociological study. One reason for such transitions lies in continual resident turn-over, but a further reason lies with the staff counteraction that may follow on the heels of resident resistance.

Some counteraction was local in the sense that the forms it took varied with the form of resident resistance and varied from community to community. Whereas non-cooperation in the permissive environment of the reality confronting community would be a focus for therapeutic work, in the instrumental community, in contrast, the staff would employ specific techniques of intervention in order to ensure resident compliance and a quick return to the supervised task.

It seems rather mystifying to talk of counteracting resident resistance in communities characterized by their permissive environments, although, of course, permissiveness is never total but always subject to limits and qualifications (Morrice 1965). However, in reality confronting communities, counteraction is frequently not a staff but a resident response to fellow resident resistance. Thus, it will be recalled that it was fellow patients who visited would-be defaulting day hospital patients (although sometimes a staff member would be included in the visiting delegation). These are reflections of the fact that in such communities staff relinquish direct control of events but nevertheless ensure that the community continues to function by other indirect means: they 'orchestrate' therapy and counteraction (Bloor 1986).

Counteraction is not always decisive. For one thing it may itself call forth further techniques of resident resistance, as in the case of the patient who refused to meet the delegation of visiting patients. But to the extent that counteraction is successful in defeating resident resistance, then we must judge that strategies of concealment are likely to be the most successful strategies of resident resistance; since concealment by its very nature may occur without associated counter-action, staff may not be aware that concealment is occurring.

Yet, although staff may be unaware of specific instances of conceal-ment, they may be very well aware of the likelihood that concealment may occur and take steps to prevent it. Thus, in reality confronting communities, staff may stress to residents the importance of 'open communications' to the successful functioning of the community and the destructive and burdensome nature of secretive pair-bonds:

> Olive (staff) raised the topic of 'nicking' . . . several of the girls were sitting around wearing new gold jewellery. This met with almost complete silence. . . . Olive said the worst thing about nicking was the way it divided the house. She illustrated this by telling about how Tony (resident) had told her that when he and a former resident had gone nicking it had glued them into a destruc-tive and exclusive pair-bond: they were forced to support each other although they ended up hating each other.

In contrast to the transient nature of resistance in therapeutic com-munities, resistance to surveillance by health visitors is more enduring. The principal reason for this, we suggest, is because counteraction is difficult in health visiting. In the first place, health visitors have no right of access to the covert activities of their clients. Second, health visitors may be unaware or unsure that concealment is taking place and therefore unable to proceed against it. A third possi-bility is that, even when health visitors are aware that things are being concealed from them, 'politeness' may prevent them from attempting to counteract it; they are hamstrung by what Strong and Horobin (1978) called 'the conventions of medical gentility'. The only available option to the health visitor who suspects concealment is to increase surveillance, although even this possibility is, of course, severely circumscribed.

CONCLUSION

Our prime objective in this paper has been to produce a typology of client resistance. The types have only a conceptual distinctiveness; empirically there is much association and overlap: for example, covert ideological dissent may be a technique of resistance in itself or may lead on to, and be associated with, any of the other techniques we listed. Nor can resistance be considered in isolation: power provokes resistance; indeed, there is a sense in which power creates resistance — resistance is itself part of a disciplinary relationship (Armstrong 1988). Accordingly, we have described local techniques of resistance in the context of local techniques of surveillance. In so doing, we think we have produced one of the first Foucaudian studies of the contemporary exercise of power in professional–client relationships using fieldwork rather than documentary materials (see also Silverman 1987).

How far our findings may be generalizable to other kinds of professional–client relationships should be an empirical question. Our study settings (health visiting and therapeutic communities) may seem somewhat arcane. However, there are many settings where the monitoring of client behaviour is a crucially important professional task. And, where surveillance is a prominent technique of professional power, then we would expect our types of client resistance (particularly concealment) to be similarly prominent.

It is arguable that, prior to Foucault's work, surveillance was an underemphasized aspect of power relations in the sociology of medical encounters. Our present analysis leads us to suggest that concealment may have been similarly underemphasized in the sociological analysis of patient or client behaviour — Goffman's *Asylums* (1968) was a honourable exception. Certainly, early interactionist studies of the professional–client relationship stressed the negotiated character of the relationship with an emphasis on overt bargaining (for example, Scheff 1968). And later studies chose to stress the constraints on the negotiability of the encounter from the clients' point of view and to emphasize the professional's dominance of the encounter (for example, Stimson and Webb 1975; Bloor 1976; West 1976).

It is a commonplace that studies of health services usually approach their topics from what is explicitly or implicitly a staff perspective. For example, to view everyday events in therapeutic communities in accordance with their bearing on therapeutic work is to view those events in relation to staff preoccupations. But in any professional–client relationship the clients are likely to have their own projects, their own immediate and long-term aims and objectives. The professional–client relationship is always a power relationship, and even in the process of professional–client *contest* the two parties are locked into a disciplinary relationship. This chapter has attempted to describe that contest between health visitors and their clients and between therapeutic community practitioners and their clients.

ACKNOWLEDGEMENTS

Michael Bloor wishes to acknowledge the support of the Medical Research Council and James McIntosh wishes to acknowledge the support of the Scottish Home and Health Department for their respective studies. An earlier version of this paper was given at a special meeting of the British Sociological Association Medical Sociology Group (Scottish Section) held in Glasgow on 31 October 1987 in memory of our former colleague, Gordon Horobin. We wish to thank the participants at the meeting and David Armstrong, Sarah Cunningham-Burley, David Greaves, Neil McKeganey, Lindsay Prior, and Victor Sharp for their comments.

Chapter Eight

PROFESSIONAL – CLIENT RELATIONSHIPS AND WOMEN'S REPRODUCTIVE HEALTH CARE

MAUREEN PORTER

INTRODUCTION

The form and nature of the relationship between doctors and patients in medical consultations has been a popular focus for sociological study for many years (Bloom and Wilson 1972). Since the early 1970s, however, concern has been expressed at the many short-comings in that relationship, especially in consultations concerned with women's reproductive health — that is, consultations occurring in gynaecological, obstetric, and family planning settings, where women interact with doctors about such matters as having or preventing babies, the menstrual cycle and female reproductive organs (Doyal 1979). Examining the functioning of the doctor–patient relationship in this context, sociologists have drawn attention to the medicalization of normal biological processes such as pregnancy and childbirth (Oakley 1975), the control and dominance over decision making exercised by the medical profession (Scully 1980), and the poverty of communications between women patients and their predominantly male medical attendants (Macintyre 1981).

In this chapter I shall discuss why medical sociological analyses of reproductive health consultations changed from an acceptance of the medical model of events to a critical, consumerist view of interaction. I shall discuss the effect that this change in perspective has had upon the delivery of reproductive health care and the problems which remain for women experiencing it. In doing so I shall draw on observations of antenatal and postnatal clinics and wards, gynaecology clinics and wards, and family planning sessions at local authority clinics and general practices. I shall also make use of interviews with the staff concerned, and with pregnant women, contracepting

182

women, and infertile women which I have completed over a number of years (Porter 1980; Hall *et al.* 1985; Porter 1986).

THE HISTORICAL AND POLITICAL CONTEXT

There is, in Britain, a long tradition of studying the pattern of human reproduction and its social sequelae. Early in the present century government bodies began making the link between maternal well-being and behaviour and the health of children. The poor standard of recruits for the army fighting the Boer War drew attention to the poverty and ignorance of the working classes and led to the setting up of the Interdepartmental Committee on the Physical Deterioration of the Population which reported in 1904. Among its other recommendations were those calling for better statistics relating to pregnancy and childbirth, the registration of stillbirths, presentation of infant mortality rates by locality, and education in infant feeding and management for mothers and young girls. The infant mortality rate, which was 154 per thousand live births in 1900, also gave rise to concern and calls for better nutrition and education of mothers. In the 1920s and 1930s government reports focused on the high rates of maternal mortality and called for wider provision of antenatal care as well as 'a general amelioration of the social conditions in which women performed their childbearing and childrearing roles' and improvements in medical care during delivery (Oakley 1982: 7). Similarly, the report of the Select Committee on Perinatal and Neonatal Mortality published in 1980 (the Short Report) called for mothers to be educated in the value of (improved) antenatal care so that they would make greater use of it (cf. Lewis 1980).

When sociologists began studying human reproduction they too took the existence and functioning of services relating to reproductive health largely for granted and focused on the social aetiology of various outcomes of conception. Concentrating on women as mothers they examined their behaviour and social circumstances to see whether these could explain observed differences in reproductive outcome as indicated by rates of live and still births, infant and maternal deaths, prematurity, complications of pregnancy and so on. Macintyre (1980) has argued that sociologists took this limited perspective because they 'worked mainly in collaboration with obstetricians and within the prevailing paradigms of obstetric and administrative orthodoxy' (p. 215). She concluded that it led to a concentration on failures in women's behaviour, such as the failure to use the antenatal services provided, to the exclusion of organizational and other failures in the services themselves.

In the mid-1970s, however, sociologists interested in human reproduction shifted their allegiance, as it were, from the doctors to the patients. They began to question medical orthodoxy and with it the existence and operation of health services and the role of the medical profession within them. Some feminist groups and sociologists felt that doctors were making the natural, normal physiological processes of reproduction — conception, contraception, pregnancy, and childbirth — into medical events to be actively managed and controlled by medical experts, who were alienating women in the process. A whole edition of the *International Journal of Health Services* (1975 (5) 2) was devoted to this topic. Two important and related themes can be identified in this theoretical critique of reproductive medicine. First, an historical shift from female-dominated midwifery to male-dominated obstetrics was held to be the result of *medical imperialism*; that is, a tendency for the medical profession to expand its sphere of competence to include more and more new areas hitherto deemed outside its remit. Many examples of this tendency have been identified; mental health (Szasz 1971), hyperactivity (Conrad 1975), the care of old people (Illich 1975). In the case of human reproduction it is argued that greedy, selfish, and careless men expropriated from caring and careful midwives and lay women the power to help women reproduce naturally, joyfully, and safely (Ehrenreich and English 1973; Donnison 1977; Oakley 1976; Versluysen 1981). Gynaecology and family planning were similarly seen as having been taken over by medical men with questionable motives (Scully 1980; Roberts 1981).

The second theme is related to the first and concerns the *medicalization of reproduction*. It has been argued that women and obstetricians have 'competing ideologies of reproduction', women seeing pregnancy as natural, normal, and a pleasurable life experience and doctors seeing it as a potentially pathological clinical event to be medically managed and controlled (Comaroff 1977; Graham and Oakley 1981; Nelson 1983). This explains the medical profession's provision of antenatal care for what is essentially a normal state of health, doctors' preference for universal hospitalization at birth and active intervention in the form of induction and acceleration of labour, and for operative deliveries (Cartwright 1979; Tew 1986). Obstetricians' reliance upon modern technology and active intervention was seen as taking away women's control and their pleasure in reproduction and making them dependent on man-made machines and obstetric expertise. Birth was seen as having become unnatural, controlled, and alienated (Fleury 1967; Oakley 1975; Cartwright 1979). Katona's (1981) review of antenatal education led him to conclude that antenatal literature is geared to making women conform to this medical model of childbirth.

Similarly, it was argued that since the invention of the pill and the Intra Uterine Device (IUD) and the widespread decline in popularity of barrier methods which accompanied this, the provision of contraception was medicalized (Porter 1986). Despite arguments that medical prescription was totally unnecessary, the most effective methods of contraception were under medical control. Doctors continued to resist attempts to make the pill available over the counter (Family Planning Association conference 1976) whilst denying women free choice of methods (Rakusen 1981). Recently it has been argued that the growth of infertility clinics and complex methods of infertility treatment have led to a medicalization of conception as well as contraception and childbirth (Arditti *et al.* 1984; Roberts 1981).

Implicit in both these themes is the notion of a dominant medical profession which exercises control over the means of reproduction — access to procedures, technology, information and so on — and thereby controls women's bodies and ultimately their lives. Much criticism of this medical dominance was to be found in the feminist health books which flourished in the mid- to late 1970s (MacKeith 1976; Phillips and Rakusen 1978) which informed women how to deal successfully with the medical profession as well as to cope with their medical problems. In these works there was a great deal of criticism of the way in which doctors had hitherto dealt with women patients and women's problems. Gynaecologists were seen by some writers as having little understanding or sympathy for women with unwanted pregnancies, period problems, prolapse, menopausal problems, and so on (Daly 1979; Ehrenreich and English 1979).

These concerns with gynaecology and infertility were not reflected in research studies of reproductive health care at that time (Homans 1985) although the focus had changed from reproductive outcome to women's experiences of services. Sociologists tended to concentrate on pregnancy and childbirth perhaps because of growing public and governmental concern with the functioning of the maternity services and because of the activities of pressure groups like the Association for Improvements in the Maternity Services (AIMS) (Hall *et al.* 1985). Allowing women to speak for themselves for the first time, sociologists graphically illustrated the disquiet and dissatisfaction among patients which consumer groups had already revealed in surveys (Robinson 1974; Garcia 1981). Among women's many criticisms of the maternity services were the impersonal production-line atmosphere of antenatal clinics, their lack of continuity of care, their long waiting times and brief examinations, insufficient information, and no opportunity to raise problems or discuss progress (O'Brien and Smith 1981; Graham and McKee 1979; Oakley 1979; Reid and McIlwaine 1980). Intrapartum care was similarly criticized, with women being particularly dissatisfied with the lack of information provided to them, lack of choice and involvement in decisions made on their behalf, and the unwanted and possibly unnecessary use of procedures such as shaving, administration of enemas, episiotomies, and pharmacological or mechanical intervention in labour and delivery (Cartwright 1979; Oakley 1980; Kirke 1980; Boyd and Sellars 1982).

In other words, research on women's experiences of reproductive health care suggested that the medicalization of reproduction was indeed experienced by women as alienating, that some use of technology and intervention was seen as unnecessary, that there were tremendous problems in communications between women patients and their doctors, and that medical dominance over information and decision making in consultations was unsatisfactory for many women.

This change in attitude among patients and sociologists has been widely noted (Chalmers 1978; Macintyre 1980; Hall *et al.* 1985), and various reasons have been put forward to explain it. Hall, Macintyre and Porter (1985) have suggested that the many changes in technology relating to reproduction — ultrasonic scans, foetal heart monitors, epidural anaesthesia, and so on — which had occurred since the 1960s had been not merely embraced but actively promoted by the medical professsion. These changes occurred at a time when the ecology movement was promoting the 'natural'; the anti-medical establishment lobby (embodied by Illich 1975) was fashionable; and the consumer movement was calling for more evaluation and control of services and a more caring attitude. Also, the newly reborn women's movement which had hitherto been uninterested in reproduction made pregnancy and childbirth into a *cause célèbre*. To sum up:

> It is possible that the coalescence of these four strands of social thought in the mid 1970s played a major role in producing a reaction against what was seen as high technology, medically (and primarily male) dominated, centralized and bureaucratized obstetric care.

(Hall et al. 1985: 3)

However, these four strands are perhaps not sufficient to account for the angry tone of much of the sociological writing on reproductive health care. That anger, I would suggest, was probably the result of sociologists' own personal experience of reproductive health care, since most of them were women, and many of them had experienced medical care relating to their own reproductive biology. Some had had babies (for example, Hart 1977; Comaroff 1977), some had tried to have them (for instance, Pfeffer and Woollett 1983), some had tried not to have them (Porter 1980). Many had experienced the pill; some had suffered menstrual problems or premenstrual tension (Laws *et al.* 1985). Others had experienced the menopause and hormone replacement therapy. These women had been radicalized. Though they did not always write *about* their own experiences, they wrote *from them* or allowed their own experience to influence the way in which they conducted and reported research. They were no longer content to be impartial observers of the medical world but became political activists, spokespersons for the patient, and champions of the underdog. Along with various political pressure groups, feminist journalists, and others they called for human relations to be brought back into obstetrics.

With the birth of the women's movement and feminist sociology that approach has become acceptable. Indeed, the completely 'objective' and impassive stance favoured by the founding fathers of empirical sociology is now rejected in favour of one grounded in the sociologist's actual experience. As a value-free sociology is impossible, sociology should be reflexive, preserving in it 'the presence, concerns and experience of the sociologist as knower and discoverer' (Smith 1987: 92). For the feminist researcher the personal is political; being in the same critical plane as the women whose experiences s/he studies, the feminist sociologist designs her or his research to meet their needs for explanation and action (Harding 1987).

These criticisms of doctors and their behaviour appear to have had some effect on the medical establishment. The Royal College of Obstetricians and Gynaecologists, for instance, has studied and reported on care in labour (1975) and antenatal and intrapartum care (1982). In the early 1970s the medical school curriculum started to include social sciences as the General Medical Council acknowledged the importance of these subjects to the creation of good doctors. In 1980 obstetricians and gynaecologists co-operated with sociologists and psychologists as well as other health professionals to discuss 'pregnancy care for the 1980s' (Zander and Chamberlain 1984), and all over Britain individual doctors or departments made efforts to improve their own practice and women's experiences. These efforts included increasing the involvement of midwives, taking antenatal care back into the community, reducing the number of unnecessary hospital visits, and so forth (Flint 1983; Draper *et al.* 1984; McKee 1984; Hall *et al.* 1985). Rates of induction, which had caused concern in the mid-1970s, declined to 35 per cent of all births by the end of the decade. Obstetric intervention in labour (forceps, vacuum extraction, caesarian section, and so on) continued to increase, however, from 13 per cent of all births in England and Wales in 1970 to 21 per cent in 1978 (Macfarlane and Mugford 1984). That proportion was unchanged in 1985 (OPCS Monitor 1985). Professional resistance to the patient-centred approach to labour favoured by obstetrician Wendy Savage was shown by the inquiry into her professional competence (Savage 1986; Inch 1988); her vindication suggests that the profession may be moving in this direction.

If the medical profession's public statements and actions relating to their own deficiencies reflect their clinical practice and if sociologists' and feminists' writings reflect most women's feelings about reproductive health care, it would be anticipated that changes would have occurred in the consulting room in the actual interaction between women patients and their medical attendants. In a later section I shall examine to what extent that is the case, but first I shall describe the sources of data on which I base my conclusions.

SOURCES OF DATA

Over the past ten years I have completed a number of studies of women's experiences of reproductive health care in Aberdeen and elsewhere in Scotland. The first, a study of childlessness, involved locating and interviewing a sample of thirty-four women who had been married for four or eight years and had remained childless (Porter 1980). Part of this research project was concerned with their experiences with the medical profession *vis-à-vis* their childlessness — namely, their experiences of pronatalism, antagonism, or sympathetic support for voluntary and involuntary childlessness.

The second study was a medical and sociological evaluation of a new system of antenatal care which was introduced in Aberdeen in 1980 and completed with Sally Macintyre and Marion Hall (Hall *et al.* 1985). The new system was expected to retain the benefits of antenatal care for mother and baby whilst reducing the number of routine visits and shifting the balance of care from obstetricians to general practitioners (GPs) and midwives. Studying the effectiveness of the new system involved the observation of antenatal clinics before and after the change, timing women's passage through them, interviewing obstetricians, GPs, midwives, and health visitors before and after the change, and women patients experiencing the new system.

The third study on which my conclusions are based was a prospective study of contraceptive decision making. The object of this study was to find out how and why women choose the methods of contraception they do and why they continue or discontinue with those methods. It involved observing women interacting with family planning providers — doctors, nurses, receptionists, and so on — in a number of different settings throughout Scotland. These settings included gynaecology clinics and wards, postnatal clinics and wards, family planning clinics, general practitioners' surgeries, and domiciliary visits. The women and medical or paramedical staff concerned were then interviewed about the consultations observed, the object being to produce an account which was acceptable to and validated by the participants (Bloor 1978).

In describing what currently happens within reproductive health consultations I shall rely on all three studies, but particularly on the latter two because of their extensive use of observation. In the antenatal care study 755 antenatal consultations were observed, mostly between women and obstetricians; in the contraception study 944 consultations were observed — 282 in general practice, 132 in family planning clinics and the remainder in hospital clinics and wards. We also attended a theoretical course in family planning, intended for doctors completing the Joint Certificate in Family Planning (of the

Royal College of General Practitioners and the Royal College of Obstetricians and Gynaecologists).

Direct observation is a particularly useful technique where detailed description of behaviour and social interaction is required rather than respondents' opinions of what they are doing or what is going on in a situation. As I argued elsewhere (Porter and Macintyre 1984), there may be some differentiation between practitioners' accounts of their behaviour and their actual behaviour. Doctors who were interviewed in the study of antenatal care, for instance, expressed concern over the poor quality of their patients' experiences at overcrowded and impersonal antenatal clinics, yet were observed regularly arriving late and rushing through such clinics, giving women very little opportunity for discussion. Equally, many doctors may believe that they have changed their attitudes and behaviour in the consulting room as a result of public criticism much more than they actually have. This would not be apparent if reliance were placed solely upon interview material.

Providing that observers are accepted in the situation studied, the data collected can be very rich, consisting not only of description of events and social processes but also recording invaluable conversations with those observed. Frequently during periods of observation medical staff made 'off-the-record' comments about patients or their practice. In the contraceptive study these were systematically recorded and analysed along with the entire content of each relevant consultation — that is, one concerned with reproductive health (see Porter 1986 for more details of research methods).

As Scully (1980) has shown, observation can be a fairly stressful and radicalizing experience for the observer who may at times wish to intervene and to right wrongs seen perpetrated. This certainly accords with my own experience and that of my colleagues. I usually refrained from interfering, but I feel no hesitation in reporting some of the transgressions observed. Indeed, as a feminist sociologist who has also been a gynaecology and obstetric patient on a number of occasions, I feel bound to publish my findings in the hope that future generations of women may receive more sympathetic treatment than did those cited here.

CHANGES IN REPRODUCTIVE HEALTH CONSULTATIONS

In this section I shall consider what has and has not changed in the recent past in doctor–patient interaction in reproductive health consultations. I will show that such changes as have occurred may not always be attributable to acknowledgement of the feminist and consumerist criticisms of care outlined above. I have insufficient data to examine all problematic aspects of reproductive health consultations and shall concentrate on those types which were observed directly — that is, gynaecology, antenatal, and family planning consultations — whether they occurred in hospitals, clinics, surgeries, or patients' own homes. I shall focus upon the main shortfalls identified earlier: namely, medicalization, communications, and medical dominance.

The medicalization of reproduction

So far as I know no attempt has been made to de-medicalize the routine provision of contraception despite criticisms of it. Indeed, doctors continue to resist any suggestion that they should not be involved in issuing the pill, and with the threat of AIDS spreading rapidly they seem likely to be more involved than previously in issuing condoms. Infertility treatment is perhaps too new, too specialist, and too threatened to respond to its critics. In a time of drastic cuts in funding of health services it is busy trying to justify its existence.

Throughout Britain changes have occurred in the delivery of antenatal care. Apparently in recognition of women's feelings about and preferences for those delivering antenatal care there has been a devolution of power from obstetricians to midwives and GPs, and a movement away from specialist hospital clinics to community clinics (Macintyre and Porter 1989). In Aberdeen this change to GP care has been welcomed by women experiencing it. They found the GP's service more convenient and more friendly and personal than the service provided by the hospital clinic. Midwives who started giving antenatal care under the new system received a more mixed reception, probably because they worked in an inconvenient hospital clinic, were often as busy as their medical colleagues, and were not involved in delivering the baby or attending women at home. Women did not complain that midwives rushed in and out with barely a word, as did obstetricians, but they did not perceive any great benefit in the midwife's care and did not think she had done anything the GP could not have done (Hall *et al.* 1985). On the other hand, simply changing the emphasis of care provided for certain patients from very specialist to less specialist — that is, obstetrician to GP or midwife — does not redefine pregnancy as a natural, normal event. It is still a medical event and it is still medically managed.

Without observations or relevant interview data it is difficult to say what changes have occurred in the medical management of labour and delivery. At Aberdeen, and probably at most hospitals, women are no longer routinely shaved or given an enema before labour. This may, however, be a response not to feminist criticism but to clinical trials which have shown these procedures to be ineffective (Romney and Gordon 1981; Drayton and Rees 1984). Several sources suggest that it is easier now to get a trial of labour or a so-called natural birth than it was ten years ago (Houd and Oakley 1986), but Britain now has the highest rate of surgical intervention in Europe (Bergsjo *et al.* 1986) and home births are still few and far between.

Some women now complain of the difficulty of getting effective pain relief in labour. It appears that many hospitals have embraced the totally 'natural' model of childbirth currently in vogue among middle-class women to the exclusion of the more technological and pain-free one favoured by working-class women (Nelson 1983; Reid *et al.* 1983). The feminist journalist Polly Toynbee has frequently complained, in the pages of the *Guardian* and elsewhere, that she has twice been denied the 'high tech' birth she wanted with effective pain relief, and forced to have a natural birth which she did not enjoy (Toynbee 1985, 1986, 1987). When the Wendy Savage trial was being sympathetically reported in the press, a woman wrote to the *Guardian* defending women's rights to have a technological birth rather than a natural birth. She says of the epidural anaesthesia she elected to have:

> Yes, epidural, some may call it cowardly, I call it common sense, I didn't have my appendix out without anaesthetic, nor my teeth filled without injections, why am I supposed to endure (no, correction enjoy) hours of pain during childbirth?
>
> (Cartwright 1986)

Further research is needed to see whether, in embracing women's concerns for a more natural birth, the medical profession has gone too far and again effectively denied them choice.

Communication problems

Attempts have been made throughout Britain to improve communications between pregnant women and their medical and midwifery attendants (Macintyre and Porter 1989). The degree of success achieved has not yet been fully reported. Observations in various Scottish locations suggest that many of the problems of communication about which women complained remain. For instance, despite the introduction of the new system of antenatal care in Aberdeen, designed to give doctors more time per patient, there was no change in the quantity or quality of interaction between women and doctors. Although no more time was available after the introduction of the new system than had been available before it, it is questionable whether doctors would have used that time to discuss women's problems or answer their questions. As reported elsewhere (Hall *et al.* 1985), we found that the time taken per patient and the number of topics covered varied by individual doctor and not by the time available, some doctors always taking more time and having more to say to each patient than did others.

Unfortunately there were too few female doctors to examine fully the relationship between time and trouble taken and sex of doctor. Many of the feminist critics of medicine seem to have assumed that if there were more female doctors, women would automatically receive more time, sympathy, and understanding, if not better medical care. In the field of reproductive medicine there are more women doctors at the junior level than there were twenty years ago but this may not be so radical an improvement as might have been hoped. Nearly all patients interviewed in the contraception study expressed a preference for women doctors dealing with 'female' problems, and the majority who had had experience of women doctors reported women to be gentler when carrying out internal examinations.

However, we observed that family planning doctors — all of whom were female — were often impatient with women's difficulties and doubts about their contraceptive methods: junior women doctors were just as likely as men to make unkind or sexist comments about patients or to lack understanding of their problems. The following conversation occurred between a male consultant and three female residents:

Over coffee the doctors discussed women's problems with the pill. Consultant said he was faintly amused at the way so many things got blamed on the pill and he often had to remind himself that men got headaches, men got fat, men got depressed too. Residents all wholeheartedly agreed and one told us of a previous resident who had heard this story so often she no longer believed anyone who presented with such symptoms. Another said it was entirely due to women's changing lifestyles at the time they went on the pill.

(Author's fieldnote: MP/GW11/8)

A female registrar was observed to be dismissive of women's problems with the contraceptive pill and unsympathetic to those who simply felt uncomfortable about using hormonal contraception. She later confided to the observer that she thought the pill was wonderful and could not see why women 'invented' all these problems with it. A female trainee in general practice remarked of a woman who had become pregnant long after her husband had had a vasectomy that she was surprised because she thought that the woman was so unattractive that no one other than her husband would want to sleep with her.

Furthermore, women doctors could be less sympathetic than men to some unpleasant symptoms experienced by many women. One senior doctor was reputed to tell patients that she too had period problems and she still came to work, so why did they not just get on with living? Another apparently had such easy labours herself that she had little sympathy for women's suffering. These comments and attitudes were not directly observed by us but reported to us by more junior doctors and residents on the wards:

Somehow the subject of neurotic women and their pelvic pain came up. The residents were very dismissive of this and said that Dr X's attitude was right and such women should learn to live with their conditions as she did. The female student said that Dr X was a pretty amazing woman and it was not fair to expect all women to be like her.

(MP/GW8/4)

Unfortunately some residents assumed that this hard line was the correct attitude towards certain problematic patients.

Observing in gynaecology wards and clinics we noticed that doctors still tend to label certain patients for whom they cannot find a solution. Women with undiagnosed and inexplicable pelvic pain tended to be labelled 'neurotic'. One senior doctor explained to the observers that women projected problems in their daily lives on to their pelvic organs and appeared at the clinic with unspecified pain. These women could often be recognized by doctors in advance by the thickness of their casenotes:

> After the consultation the doctor told the observer the patient had been in and out of hospital over the years always with unidentifiable pains in the abdomen. Consultant had left explicit instructions not to do a hysterectomy because it would not solve her problems and she would blame the doctors.

> (MP/PC22/11)

Unfortunately, junior doctors on the wards often accepted this view unquestioningly and were observed to baulk at thick files. One resident picked up a thick file and said that he was 'off to see another neurotic patient'. Sympathizing with the women, we tended to see this labelling of problematic patients as doctors' ways of coping with the failure to diagnose or rectify the condition.

Similarly, doctors at family planning clinics tended to label women who had tried but could not find a satisfactory method of contraception as 'neurotic' and to be visibly impatient with them. Although they acknowledged in interviews that all methods had flaws and the choice for some women was very small, they thought that the normal, reasonable woman ought to be able to find *something* to suit her. Thus despite the public criticisms and their acknowledgement by the establishment, little seems to have changed in this respect since Stimson (1976) reported GPs categorizing certain women patients as 'trouble'.

This labelling of problematic patients was symptomatic of doctors' tendency to work with ideal types. These ideal type patients were described to us in formal and informal interviews and held up as the standard against which all such patients should be judged. For example, the ideal type sterilization patient was a woman in her early thirties, happily married with two or three children. The ideal type depo provera patient was a woman in her early twenties with a large number of unwanted pregnancies, not in a stable relationship and living in local authority housing in a poor part of the city. The quotation below is from an interview with a female registrar:

MP: Do you very often get asked for the injection, depo provera?
Dr: No, not really asked for it. It's more something you suggest for

the sort of girl I was talking about earlier, who is single and unreliable and likely to be exposed to venereal infection so the pill would not be very suitable for her. And you know it's quite a good idea for that sort of girl.

We found that in some cases the majority of patients conformed to type whereas in others the ideal bore surprisingly little resemblance to reality. The average or typical sterilization patient in Aberdeen was indeed a woman in her late twenties or early thirties with two or three children, although she might not have had a particularly happy marriage. The typical depo provera patient, on the other hand, was in her mid-twenties and had only two or three children and simply could not be bothered taking the pill every day. She was certainly living in a poorer part of the city but might or might not be in a stable relationship.

Unfortunately, doctors' use of such stereotypes effectively limits the options available to patients in that those not conforming to type tend to be denied that option. This was true not only of gynaecology but also family planning patients. Many middle-class women in the contraceptive study knew nothing about depo provera and asked the interviewers for further details: one, who was observed asking a doctor for it, was told simply that it was unsuitable for her. On the other hand, doctors had the idea that cap users were mainly educated, middle-class women in stable relationships who could be relied upon to insert the cap regularly before intercourse. In many cases this was true, but it means that doctors rarely offered the cap to women not in this category or actively dissuaded those who asked for it and were deemed unsuitable (Porter 1986).

Our observations show that doctors still tend to disbelieve patients if their explanation or information does not fit with the doctor's own assessment of the situation:

> Doctor asked patient how often she had intercourse with ex-boy-friend. Patient said only once. Doctor shouted that he knew that was a lie. Told her that 'they' all say that and it did not matter to him how often it happened, it would not affect his decision but it was important for future contraception that she admit to frequent sex.
> (MP/GC89/4)

Doctors' view of procreation seemed to have changed little since Macintyre described in 1976 the 'social construction of instincts' —

196

namely, the notion that married women instinctively want children and unmarried women do not. Thus women who claimed to have conceived the first time they had unprotected intercourse were likely to be disbelieved if they were young and single but not if they were married. Women who were seeking an abortion and who claimed that pregnancy was due to contraceptive failure were less likely to be believed than those continuing with the pregnancy. One gynaecologist said that sheaths did not burst so much as 'remain in handbags'. Young women requesting abortion who claimed to have a regular boyfriend were sometimes disbelieved, as were those who claimed to have split up with the father of an unwanted child. Most gynaecologists worked, perhaps rightly, on the assumption that women tried to present an acceptable account in order to get a termination. Young single women whose account was what the staff saw as too acceptable were therefore likely to be disbelieved. Such an account might portray an innocent or unlucky girl caught out in a single transgression with no man to marry or support her; this is little different from the acceptable stories Macintyre (1977) had described ten years earlier.

In antenatal clinics pregnant women were still being treated as unreliable observers of their menstrual cycles (cf. Oakley 1980), and scans were often taken as giving the 'true' gestation of pregnancy rather than the woman's recollection of her last menstrual period. Doctors seemed unaware of the distress it could cause a woman suddenly to find her pregnancy put back a month because her dates did not agree with the scan. Similarly, contracepting women were not always treated as reliable witnesses to the side effects they experienced. Weight gain, depression, loss of libido, and so on were often put down to women's lives rather than the effects of the contraceptive pill. Admittedly, they seemed to us to be offered rather tentatively, in many cases, as though the women did not really believe it themselves (or feared that they would be disbelieved). Yet some family planning doctors were observed warning women to expect these very symptoms when they first started the pill.

Elsewhere we have argued that many doctors and para-medical workers seem to have a low opinion of the women patients with whom they came into contact, distrusting them or treating them as ignorant (Macintyre and Porter 1989). We based this argument on our experiences in completing the antenatal care study (Hall et al. 1985) and reports of doctors' lack of appreciation of patients' medical knowledge (McKinlay 1975). Also Reid (1983) reports that patients in a Glasgow community clinic were expected to steal the toys provided for their waiting children. The aforementioned tendency to disbelieve patients may be part of the same lack of respect for them. Thus obstetricians and GPs interviewed in the antenatal study were mainly of the opinion that women could not be trusted to carry their own notes, although studies have shown that they are more reliable than a medical records department (Taylor 1984). Similarly, patients at antenatal, gynaecology, and family planning clinics were believed to be unreliable timekeepers and to fail to keep appointments. The default rate has always been a big issue with the providers of antenatal care (Parsons and Perkins 1980), and bookings at the antenatal clinics studied were organized on the assumption that one patient in four would default. A careful check of attendance records revealed, however, that very few women defaulted and those who did usually had very good reasons for doing so (Hall *et al.* 1985).

The amount of information given out by doctors and knowledge of the workings of women's bodies shared with them are still minimal in all the settings studied. The patient in the consultation below was dissatisfied with the information she had received but apparently felt too inhibited to ask questions:

> Patient said she felt something coming down. Dr examined and said he could not detect a prolapse; said he would write to her GP and tell him to prescribe cream for the area. Patient said she had been using cream for several months. Doctor said OK and told her to go and change. Said he would see her again in six months. Patient said 'Is that all?' and left looking very subdued.
>
> (MP/GC47/3)

The women's movement has argued for a sharing of knowledge and expertise on the grounds that knowledge is power (Fee 1975). A large proportion of gynaecologists and some family doctors routinely gave women so little information that we questioned the practice in interviews with them. We were usually told that patients would not take in or understand what was said to them or that the majority had no wish to know.

The doctors' belief that women did not wish to know may be based on their behaviour in consultations. We observed that relatively few women asked questions — 49 per cent of gynaecological clinic patients asked one or more questions, 37 per cent of patients asked questions in antenatal clinics, as did only 28 per cent of postnatal patients — and when interviewed few women said they had had questions they had wanted to ask but had not done so. In gynaecological clinics we observed women being told they would have to have a D and C (dilation of the cervix and curettage of the womb) to find the cause of a problem or confirm a diagnosis based on vaginal examination. None of the women ever argued with these suggestions and very few asked for further details. The women seemed more concerned with how long they would have to be in hospital or off work than with the decision or the operation itself:

> Examining the patient the doctor said she had a small polyp on the cervix which bled when touched. He then said that she had fibroids but that would not explain her erratic periods, only heavier periods which she was not having. Doctor said they would have her in for a small operation and she would receive tablets later on to regulate her periods. Patient asked if it could be done today. Doctor said not and she would receive a card telling her when to come in. Patient left.

> (MP/GC68/3)

Similarly, patients requesting sterilization were more interested in whether they could be done as day patients than in the details of the operation. Even those women who were told that a hysterectomy would be best for them never questioned this diagnosis or asked about alternatives, though some doctors punctiliously went through the alternatives available.

It may be that women did not find the atmosphere at specialist clinics conducive to asking questions, or feared that they would not be treated sympathetically if they did so. They did not appear to be saving them up for consultations with family doctors, however. As we have argued elsewhere (Porter and Macintyre 1989), medical responses to questioning women were often very poor. Pregnant women who followed the advice literature and saved up all their questions to ask at the antenatal clinic were likely to be labelled 'anxious'. Women who took an interest in the results of their routine measurements — blood pressure, haemoglobin, weight, and urine — were also likely to be seen as neurotic. This suggests that little has changed in this respect since Hart (1977) noted that obstetricians labelled vocal, demanding women 'difficult'.

On the other hand, doctors sometimes withheld information for which they were pointedly asked. One woman was diagnosed as having cancer of the cervix. Upon finding it the doctor became very agitated and insisted that the sociological observer look at it, but he refused to discuss the possibility of cancer with the woman even though she asked, 'What if it's cancer, doctor?' He arranged for her to come in for a biopsy the next day, and when she had gone he told the observer, the midwife, and a medical colleague that it was cancer. He then dictated a letter to the woman's GP saying he was sure it was cancer. Thus everyone but the patient concerned was aware that a cancer was present.

On quite a number of occasions women raised topics which were simply ignored by the doctor because, it seemed to us, the topic was not defined as relevant by the doctor. The patient in the following example was referred to the gynaecology clinic with menstrual irregularity:

> Patient said that one of her problems was that she felt everything was falling out after her periods. Doctor said a D and C would not do much good at this stage. Discussed her hormones and the drugs she had taken to sort them out. Patient said she was very shaky and was sitting weeping for nothing these days. Doctor said he would give her some tablets and explained when she should take them. Patient asked him to write it down because she would forget but the doctor merely repeated his instructions. Patient asked if shaking was due to the change of life. Doctor said that the menopause would not cause her to be shaky and then described the (healthy) condition of her cervix.

> (MP/GC/4)

In other cases women referred with menstrual problems mentioned intolerable side effects of some contraceptive method they had been using or the length of time they had been trying for a family without success. Some doctors ignored such 'irrelevancies' completely, whilst others acknowledged but did not explore them. This behaviour is contrary to modern notions of good medical practice; analysts of patient–doctor communications have long stressed the importance of the 'hidden agenda', particularly in consultations of this sort (Zola 1963; Balint 1964).

These data suggest that knowledge sharing remains a feminist ideal, as is the idea of self-examination. Very few of the women interviewed said that they examined their own breasts although younger hospital doctors and family planning clinic doctors tended to encourage it. Doctors also encouraged coil wearers to check for the threads of the coil though few women reported doing so when interviewed. No doctors encouraged women to examine their own cervixes. When interviewed, most doctors said they thought it a futile practice: yet, many of them felt that the recommended time of five years between smears was too long; cancer could develop in less than one year. This gap between what doctors say and do has been discussed elsewhere (Porter and Macintyre 1984).

Medical dominance

In the foregoing discussion of the poor communications still occurring within reproductive health consultations it is apparent that in controlling information, the medical profession also controls access to the means of reproduction — contraception, conception, abortion, sterilization, and pregnancy and childbirth. That control has remained virtually intact despite the many criticisms which have been levelled at it. This medical dominance operates at two levels. First, doctors have the power *directly* to deny women access to procedures such as abortion, sterilization, and epidural anaesthesia, treatment such as hormone replacement therapy and infertility drugs or methods of contraception and assisted conception. Second, they are in a position to do so *indirectly* by limiting the range of options from which women may choose. This practice was particularly prevalent in family planning consultations where doctors not only worked with stereotypes of 'suitable' patients, imposing rigid, non-medical criteria for certain methods but also described favoured methods in such a way as to deny women choice.

As was shown earlier, doctors often work with notions of ideal type patients. As a result they offer certain women certain methods of contraception and withhold information from others. The following example is from notes taken during a gynaecology clinic:

Doctor said the problem was to find the patient a satisfactory method of contraception if she did not want the coil and husband did not like the sheath. Patient said it looked like sterilization. Doctor said 'there is the cap but it's an awful scutter.' Said he didn't know how organized she was but it had to be put in so many hours

201

before and not taken out until so many hours afterwards. Woman laughed and said she didn't fancy that at all.

(MP/GC27/5)

One doctor told us that she did not like the statistics for the contraceptive sponge's effectiveness and could not recommend it. She told women who wished to try it that it contained so much spermicide that it ran down the user's legs. Other doctors who felt the same way about its effectiveness simply said (inaccurately) that it was little better than using no contraception.

In addition to describing methods they did not favour in a very negative way, family planning personnel emphasized the good aspects of methods they approved and played down their shortcomings. This was particularly noticeable with respect to the pill, which seemed to be the method favoured by the majority of doctors. Women who asked about the risks or side effects were often told not to worry because they were not in a risk group — for example not smokers or not over 35. Side effects were usually described as 'very minor' and experienced by an unlucky few whereas those of the IUD seemed to be seen as serious, universal, and unavoidable. One gynaecologist explained his attitudes as follows:

'I prefer not to use coils if possible. As I say it's the pill unless there is some reason a woman can't have it. And then I would prefer to use some other method to the coil for women who have never been pregnant because of the risk of infection and subsequent infertility which I think is a total disaster because infertility is my special interest. I would do anything in my power to persuade a woman who didn't have family that she should use the pill.'

Women responding to pill scares often had their doubts dismissed or were presented with so few acceptable alternatives they felt obliged to continue with the pill against their own better judgement. In such ways as these family planning doctors indirectly controlled women's access to methods of contraception and effectively limited their choice to those they favoured.

In most areas of Scotland women requiring terminations or sterilizations have to gain the consent of a gynaecologist. Thus doctors still control access to these means of fertility control just as they do to the most effective methods of contraception (that is, the non-barrier methods). It appears to be easier to get a termination now than it was ten years ago, even in Aberdeen which has had a liberal attitude to abortion and sterilization since the 1960s when hospital policy was to ensure that every child should be a wanted child (Baird 1965). A number of women in the contraception study commented in interviews on how much easier it had been than they had expected. We only saw one woman refused out of forty termination requests observed, whereas only 55 per cent got them in 1975 (Fullerton 1985). The woman who was refused was married and in good health but did not feel that she could cope with another pregnancy. The doctor told her she did not have grounds for a termination under the Act. That may well have been true, but many other women in the same or similar circumstances got their terminations. And it is very likely that, had the woman seen a different doctor, she would have been granted the termination.

It would appear that the seemingly arbitrary nature of the decision to grant a termination or not, about which women complained in the mid-1970s, remains, although doctors may no longer be *fully* exercising the power over women's lives and destinies which the 1967 Abortion Act gave them. Several explained to us that they left the decision entirely to the woman and that this enabled them to reconcile the abortion with their own consciences. On the other hand, certain gynaecologists took the opportunity to lecture women on sleeping around, having repeat abortions, or claiming to have taken risks only once:

> The doctor asked the patient if she had felt guilty after her last termination. She said that she had but knew it was the right thing to do. The doctor pointed out the risks of termination and the risks of infertility after repeat terminations. He told her they could advise her what to do, what method of contraception to use but they could not make her use it and that there was some risk of her not being able to become pregnant when she wanted to if she kept having repeat terminations. The doctor asked her 'in the light of that wee lecture' what she would do this time and she said she would go on the pill.
>
> (EA/GC60/4)

Another way in which gynaecologists exercised their power over termination patients was to send them for a scan. The justification for this was invariably that the doctor thought the woman was further on with her pregnancy than she said. We interviewed only one woman to whom this had happened. She proved to have accurately estimated her gestation and described the scan experience as 'cruel'.

Continuing to control women's access to sterilization, doctors sometimes seemed to exercise their power in a sexist way owing partly to their adherence to rules based on ideal types. It was no longer the case, as Jean Aitken-Swan (1977) found, that it was virtually impossible for the nulliparous to get sterilized. On the contrary, doctors described themselves as willing to consider the case of intelligent couples who definitely did not want children. It was the married multiparous woman of only 25 who raised problems for them and attractive single women of any age. One 25-year-old estranged wife of a prisoner with four children and two terminations behind her was told that she could not be sterilized until she was 30 because she was young and attractive and might remarry and want more children. Doctors justified such attitudes by referring to the number of reversals requested. Quite apart from the fact that a woman of 30 still has time to meet another man and have another family, it suggests that the decision might have been different had the woman been assessed as less attractive.

Whereas men used to be discouraged, the presence of the baby's father at the birth is now virtually mandatory. This change in attitude to men in the labour ward may not be a response to women's complaints about being left alone in labour, however. If a woman does not have a partner to hold her hand and mop her brow a midwife has to be freed to perform these tasks, and this can be a problem in times of staff shortages. Furthermore, our observations suggest that men may still be *personae non gratae* at some gynaecology clinics.

DISCUSSION

The foregoing data suggest that women's experiences in reproductive health consultations have not changed greatly as a result of feminist/ sociological criticisms of them and that many of the shortcomings highlighted in the literature review remain. It is therefore slightly surprising that we observed little overt conflict or disagreement and recorded very few instances of disharmony. Even where male doctors were fairly provocative — for example, suggesting that vaginal discharge, premenstrual tension, or period pains were a normal part of being a woman, and must therefore be accommodated — women did not show any signs of annoyance or even surprise:

Doctor said this (dysmenorrhoea/discoloured bleeding) was not a surgical problem but a hormonal one and he wasn't very hopeful of finding a solution. It just happened to some women from time to time. Patient asked if it was anything to do with the premenstrual syndrome. The doctor repeated that is was hormonal and they could try lots of things. He said he did not mean to be a male chauvinist pig but it would be a good idea to learn to live with things, for example getting round the problem by facing up to it or avoiding things that might irritate her. The patient said she just swells up anyway, goes from a twenty-four inch waist to a thirty-four inch and can't get her shoes on. Doctor said he would see her again about the black bleeding and patient left.

(EA/GC47/5)

When interviewed afterwards patients rarely expressed dissatisfaction, or recounted the sort of stories described by Stimson and Webb (1975). In these accounts of consultations which had recently occurred, patients often cast themselves in the role of hero or heroine and, putting the doctor in his or her place, they gained the power and effectively redressed the balance of right and wrong. Although our respondents appeared to us to have 'wrongs to be righted', one reason they may not have told such stories to us may have been because we were often present at the consultations and so any elaboration, by them, of what happened would have been seen as a fabrication. It was rare for a woman to express annoyance or dissatisfaction with even the most untoward events. For example, the woman who was refused a termination was asked about how she felt about it:

'Well I was a bit surprised. My own doctor said it was all right and all I had to do was to see the gynaecologist. I wasn't expecting this. I don't know what I'm going to do.'

In fact she was subsequently allowed to see another gynaecologist. In Edinburgh I observed a woman of 30 who was told by a family planning doctor that it was perhaps time she thought about starting a family. The woman looked totally taken aback, and said, 'I'd like to be married first.' When interviewed she merely expressed surprise at this occurrence, whereas a few years ago, in Aberdeen, childless women experiencing such medical pronatalism were furious, as the following extract shows:

When I went back the last time to get my prescription for the pill he (the doctor) told me he wasn't going to give me them. So I just promptly went to the lady doctor. Och I'll have no bloody man telling me I can't have my pill.

(Porter 1980: 279)

Like other researchers in this area (Kirke 1980a; Macintyre 1984), we found that women were most unwilling to comment on what the doctor had said or done although they complained at length about waiting times, having to undress, being practised on by medical students and nosey or obstreperous receptionists. This silence was not a result of deference to the medical profession because they were happy to criticize other doctors or the same doctors in circumstances other than those observed. But women's criticisms were not really about medical decision making so much as *being* a doctor or family planning nurse or good medical practice. For example, GPs were criticized for not doing vaginal examinations or smears. Many women felt that a 'proper' doctor would do them if he were issuing women with the pill:

When I went to go for the pill, I thought first of all you'd have to have an examination, I mean I didn't even get my blood pressure taken. It was just a case of he signed the prescription for the pill. . . . I used to just write away for one six month batch and then I used to go for the other . . . just in case he wanted to see me.

Do you think he should have done more?

Well I thought I should have had a bit more than that. I mean I should have really insisted I suppose but I felt fairly healthy within myself and I just thought well you always rely on them to know best don't you?

Family planning nurses were criticized for being indiscreet about the women they were seeing — for example, shouting patients' names in Glasgow tenements or posting contraceptive supplies through the letterbox.

There are several possible explanations for women's compliance with unhelpful or sexist doctors and their apparent lack of overt anger about the continuing poor quality of experiences in consultations such as these. First, these criticisms may never have reflected women's own feelings about such consultations, but been a preoccupation with feminist journalists and sociologists removed from ordinary women's experiences. As sociologists tend to talk mainly to one another and to other educated and radical women, they may be unaware of the feelings of ordinary women with quite different concerns or 'purposes at hand'. This possibility is supported by research on working-class women's perceptions of pregnancy and childbirth which shows them to be closer to the medical ideology than the natural, normal one that feminist sociologists claim women hold (Nelson 1983; Reid *et al.* 1983).

On the other hand, perhaps it is expecting too much of such women to contest the authority of the doctor, to criticize behaviour which is simply symptomatic of much more sexist behaviour in our society. Indeed, acquiescence may be in a patient's own best interests. Thus, second, patients may not question the doctor's authority or behaviour because they believe that they will end up receiving worse treatment if they do.

This would not explain, however, why patients did not express annoyance or dissatisfaction to us in interviews even when pressed to do so. This could be, third, because they identified us with the hospital or the medical establishment having first met us in that context, and were reluctant to be overtly critical and appear rude. Though we tried to make it clear that we were critically studying the staff and events occurring at the various settings, this may have worked against us. Patients may have believed that their criticisms would somehow get back to the staff concerned and affect any future treatment they received.

Fourth, patients may not have felt 'qualified' to argue with or criticize the doctor. We observed that doctors were expert at offering patients what appeared to be very good reasons for everything they do and it is virtually impossible for a non-medical person to argue with them. As this has important implications for the feminist and socio-logical demand for greater patient participation in decision making I should like to give some examples to illustrate this point.

In antenatal clinics we observed a few women asking for a home confinement. None of the obstetricians favoured home confinements, and, while they told such women that it was 'a possibility', they also pointed out that it would entail having to find a midwife and GP willing to do it. As the obstetricians knew, at that time such midwives and GPs were few and far between. Similarly, women asking for a Leboyer-type delivery were told that they could have a modified Leboyer delivery if everything was normal; that is, they could have dimmed lights, no loud noises, and the cord need not be cut immediately, but the new-born baby could not be bathed because it is too cold in Aberdeen. Regardless of the outside temperature the labour ward is always like an oven, but few mothers would probably be brave enough to argue that it is not too cool to bath a new-born baby.

Similarly we observed women asking for a natural childbirth, and nearly all of them were told they could have a natural childbirth if the labour appeared normal and there were no contra-indications to it. Some doctors explained that they would monitor the contractions and the baby's heart rate and check the fluid and interfere no further if all appeared to be well. If there were problems such as the baby becoming distressed they would however have to intervene and help the baby out. In my opinion no woman told that her baby is becoming distressed will lightly refuse the forceps, episiotomy, or caesarian section. Few women will refuse to be induced or accelerated if they are told that it is in their baby's best interests. These are matters of clinical judgement which most women would probably feel powerless to challenge. The natural vaginal delivery is bound to go by the board if the doctor tells the labouring woman the baby cannot get out that way. She has not the knowledge, understanding, or confidence to argue or the wish to endanger her child's life. Perhaps the best that women can hope for is to be given full explanations of medical decisions rather than involvement in them.

As we have already said, women in gynaecology clinics often seemed uninterested in quite major decisions being made about their health and bodies, such as decisions about sterilization or hysterectomy. They may have felt that there was nothing effective they could say or do. In family planning clinics women were sometimes required to play an active part in decision making, and this they often seemed to find hard to do. In most routine family planning consultations no choice or decision was involved; the woman simply said that she wanted a repeat prescription of the pill. The doctor asked if she had any problems, and upon hearing that she had none issued six months' supply. Where a choice was to be made it was often small; for example, doctors would not fit IUDs in women who had no children, so a woman wanting to come off the pill might only be able to choose the cap. Even so, when doctors explained the risks or the side effects or details of a method, women sometimes asked the doctor what she thought they should do:

Doctor told the patient (who wanted to come off the pill) that the snag with the cap was that it was not quite so effective i.e. two or three pregnancies per hundred women per year. Patient was horrified to hear this. Doctor discussed with her how important it was not to get pregnant. Patient asked doctor what she should do in the circumstances.

(MP/E/6,10)

In these circumstances doctors usually said that it was up to the woman to decide for herself and that she would only be happy with the method if she chose it.

CONCLUSION

During the last ten years there has been little change in the medical profession's tendency to expand its remit or to define natural, normal processes such as pregnancy and childbirth as medical events. On the contrary, demands for an expansion of pre-pregnancy care and for routine use of HIV screening in antenatal clinics suggest that medical domination of women's lives and lifestyles is increasing. Furthermore, evidence is now coming from the USA that obstetricians are taking patients to court to ensure that they have the (usually hospitalized, technological) type of confinement the obstetricians prefer (Hughes 1987). The changes which have occurred in reproductive health consultations since the mid-1970s, when criticisms first started being voiced, are few, and quite probably owe very little to the feminist or consumer movements. Not only does medicalization of reproductive health continue virtually unabated, but also communication between patients and doctors often remains poor and the dominance of the profession over information and decision making is unremitting. Consultations would need to change both their content and form much more in order to satisfy the critics of the medical profession.

This chapter has questioned whether those criticisms are really representative of the feelings experienced by the majority of patients, or whether they are those of the vocal and largely middle-class minority. If the majority of women do wish for more information and involvement in decision making, research should be directed at how this can be achieved, as there seems to be some doubt about how active that involvement can be, given the different power and knowledge bases of patients and doctors. Doctors may not be willing or able to furnish patients with non-technical explanations which enable them really to participate in decision making, and patients may be uninterested in becoming 'informed' consumers of services. It may be that patients need a truly independent medical expert to intervene and interpret for them. In the absence of such a patient advocate, medical sociologists and feminists may be able to speak for patients' needs but they must take care to represent the interest of all women experiencing reproductive health care.

ACKNOWLEDGEMENTS

This chapter is based on a number of research projects carried out at the University of Aberdeen and funded by the Medical Research Council, the Scottish Home and Health Department, and the Family Planning Association. I am grateful to the women, their partners, and the health service staff who took part in the various studies. I am also indebted to Marion Hall and Sally Macintyre with whom I have collaborated in the past and whose work forms part of the basis of the chapter.

Part Five

HEALTH-CARE ORGANIZATION

Chapter Nine

ORGANIZING AND MANAGING HEALTH CARE: A CHALLENGE FOR MEDICAL SOCIOLOGY

DAVID HUNTER

INTRODUCTION

It has been suggested that health service policy-makers and managers devote much of their time to problems that are less amenable to the knowledge and technology of medicine than they are to the research findings and methods of the social and behavioural sciences (Levine and Sorenson 1983). If there is any salience in this view then the conceptual, empirical, and methodological approaches provided by medical sociologists are highly relevant for health-care policy-makers and practising health service managers. However, there is little evidence that medical sociologists regard their discipline in this light, or that policy-makers and managers explicitly value the contribution of medical sociology in understanding better the policy and organizational settings they inhabit.

The theme of this chapter is that medical sociologists do have an important contribution to make but that it remains in danger of not being made. The chapter assesses the potential contribution of medical sociology to the understanding of organizing and managing health-care services in the UK. It argues that with few exceptions this has been, and continues to be, an area neglected by medical sociologists. The chapter refers to work that has been carried out in the UK, mainly stimulated by successive reorganizations of the National Health Service (NHS) commencing in 1974 and culminating in the introduction of general management a decade or so later. Most research into organizing and managing health care has been conducted by those working in disciplines other than medical sociology, notably health economics, which raises the question of why medical sociology has been eclipsed. It is important to address this question and to seek explanations for medical sociology's weak contribution. Some of these relate to particular preoccupations within medical sociology itself; others concern the wider socio-political environment in which research is conducted. There is a section which reports on some of the author's own recent work by way of illustrating the importance of sociological insights into the organization and management of health care. The chapter concludes with a portfolio of the kinds of research and policy concerns which might merit attention from medical sociologists.

CONTRIBUTION OF MEDICAL SOCIOLOGY

Illsley (1980: 162) laments the dearth of research by medical sociologists 'at the policy and system level, on health planning and the organization of health care'. He posits that the vacuum may be caused by selective funding from central government and difficulties of access for detailed observational and interactionist work on the policy and planning process. It may, however, also reflect a lack of interest among medical sociologists themselves, most of whom continue to inhabit the heartlands of the discipline comprised of, *inter alia*, the following issues: health inequalities, the professionalization of medicine, and the sick role. Illsley cites policy and its implementation as a major gap in understanding how health-care systems operate. He contrasts the absence of policy research with the relative abundance of research completed by medical sociologists on professionals and their work reflecting a more general sociological stream of activity embracing, for example, education and teachers, the law and the police. This gap is evident in the British collection of readings in medical sociology assembled by Tuckett and Kaufert (1978). There is no section on health policy or organization and management — only a section on the organization of hospitals. A similar gap exists in Robinson's (1978) introduction to medical sociology. The sociological approaches to health and medicine reviewed by Morgan, Calnan, and Manning (1985) also contain no mention of health policy although the authors implicitly acknowledge the gap in the final chapter on future directions. In contrast, in the United States, Mechanic's (1980) collection of readings on medical sociology has an entire section devoted to health care and social policy with chapters on health planning and the political economy of health care.

Medical sociology tends to be of either a macro (for example, identifying structural determinants in health inequalities) or micro (such as penetrating doctor–patient relationships) nature. The meso level — the intermediate layer where policy and organizational and managerial processes tend to be concentrated — is perhaps considered not to be legitimate territory for medical sociologists. It is certainly territory where medical sociologists are thin on the ground. Work in this area, limited though it is, has become almost the exclusive preserve of social administration, public administration, and some branches of political science.

Medical sociologists, with their traditional preoccupation with macro and micro themes and issues in health care, are well placed to bring a distinctive and well-informed perspective to bear on policy, implementation, and management issues. As Illsley observes, work on the health professions over the past twenty years or so has provided sociologists with a valuable entrée to the health-care arena and has taken the discipline away from abstract theorizing. But Illsley believes, as does the writer, that it is unfortunate that a concentration on the interface between service providers and users (for example, see Davis and Horobin 1977), important though it is, has led to the 'relative neglect of the general health system within which professionals work and which, in turn, influences the nature and distribution of services' (Illsley 1980: 166). Allied to this neglect is the absence of a research focus on 'informal and formal decision-making at each layer of the health system from the point of delivery through the administrative structure to the development of policy in government' (Illsley 1980: 166).

Smith (1986) echoes Illsley's concern about the absence of research of a 'middle range' type. Both the impact of organizational structure upon service delivery and the importance of interorganizational relations on the overall system of care merit attention. Smith also believes there is further scope for micro level research on the ideology and impact of front-line workers in service delivery and that the importance of interorganizational relations on the overall system of care merit attention. Although it is possible to point to a considerable body of work on professional decision making in relation to issues such as access to care by users, there is a gap at the meso level in linking provider discretion and resource use to policy, organizational, and managerial structures. As Lipsky (1980) and others (for example, Prottas 1979; Hill 1981; DHSS 1986) have observed, front-line providers through their discretionary decision making commit

215

resources and make policy. Therefore, research which combines a middle range, or meso, focus with a micro focus is much needed.

The lacuna described above represents a key challenge to medical sociology. Despite the plethora of management consultants and others who may claim such territory for themselves, and who would argue that whereas medical sociology is likely to raise further questions they offer solutions to problems, it is not too late for medical sociology to contribute to understanding and improved performance in these areas. There is, however, a further obstacle to be addressed. It also goes some way possibly to explaining why medical sociology has been left out in the cold. Increasingly, over the past decade or so, the value of social science research in general has been perceived by funding bodies and policy-makers in narrow, functional, and instrumental terms. For example, reviewing the contribution of social science research to the 1976–9 Royal Commission on the NHS, Taylor (1981) points out that in calling for an increase in the contribution of research, the Commissioners' conception of research differed from that traditionally carried out by university-based social scientists:

> There has been a fairly widespread view that the main task of social science research was to put specific problems into a broad context in relation to general theoretical notions. According to this view, social science research provided the policy-makers with generalized understanding rather than narrow technical solutions. The Commissioners clearly have a different view. Instead of descriptive studies of structure, process and decision-making, they want closely specified studies which will evaluate the effectiveness and efficiency of services.
>
> (Taylor 1981: 546)

Despite the dangers of an overly narrow 'technocratic' research agenda, it does not constitute grounds for medical sociologists, or indeed, other 'softer' social sciences, to opt out of attempts to make a contribution. Subsequent sections of the chapter endeavour to demonstrate what is possible and what remains to be done. The remainder of this section aims to show how medical sociology can contribute to a better understanding of, and improvements in, policy and management in ways that are of practical relevance but which do not do violence to the discipline and its illuminative rather than prescriptive perspective.

With possibly the sole exception of social anthropologists, medical sociologists have remained sensitive to the importance of ethnographic methods of enquiry. Illsley claims that empirical work on the health professions has been pursued through interactionist, ethnomethodological, and phenomenological approaches 'favoured by the current cohort of sociologists' (Illsley 1980: 166). Thompson (1986: 6) believes that 'these methods can legitimately claim a significant place in the research repertoire needed to analyse the development, evolution, and outcomes of public programs' in health policy. Moreover, a focus on the micro and meso levels 'serves as a useful corrective for the centralist and often simplistic perspectives of those who dominate policy-making networks' (Thompson 1986: 6).

Research of both a middle range and micro variety becomes more relevant in health-care systems in developed countries as they move from what Thompson terms 'breakthrough politics' toward 'technical politics' (Thompson 1986: 8). Breakthrough politics evolves around basic reforms where governments launch major new initiatives or presage major changes in the role of the medical sector. Technical politics, on the other hand, involve efforts to improve the delivery of services to ensure more cost-effective care. Organizational and management reforms would come into this category. Taking the British NHS as an illustration, its creation in 1948 is an example of breakthrough politics. Successive reorganizations in 1974, 1982, and 1984, together with a battery of initiatives designed to improve the performance of the NHS (for example, Rayner scrutinies, performance indicators, annual performance reviews, cost improvement programmes) constitute examples of technical politics. Since the start of the 1980s the NHS has been subjected to numerous examples of fine tuning all based on an overriding concern with value for money and the three 'Es': Economy, Efficiency, and Effectiveness.

Looking ahead, at the time of writing the NHS has been subjected to a major government review into its future funding and organization. If the NHS were to be replaced by, for example, a system of social insurance then breakthrough politics would have triumphed. But since the proposals in the White Paper centre on giving more opportunity to the private sector to expand, to stimulating provider competition in the NHS, and to improving the clinical management of resources, then technical politics can be said to have triumphed (Secretaries of State for Health, Wales, Northern Ireland and Scotland 1989). Of course, a series of reforms of a technical politics variety could over time lead to a fundamental transformation of a health-care system. Indeed, critics of the NHS White Paper have pointed to its destabilizing character and to the government's 'hidden agenda' which is to make the NHS a residual service fit for those who cannot afford to pay for health care. As Thompson states, 'despite its emphasis on marginal adjustment, technical politics is by no means trivial politics' (Thompson 1986: 9). The main point is that while technical politics can profoundly shape who gets what in the health-care arena, the language of this politics emphasizes tinkering and the rationalization of existing arrangements.

At a time when technical politics reigns supreme, it is scarcely surprising that 'economics ranks as the dominant social science in health policy circles' (Thompson 1986: 11). Although no one would deny that the discipline of economics (and health economics in particular) has contributed important insights, economists have often been insensitive to the political and organizational issues involved in implementing public policies. Similar issues are alive in all developed health-care systems. In the United States, for example, Himmelstein, Woolhandler, and Bor (1988) point out how cost-effectiveness analysis (CEA) is increasingly advocated as a basis for health policy. In the UK, a similar concern is evident in the requirement placed upon health authorities to conduct option appraisals on major capital schemes and service developments. The assumption underlying the application of CEA is that resources can be released from inefficient practices and reallocated to efficient ones. However, the work of Himmelstein and his colleagues demonstrates how CEA ignores the political restraints in health-care decision making. Merely freeing up resources devoted to inefficient practices is no guarantee that they will find their way to preferable alternatives. They could, for instance, be shifted to other services of dubious cost-effectiveness. The solution, according to Himmelstein and his colleagues, is to have a rational system of decision making, possibly along the lines of the British NHS. However, although the problems to which Himmelstein and his colleagues refer may be more acute in the United States because of that country's fragmented 'non-system' of health-care delivery, similar concerns, albeit on a smaller scale, are evident in the British NHS. Himmelstein and his colleagues assert that 'health policy analysis should take into account not only the relative cost-effectiveness of services, but also the complexity and frustrating irrationality of current mechanisms of resource allocation' (Himmelstein, Woolhandler, and Bor 1988: 2). But the problem goes deeper and to the heart of health economics. 'Cost-effectiveness analysis frames difficult health policy questions in appealingly simple and objective equations' (Himmelstein, Woolhandler, and Bor 1988: 7).

The point about CEA and related techniques, and the problems to which they are applied, is that no single social science discipline can successfully address the complexities posed by the problems in the health policy arena. Increasingly, health-care policy problems demand multiple disciplinary approaches. 'Most health care policy issues do not occur as simple economic, psychological, sociological, epidemiological, or clinical problems, but as mixtures of all of these' (Shortell and Solomon 1982: 693). For these reasons medical sociology has an important contribution to make.

Medical sociology can be helpful in providing knowledge and sensitizing perspectives to policy-makers and managers. It will rarely provide 'right' answers to aid decision making; nor will it directly contribute to better or more efficient management (though it may do so indirectly). Often those who believe otherwise confuse medical sociology with management consultancy or management development. What medical sociology can contribute is greater awareness about interprofessional and interorganizational dynamics and power-dependence relationships. Health-care organizations will not be seen as simplistic, monolithic entities, but rather as complex pluralistic constellations of highly variegated groupings which do not necessarily all subscribe to a shared view of the organization's mission. Perhaps most important, as Levine and Sorenson (1983) point out, problems will be less likely to be defined as *thing* problems when they may in fact be *people* problems.

At this stage in the argument it is appropriate to refer to the research record in the UK with regard to health policy, organization, and management.

REVIEW OF RESEARCH

This section reviews research of relevance to health policy, organization, and management. Some of it might not strictly speaking be regarded as medical sociology nor as having its origins in this discipline. Indeed, most work in this field has been completed by social scientists whose roots lie in other disciplines but who have either wandered into medical sociology or brushed up against its boundaries. Actual work undertaken by 'pure' medical sociology is rare indeed.

Moreover, as Shortell (1983) has acknowledged, the boundaries within the social sciences are becoming increasingly blurred, both theoretically and empirically. Mechanic (1980: 1) states, in similar vein, 'medical sociology by its very character depends on the efforts of many disciplines, because its concerns are broad and largely problem oriented'. It is not uncommon for similar types of study to be carried out under different rubrics. The discussion which follows, therefore, draws on closely related disciplines while endeavouring to tease out what medical sociology in particular has to offer.

As mentioned in the introduction, the British NHS has undergone a succession of major structural and managerial reforms over the last fourteen years or so. Social science research, even where pertinent findings have existed, has played a negligible role in these reforms. Generally, research is perceived as offering little to policy, a state of affairs, which Bulmer (1983: 10) suggests may reflect the bias of British public life 'towards knowledge derived from the experience of the practitioner: "He who does, knows"'. Running through much of the thinking behind the three major reforms in the NHS which took place in the 1970s and early 1980s is an adherence to an outmoded, narrowly Weberian, and apolitical rational-legal-institutional model of organization. This essentially naïve model perceives organizations as conflict- and value-free. Most earlier writings on organizations, as well as later reforms of them, subscribe to a monolithic conception of organizations, the principal components of which are that they share a homogeneous structure and process, culture and behaviour (Pfeffer 1981; Jenkins and Gray 1983). The micro aspects of how organizations in fact operate are overlooked.

Largely because organizational and managerial reforms have been dominated by simplistic views of bureaucracy, the study of power and the concept of organizations as 'politically negotiated orders' (Bacharach and Lawler 1980) have received scant attention. To treat organizations as political systems does not entail a rejection of a classical or orthodox bureaucratic approach, but to see it as too narrow and one-dimensional. The work of sociologists like Pfeffer on power, and political scientists like Allison (1971) on bureaucratic politics has done much to develop and round out the classical, naïve model of organizational functioning adhered to by 'scientific management' theorists like Taylor and by other more recent writers such as Stewart (1985). Some researchers have argued that Griffiths' prescriptions for the management of the NHS are essentially informed by just such a model (Hunter 1984). Barnard and Harrison (1984) state that although the Griffiths report on the management of the NHS says much about responsibility, it says nothing about power or authority. More generally, Gunn (1985) is critical of popular texts like that of Peters and Waterman (1982) whose simple (and simplistic) nostrums have permeated the management reforms in the NHS. As Gunn (1985) states, 'words like politics, power and conflict are virtually outside the gung-ho vocabulary of Peters and Waterman'.

More recent organizational analysis drawing on political concepts like power, authority, and conflict can be of practical value in demonstrating how complex organizational life really is. The tendency for organizational and managerial reforms to fly in the face of organizational reality has been exposed in the NHS and elsewhere, even if it is rarely, if ever, acknowledged. A reformulated model of how organizations operate drawing on sociological concepts would lead to the conclusion that many of the prescriptions for administrative reform have been founded on conceptions of health service organization which have failed to appreciate sufficiently the NHS's power structure, the capacity of groups to bargain and influence (notably sections of the medical profession), and the development of policy at the front-line level rather than solely at higher levels.

It has been argued that much of the failure of structural and managerial reforms within the NHS over the past fourteen years or so stems from the invalidity of the conceptual framework. A major concern of policy-makers has been the so-called 'implementation gap' (Hill 1981). Since the early 1970s there has been mounting concern over the weaknesses of policy implementation. Why, commentators ask, is it that centrally pronounced policy does not get implemented as described? Why are top-level actors failing to get lower level actors to comply with their wishes? Why is change in policy or service which is deemed desirable by central government or higher levels of the NHS often so difficult to achieve at local or front-line levels? Such problems are not unique to the NHS although possibly particularly acute in a system which professes to exhibit a high degree of uniformity and centralized control while being highly decentralized in operational terms.

In the conventional wisdom there are a number of challengeable assumptions underlying the questions posed above, including, first, the assumption that policy-making and implementation are quite separate activities and, second, the assumption that they conform, or *should* conform, to a top down (that is, hierarchical) managerial model in which policies are handed down from above to be implemented by those providing services on the front-line. As mentioned, this view about how policy develops, and is enacted, betrays a grossly over-simplified conception of the complexity of organizations and policies. The NHS is not a monolithic entity, as a clutch of studies has shown (Haywood and Alaszewski 1980; Hunter 1980; Ham 1981). It is a pluralistic, sometimes confused, and often loose federation of group-ings and sectional interests (Taylor 1977, 1978). Success and failure in policy can, therefore, be differentially perceived by the various interests occupying positions in the NHS (Smith and Cantley 1985).

A growing corpus of research on health service organization and management has sought to address many of the issues considered above, but its findings have not had any observable impact on the changes which have taken place in the NHS. Perhaps the message is not one that policy-makers wish to hear. Indeed, this is the pattern with many social science research findings which challenge cherished assumptions and appear destabilizing. The reforms of the service mentioned earlier have been inspired by organization theories drawn primarily from industrial models of management and by advice proffered by a select group of advisers brought into government from the commercial and academic worlds.

Much of the work referred to has focused on three broad, over-lapping areas; for a more extensive review see Hunter (1986):

1 NHS reorganization: impact of structural and procedural changes; cost of reform;
2 Central – local relations in the NHS: levels of responsibility; power and authority;
3 Policy making and implementation: management styles and skills; change and innovation.

To illustrate ways in which medical sociology and related disciplines can contribute to an improved understanding of health policy, organization, and management, examples are given of two studies in which the author has been involved. The examples have been chosen to illustrate policy concerns on the one hand and organization and management concerns on the other, although a clear distinction between these does not exist in reality. The first example is a recently completed study of the evolution of community care policy in Britain; the second is a study of the introduction of general management into the NHS following the NHS management inquiry by the government's health adviser, Sir Roy Griffiths, in 1983.

COMMUNITY-CARE POLICY IN BRITAIN

For at least thirty years, the policy of successive governments has been to give priority to services for mentally ill, mentally handicapped, elderly, and physically disabled people and to shift the emphasis from institutionalized care to domiciliary care. Not only has implementation of the policy been slow and uneven across the country but it differs quite markedly across Britain both in substance and in the pace of implementation. Although it is claimed that a uniform policy of community care is adhered to in England, Wales, and Scotland, research shows that in fact three rather different policies are in operation in each of the three countries (Hunter and Wistow 1987a). Why this should be so is imperfectly understood. Work completed separately by each of the authors has documented the problems of developing community care at local level but no systematic attempt has been made to chart the differences in policy between the three countries at national level, to offer explanations for them, and to link the findings with developments at local level.

The study design was kept simple. It entailed a search of the literature on the central administration of the NHS in each of the three countries, supplemented with interviews with senior officials in the Welsh and Scottish Offices. Generally speaking, and in contrast to England, less published material is available on the workings of the administrative machine and policy processes in either Wales or Scotland. Various official policy statements and circulars were also analysed for the light they shed on the evolution of community-care policy and on differences in approach. The study produced both quantitative and qualitative evidence to show clearly that community-care policy had different meanings in England, Wales, and Scotland. The reasons for the differences were complex and cannot be explored in detail here (see Hunter and Wistow 1987a, b, c). Among the explanations offered were the existence of different political, cultural, administrative, and economic factors which shaped the respective approaches to community-care policy adopted by each of the three countries. The study demonstrated unequivocally that although a symbolic attachment to a uniform policy of community care was evident across Britain, it only served to conceal quite sharp differences in philosophy, approach, and even commitment.

The Scottish Office, for example, has never pursued community care with anything like the degree of enthusiasm and conviction shown by the then Department of Health and Social Security (DHSS) and the Welsh Office. A review of expenditure and service patterns demonstrated the marked bias towards hospital provision in Scotland. At the same time, the Welsh mental handicap initiative represents a radical departure from the common policy framework within which England and Wales operated during the 1970s. Since both Wales and Scotland have proceeded in quite opposite directions from each other and display major differences from England, the evidence points to a substantial degree of independent policy determination within a general but flexible framework. Substantial divergences exist between England, Scotland, and Wales not simply in the area of implementation but also in the fundamental goals, values, and outputs associated with community care.

As mentioned, the explanation for such differences is not straightforward and could be firmly established only by more intensive study. Some pointers can be identified, although establishing causal relationships between different factors would be premature on the basis of the evidence collected. However, there appears to be some association between organizational structures, financial arrangements, and policy outputs. Equally, the impact of historical, cultural, environmental, and ideological influences cannot be overlooked. It could be that the rather more fragmented, departmental arrangements found in the Scottish Office which militate against close working relationships across service boundaries may themselves reflect the lower priority attached to such activity.

Sociological insights were especially important in arriving at plausible explanations on the basis of the data collected. It was evident, for instance, that different professional views on community care constituted an important variable, as did the distribution of power and influence across key groups of actors. Key individuals also proved decisive, as in the case of the All Wales Strategy for the Development of Services for Mentally Handicapped People where the role of the Secretary of State for Wales was crucial (Welsh Office 1983). The particular approach to community care adopted in each country seemed also to reflect the general resource position as far as health services were concerned. For instance, in England the focus of community-care policy was on running down and closing long-stay hospitals in order to release resources to build up community alternatives. This approach was less evident in either Scotland or Wales. In Scotland there was greater commitment to retaining long-stay hospitals, whilst in Wales more attention was given to preventing people in the community having to go into hospital in the first place. It may, or may not, have been significant that in both Wales and Scotland expenditure on health services was at a higher *per capita* level than in England. In Scotland, in particular, with its high levels of bed provision and other health resources, this may have served to minimize cost-push and demand-pull pressures for the development of alternatives to hospital provision.

The study of community-care policy demonstrated that it is an area marked by diversity rather than by uniformity. But such a finding is of more than academic interest. In particular, three practical implications for policy-makers emerged. First, the study suggested the limited importance of structure in determining policy outputs. Although structural factors may have appeared to be important determinants (for example, fragmentation at the centre in Scotland compared with more integrated arrangements in England and Wales), structural configurations were themselves a reflection of more pervasive and underlying process factors. For example, the DHSS client group structure devised to formulate policies for the priority groups reflected a commitment to unified policy making across health and personal social services which was, in large part, based upon a prior commitment to promote community care. In Scotland, where the key professional interests and values appeared less oriented towards community care, it should be seen as no accident that structural arrangements (or their absence) reflected such an orientation.

Second, a common belief that getting the structure right will in itself lead to successful policy outcomes is misconceived. The indisputable need for appropriate enabling structures should not be allowed to obscure the prior, and ultimately more important, need to be clear about the purposes that such structures are intended to serve. One of the lessons from the All Wales Strategy is the overriding importance of clarifying policy objectives in the first instance and of only subsequently securing financial and planning arrangements which seek to realize these objectives.

Third, the review of community-care policy and its various permutations afforded an opportunity for policy learning. Different models of care and service mixes in the three countries offer opportunities to explore the costs and benefits of each. There may be much of practical value to gain from such an exercise informed by sociological insights of the kind produced by the study.

GENERAL MANAGEMENT AND THE NHS

The introduction of general management into the NHS in 1984 was a direct consequence of ministers' acceptance of the recommendations of the Griffiths report on the management of the health service (NHS Management Inquiry 1983). Griffiths saw major management problems residing in the lack of clear responsibility at all levels of the NHS, from the central department to the individual hospital or grouping of services. In the consensus management teams which existed from 1974 until the Griffiths reforms in 1984, no single person was in charge. All decisions had to be unanimously agreed to by all members of the consensus teams which assumed collective responsibility for all decisions. Griffiths did not believe that such a cumbersome arrangement was conducive to good management, particularly where difficult or unpalatable decisions were required to be taken. Too often, Griffiths concluded, consensus management led to slow, lowest common denominator decision making.

The Griffiths changes have been heralded as the most significant since the NHS was established. For many managers and observers they constitute a cultural shift of considerably greater magnitude than the structural changes of 1974 and 1982. Unlike earlier reforms, the Griffiths changes were aimed at altering managerial processes. From a research point of view, it seemed important to monitor the progress of general management from its inception in order to establish what lessons could be learnt both from the implementation of such an initiative and from whether or not it was successful in terms of achieving its stated objectives.

The most obvious way of assessing the impact of general management was to undertake a study which would endeavour to assess the influence of the changes both on general manag*ers* and on general manage*ment* in terms of the claims made for them and to conduct the assessment through a variety of qualitative methods: documentary analysis, semi-structured interviews, and observational work. The sample of health authorities was chosen for study to reflect different types of general managers as well as authority. An Anglo-Scottish comparative perspective was built in because of important differences between the two countries in the manner of implementing the Griffiths changes and in the environment in which general management was to operate. A two-year study funded by the Economic and Social Research Council was mounted to address these concerns. Data collection is complete and the analysis is well under way.

Although the study is concerned with a number of sociological questions about the functioning of complex organizations, it is also concerned with practical questions about the management of such organizations. In particular, the researchers have sought to distinguish between the *form* and the *substance* of management. Whilst any evaluation of the introduction of general management must take into account the formal changes (for example, the designation of an officer as general manager), it must also go beyond them and consider their impact. The extent to which the infrastructure derived from the Griffiths proposals has been put in place is of interest in an evaluation of the changes, but only to the extent that it is the means of achieving the objectives of improved performance, greater consumer orientation, and better implementation of plans. It is all too easy to create the illusion of change, as Griffiths himself recognized. Therefore, the central focus of enquiry ought to be the achievement, or otherwise, of these objectives.

In line with various political and organizational theories, the research is exploring a range of possible determinants of general manager performance. These include: the cognitive and behavioural styles of individual general managers; the local setting and pattern of organizational policies within the general manager's authority; the formal organizational structure within which general managers have to work; the policy environment and the objective, infrastructural, and socio-economic environment in which a particular health authority operates. Also of importance is the 'assumptive' and symbolic cultural aspects to the implementation of the Griffiths changes. In endeavouring to capture what is happening, a process of 'triangulation' was adopted so that through documentary analysis, semi-structured interviews, and observation it would be possible to check for convergence between the different data sources (Young and Mills 1980).

Of particular interest from a sociological perspective is the issue of the strengthening of the management function in the context of a highly professionalized and decentralized service. The NHS is possibly unique in being a split organization with a bureaucratic component and a professional one.

Work in hand illustrates the point. The Griffiths inquiry team was anxious to 'involve the clinicians more closely in the management process' (NHS Management Inquiry 1983: 6). It is widely acknowledged that clinicians play a crucial role in the day-to-day commitment of resources through their decisions on who to treat and how, and on who not to treat (Haywood and Alaszewski 1980; Hunter 1980). On the surface it makes perfect sense for clinicians to be given management responsibility for the deployment of resources, but in practice, the issue is extremely complex and fraught with difficulties. The suggestion that clinicians should become budget holders with direct management responsibility for their use of resources raises both ethical and political questions and has been greeted with suspicion and even outright resistance in some sections of the medical profession (Pollitt, Harrison, Hunter, and Marnoch 1988).

Early experiments with management budgeting at around the time of the implementation of the Griffiths changes demonstrated that what was seen largely as a technical exercise failed because insufficient attention was paid to the political and behavioural issues involved. These were central to the success (or failure) of attempts to modify clinician behaviour. Certainly, insufficient attention was paid to winning the support of those on whom the success of the venture depended. Little appears to have changed with the successor to management budgeting – the resource management initiative.

The NHS is a good example of what La Porte (1975) terms 'organized social complexity' in which many groups are involved in budgeting issues, each with its own preferences, priorities, and so on. The management budgeting arena is inhabited by ten groups of participants: district general managers, unit general managers, other managers and administrators, nurses, consultant medical staff, trade unions, health authority members, central government, patients, management consultants. The analysis has sought to map the different weightings assigned by the various groups to management budgeting and to the outcomes expected to flow from it. Costs and benefits do not all flow in the same direction for each of these groups. Participants in the fieldwork sites had their own assessments of the potential costs and benefits of management budgeting. Few of the participants in this particular arena gave it a high priority even when they were generally in favour of it. Some consultants, especially the younger ones, saw it as a vehicle for more rational resource bidding but were in a minority in most places. Many others were suspicious of management budgeting, feeling it would be used to divide the consultant body and/or to rationalize cuts in budgets. Most consultants were especially cautious about the production of comparative workload information. Other participants were only weakly or occasionally in favour (nurses, senior finance staff). For others (health authority members, trade unions, patients) it was not a significant or widely understood issue. The most likely prospect for management budgeting initiatives on the basis of this evidence is a slow and patchy process.

Such findings are of major practical importance if appropriate incentives are to be devised to secure the support of key actors like consultants. If not, management budgeting, and its successor resource management, run the risk of withering on the vine as earlier initiatives have done owing in part to a failure to comprehend the behavioural and socio-political dynamics at play in any policy issue. The success of reforms such as management budgeting does not hinge upon technical issues such as ensuring that appropriate information systems are in place. Of course these are important matters, but they are secondary to winning the support of the key actors upon whom success ultimately depends.

These two brief examples of research on which the author either has been, or is, engaged illustrate areas where, and ways in which, medical sociologists can contribute to an understanding of policy, organization, and management in health care. Although medical sociologists cannot claim to have a monopoly of expertise in these matters, equally they should not allow other disciplines to colonize them exclusively. Medical sociologists, as was mentioned earlier, are uniquely well placed on the basis of their traditional concerns within health-care systems to link these with processes at a meso level that have hitherto remained somewhat neglected. Other disciplines do not always have the grasp or depth of understanding of the health-care environment that is the basis of medical sociology. Moreover, there are various areas of concern where medical sociology, possibly in conjunction with other social scientists, may be able to make a particular contribution. These are briefly outlined in the next and final section.

AREAS FOR RESEARCH

Policy-makers and managers of health services in the UK are confronted by a series of ambiguities, contradictions, and tensions which go to the roots of what the NHS exists to do. Underlying these tensions are a number of major organizational issues, including the ability: to adapt to changing demands and priorities; to adopt innovation and implement change; to manage external factors impinging on the environment; and to restructure internal relationships as the organization is reshaped to tackle the changed nature of its environment (for example, a shift from institutional to community care, an altered demographic profile). The intention in this final section is to consider what kinds of research might be best suited, though not exclusively, to a medical sociological perspective. Five issue areas, which to some extent overlap, are considered: (1) environ- mental impact; (2) improved management performance; (3) medical technology and innovation; (4) organizational relationships; (5) intra-UK differences. These themes have been selected in part because of their importance for future health policy.

1 Environment

Too often NHS management is divorced from its setting and examined in relation to management in other, different settings. The history of the service is replete with examples, the most recent being the Griffiths management inquiry, mentioned in the previous section, where scant regard is paid to the actual setting in which managers have to operate. Instead, comparison is made with management in industry or the commercial service sector. Without going so far as to say that the NHS is unique, it is at least arguable, on the basis of contingency theory, that such comparisons are of limited usefulness. If attention is confined to certain managerial and organizational characteristics and their association with performance, then the adoption of such a narrow, comparative framework may be in order. However, an alternative theory of performance stresses the importance of those attributes which enable an organization to cope better with its particular operating conditions and culture. In short, the factors associated with high performance are expected to vary along with differences in an organization's operating context. This seems especially important in the NHS, where 'the need to meld the key professional groups — particularly medical and nursing — into general management' was underestimated by Griffiths (Maxwell and Evans 1984: 184).

Back in the early 1960s, Burns and Stalker (1961) argued that different organizational designs are more effective according to whether the environment is variable and complex in nature (to which an *organic* organizational response was best suited) or stable and simple (to which a *mechanistic* organizational response was preferable). The challenge for managers in the NHS is to decide which organizational components might best be organized along bureaucratic, mechanistic lines and which might best be organized in other ways, possibly along more flexible, organic lines.

As mentioned earlier, the NHS is marked both for its complexity (multi-levelled, multi-professional, multiple objectives) and its uncertainty as a result of the variable environment it inhabits where changes in resources, expectations, medical advances, and so on cannot easily be predicted. In such a setting, successful performance is likely to depend on an organization having the capacity for intelligent adaptation to changing circumstances. There is ample documentation of a variety of barriers to successful policy change in organizations. Individuals within organizations may view change negatively and act to resist it. The most common personal barrier to policy change is the problem of goal displacement — that is, the tendency of members of an organization to interpret any policy statement not in the context in which it was written, or for which it was intended, but rather in terms of the personal goals of the individuals themselves. In short, members continue to pursue their own goals, which may well differ from those of the organization that they ostensibly exist to achieve. Moreover, each member, or group of members, will have their own goal preferences, thereby bringing about the pluralistic setting to be found in organizations including the NHS as referred to earlier.

Intra-organizational barriers are compounded by inter-organizational ones. Few public agencies have policies which do not interact with other organizations. The NHS is no exception unless health care is viewed in very narrow terms. Even then it would be difficult to set clear boundaries upon which full agreement could be obtained. It is accepted that health care is not the preserve of the NHS alone but is also the responsibility of other agencies and services, particularly those run by local government. The NHS does not exist in a vacuum.

Just as the problems it has to tackle are in part shaped by the activity, or inactivity, or other services, so are other agencies affected by what the NHS is, or is not, doing. At a much broader level, deeper environmental influences are at work. Many of the difficulties afflicting the NHS are part of a wider crisis of adjustment in Britain to the fact of a new political climate centred on a monetarist, free-market philosophy.

The 'business society ethic', as one commentator has termed the phenomenon, favours the private sector and self-help. As a consequence, the NHS is caught up in a debate about the future of the welfare state and public provision. This calls for research of a macro kind to try to trace the connections between these broader social movements and their precise impact on a service like the NHS the whole *raison d'être* of which belongs to a different era. Such research is required to complement and balance the meso- and micro-level studies of operational management which the other issues listed above, and elaborated below, call for.

2 *Improved management performance*

Any discussion of health service performance and the demand for 'better' management to achieve this is plagued by the absence of explicit notions of what constitutes better management. Little attention has been devoted to this area of concern. In particular, the concept of effectiveness is a difficult one in health care generally and even more so when applied to management. There is, as Haywood (1983) states, little hard evidence to link different management styles (such as more or less delegation of decision making; general managers or consensus management teams) to specific improvements in health care. Much the same applies to the internal organization of health authorities: it is not yet possible, if it ever will be, to relate improvements in care to different ways of organizing the work of health authorities and professional groups.

A possible way of coping with this problem may be to develop acceptable indicators of good practice which might be kept under regular review so that they remain relevant to all those involved in service provision. A prerequisite is to establish what managers are actually doing or think they are doing. Prior to, but not to the exclusion of, prescriptive work is a need for robust descriptions of the management role. Without prior knowledge of how the manager sees and does his job, attempts to effect change may have unsought consequences or none at all. Through such studies it may then be possible to go on to examine the link, if one exists or can be made, between what these same managers appear to be doing and organizational outputs.

3 Medical technology and innovation

An issue that cuts across macro, meso, and micro concerns and embraces environmental and organizational factors is the introduction and management of new technology. It has an impact on the external environment, often involves increased inter-organizational activity, and may affect the internal workings of health-care facilities and role relationships. It is for this reason that Banta (1983) favours multidisciplinary work by social scientists and argues strongly against economists dominating research. Asserting that medical technology has become a major policy issue, he argues that 'the use of technology is not merely a technical question, but is embedded in a broader framework of culture, attitudes, values and beliefs' (Banta 1983: 1363). It is assumed by and large that clinicians dominate decision making in this area. Although this is partially true in respect of teaching hospitals, Banta cites research which found that acquisition of medical technology was also likely to result from the actions of hospital administrators. It is likely that a similar situation obtains in the UK, but there is only limited documented evidence of it. In general, organizations responsible for implementing policies towards medical technology remain little studied.

4 Internal organizational relationships

Within the NHS there remain key issues surrounding relations between health authority members and managers, between clinicians and managers, and between consumer groups and managers. Particularly in respect of members and clinicians and their respective relationships with managers, work is necessary which attempts to determine what these groups already believe they are doing, how they are regarded by significant others, and, in time, to begin to identify strategies for modifying behaviour.

In terms of relations between clinicians and managers, and of attempts to fuse the two by encouraging the development of clinical managers, there are many significant issues buried in the rhetoric over better resource use. As mentioned in the previous section, Griffiths refers to the need for doctors to become more management- and resource-conscious. What might the effect be in modifying the behaviour of clinicians in this way? If they become effective resource managers could patient care suffer (the assumption is that it will not, but might there not be a case for turning the question around)? Or might patient care improve if only effective treatments are offered rather than unproven ones which may give rise to iatrogenic illness? These sensitive and contentious issues strike at the heart of the nebulous concept of clinical freedom (Harrison, Mercer, and Hedeen-Pohlman 1987). It is a concept that itself is worthy of further attention. What does it actually mean to those who actively seek its protection? Is it a shibboleth devoid of precise meaning but invoked in times of perceived danger? Or does it denote a special type of one-to-one relationship that is of peculiar quality which should not be lightly jettisoned? Systematic work into the nature of clinical freedom seems to be a necessary prerequisite of work intended to modify what-ever it is, or is thought to be.

Unless there exists a certain understanding of the current dynamics of a management system and of the assumptions, views, and behaviour of its participants then attempts to effect sought-after changes could founder. As was mentioned in the previous section, and as Maxwell and Evans (1984) express it:

> There is a tendency to think of clinical budgeting as though the challenges were primarily technical, and hence as though what is needed is primarily accountancy tricks of cost recording, cost apportionment or setting internal prices. On the contrary, the greater task is that of persuading and accustoming doctors to managing resources consciously and deliberately rather than unconsciously, and the development of social processes through which their activities and uses of resources can be evaluated.
>
> (ibid.: 188–9)

This, then, is the challenge facing medical sociology — indeed, *all* social science disciplines — in the particular domain of health-care management.

5   Intra-UK differences

It is not widely appreciated that the NHS operates differently in each of the four countries making up the UK in ways which might affect management performance. In the previous section, work was reported which has sought to establish such differences in the context of community-care policy. The importance and practicalities of intra-UK comparative work in health and other areas was the subject of two Social Science Research Council (now the Economic and Social Research Council) workshops in 1979 and reported in Williamson and Room (1983).

In some respects this whole research area underlies the others because a number of research questions might be addressed adopting such a comparative perspective. Given the variations that exist, there could be implications in these for the organizing and managing of health care. It might be that such differences are merely a matter of form rather than of substance and exert minimal influence over health outputs or even over the way in which decisions are taken and implemented. Or it may be shown that restructuring is a ritual of symbolic importance designed to give only the appearance of improved performance. But findings of this kind might still be of interest and possibly of value, given the apparent attractions of constant institutional rejigging in the expectation that this will improve performance. The point is that there exist unexplored and unexplained variations that seem to merit closer scrutiny from medical sociologists.

CONCLUSION

Truth is conflictual, and 'illuminative evaluation' (Illsley 1980) seems best able to expose the plurality of meanings that exist in any organizational, or human, setting. This type of evaluative research can be useful to policy-makers in identifying issues and clarifying assumptions even if it does not resolve problems or produce solutions. Nor does it rule out other types of evaluation — for example, option appraisal and other health economics techniques, once the dynamics of the organizational context are sorted out and understood. A number of concluding themes flow from the preceding discussion of the role of medical sociology in understanding the organization and management of health-care services. First, management in a human services organization like the NHS presents a challenge to researchers because of the wide dispersion of authority and responsibility, the central role of professions, the difficulties inherent in measuring outputs and impact on health status, the long lead time between interventions and results, and the subordination of technology to subjective judgements by all involved in delivering and receiving health care.

Second, research (especially that adopting a medical sociology perspective) needs to move more firmly and swiftly in the direction of understanding and interpreting organizational behaviour, professional motivation, and the process of innovation. Researchers need to be concerned less with the formal relationship between agencies and organizational structures as expressed in the planning and priority-setting machinery and concerned more with the structure of power and incentives that shape decisions at all levels in the NHS. It may be that factors which inhibit action in one part of the system are precisely those which inhibit it elsewhere.

Third, closer links need to be forged between the research community and the health policy community to ensure that the issues selected for management research are important and that the results of research may stand a chance of entering the organizational bloodstream and impacting upon practice either directly or perhaps through management development activity.

Fourth, too compartmentalized an approach to theoretical and disciplinary enquiry in the field of health policy and management studies is likely to result in losing sight of the ways in which various schools of thought are related to one another. Medical sociology, however, should not be excluded from such synergy.

Fifth, while theoretical and disciplinary pluralism are to be encouraged, there is a simultaneous requirement for synthesis between various theories and disciplines to avoid total anarchy. A central challenge is to meld the language of politics and power with the language of organizational analysis. Until recently the latter has been preoccupied with unhelpful, rationalistic accounts of how organizations ought to function. If medical sociology has a particular contribution to make it is in illuminating the realities of organizational life in health-care systems.

BIBLIOGRAPHY

Abbott, P. (1987) 'Policing the family? the case of health visiting', *Paper presented at the BSA Medical Sociology Group Conference*, York (Sept.).

Aggleton, P. and Homans, H. (eds) (1988) *Social Aspects of AIDS*, Basingstoke: Falmer Press.

Aitken-Swan, J. (1977) *Fertility Control and the Medical Profession*, London: Croom Helm.

Aitkinson, P. (1981) *The Clinical Experience: The Construction and Reconstruction of Medical Reality*, Farnborough: Gower.

Allison, G. T. (1971) *Essence of Decision*, Boston: Little, Brown & Co.

Alonzo, A. E. (1979) 'Everyday illness behaviour: a situational approach to health status deviations', *Social Science and Medicine* 13A: 397–404.

Alpert, J. J., Kosa, J., and Haggerty, R. J. (1967) 'A month of illness and health care among low income families', *Public Health Reports* 82: 705.

Anderson, R., Davies, J. K., Kickbusch, I., and McQueen, D. V. (eds) (1988) *Behavioural Research in Health Promotion*, Oxford: Oxford University Press.

Antonovsky, A. (1979) *Health, Stress and Coping*, San Francisco, Washington, and London: Jossey-Bass Publishers.

Arber, S., Gilbert, N. G., and Dale, A. (1985) 'Paid employment and women's health: a benefit or a source of strain?' *Sociology of Health and Illness* 7(30): 375–400.

Arditti, R., Klein, R., Minden, S. (eds) (1984) *Test-Tube Women: What Future for Motherhood?* London: Pandora.

Armstrong, D. (1983) *The Political Anatomy of the Body*, Cambridge: Cambridge University Press.

———— (1988) Personal communication.

Askham, J. (1975) *Fertility and Deprivation*, London: Cambridge University Press.

———— (1982) 'Telling stories', *Sociological Review* 30(4): 555–73.

Bacharach, S. B. and Lawler, G. J. (1980) *Power and Politics in Organization*, San Francisco: Jossey-Bass.

Backett, K. C. (1982) *Mothers and Fathers: a Study of the Development and Negotiation of Parental Behaviour*, London: Macmillan Press.

———— (1987) 'The achievement of health: the middle classes discuss health in families', *Working Paper* No. 13, Research Unit in Health and Behavioural Change: Edinburgh.

———— (1988) 'Public health and private lives', in C. J. Martin and D. V. McQueen (eds) *Readings for a New Public Health*, Edinburgh: Edinburgh University Press.

Baird, D. (1965) 'A fifth freedom?' *British Medical Journal* 2: 1141.

Balint, M. (1964) *The Doctor, his Patient and the Illness*, 2nd edn, London: Pitman.

Banta, H. D. (1983) 'Social science research on medical technology: utility and limitations', *Social Science and Medicine* 17(18): 1363 – 9.

Barnard, K. and Harrison, S. (1984) Memorandum Submitted to House of Commons Social Services Committee, *Griffiths NHS Management Inquiry Report*, First Report Session 1983 – 4, HC 209, London: HMSO.

Barrett, M. and McIntosh, M. (1982) *The Anti-Social Family*, London: Verso Editions.

Becker, H. (1967) 'Whose side are we on?' *Social Problems* 14(3): 239 – 47.

Bell, R. A. and Harper, L. V. (1977) *Child Effects on Adults*, Hillsdale, NJ: Lawrence Erlbaum.

Bellaby, P. (1984) 'What is ''genuine'' sickness? complementarity and contradiction in the relation between work discipline and illness and healing', Paper presented to BSA Medical Sociology Conference, Sheffield.

Benson, D. and Hughes, J. A. (1983) *The Perspective of Ethnomethodology*, New York: Longman.

Bergsjo, P., Schmidt, E., and Pusch, D. (1986) 'Differences in the reported frequencies of some obstetrical interventions in Europe', in J. Phaff (ed.) *Perinatal Health Services in Europe*, Beckenham: Croom Helm.

Bernard, J. (1972) *The Future of Marriage*, London: Souvenir Press.

Biswas, B. and Sands, C. (1984) 'Mothers' reasons for attending a child health clinic', *Health Visitor* 57: 41 – 2.

Bittner, E. (1973) 'Objectivity and realism in sociology', in G. Psathas (ed.) *Phenomenological Sociology: Issues and Applications*, New York: John Wiley & Sons.

Blaxter, M. (1978) 'Diagnosis as category and process: the case of alcoholism', *Social Science and Medicine* 12: 9 – 17.

———— (1981) *The Health of the Children: a Review of Research on the Place of Health in Cycles of Disadvantage*, London: Heinemann Educational Books.

———— (1983) 'The causes of disease, women talking', *Social Science and Medicine* 17(2): 59 – 69.

Blaxter, M. and Paterson, E. (1982) *Mothers and Daughters: a Three Generational Study of Health Attitudes and Behaviour*, London: Heinemann Educational Books.

Bloom, S. and Wilson, R. (1972) 'Patient – practitioner relationships', in H. Freeman, S. Levine, and L. Reeder (eds) *Handbook of Medical Sociology*, Englewood Cliffs, NJ: Prentice-Hall.

Bloor, M. (1976) 'Professional autonomy and client exclusion', in M. Wadsworth and D. Robinson (eds) *Studies in Everyday Medical Life*, London: Martin Robertson.

———— (1978) 'On the analysis of observational data: a discussion of the worth and use of inductive techniques and respondent validation', *Sociology* 12(3): 545–52.

———— (1985) 'Observations of abortive illness behaviour', *Urban Life* 14(7): 300–16.

———— (1986) 'Social control in the therapeutic community: re-examination of a critical case', *Sociology of Health and Illness* 8: 305–23.

Bloor, M. and Horobin, G. (1975) 'Conflict and conflict resolution in doctor/patient interaction', in C. Cox and A. Meade (eds) *A Sociology of Medical Practice*, London: Collier-Macmillan.

Bloor, M., McKeganey, N., and Fonkert, D. (1988) *One Foot in Eden, a Sociological Study of the Range of Therapeutic Community Practice*, London: Routledge.

Blumer, H. S. (1969) *Symbolic Interactionism: Perspective and Method*, Englewood Cliffs, NJ: Prentice-Hall Inc.

Blumhagen, D. (1980) 'Hyper-tension: a folk illness with a medical name', *Culture, Medicine and Psychiatry* 4: 197–227.

Boyd, C. and Sellars, L. (1982) *The British Way of Birth*, London: Pan Books.

Brannen, J. and Wilson, G. (1987) *Give and Take in Families: Studies in Resource Distribution*, London: Allen & Unwin.

Brenner, M. (1978) 'Interviewing: the social phenomenology of a research instrument', in M. Brenner, P. Marsh, and M. Brenner (eds) *The Social Context of Method*, London: Croom Helm.

Brown, A. (1982) 'Fathers in the labour ward: medical and lay accounts', in L. McKee and M. O'Brien (eds) *The Father Figure*, London and New York: Tavistock Publications.

Brown, R. H. (1977) *A Poetic for Sociology: Toward a Logic of Discovery for the Human Sciences*, Cambridge: Cambridge University Press.

Bulmer, M. (1983) *Royal Commissions and Departmental Committees of Inquiry*, London: Royal Institute of Public Administration.

Burgoyne, J. and Clark, D. (1983) *Making a Go of It: a Study of Step Families in Sheffield*, London: Routledge & Kegan Paul.

Burns, T. and Stalker, G. M. (1961) *The Management of Innovation*, London: Tavistock.

Burr, W. R., Hill, R., Nye, F. I., and Reiss, I. L. (eds) (1979) *Contemporary Theories about the Family* (vols 1 and 2), New York: The Free Press, Macmillan.

Calnan, M. (1987) *Health and Illness: the Lay Perspective*, London: Tavistock.

Calnan, M. and Johnson, B. (1985) 'Health, health risks and inequalities: an exploratory study of women's perceptions', *Sociology of Health and Illness* 7(1): 55–75.

Campion, P. D. and Gabriel, J. (1984) 'Child consultation patterns in general practice comparing "high" and "low" consulting families', *British Medical Journal* 228: 1426–8.

Camprubi, J. (1987) 'SIDA: prevalencia de la infecion por VIG en los ADVP, situacion actual y possibilidades de autuacial', *Communidad y Drogas* 2: 9–22.

Cartwright, A. (1979) *The Dignity of Labour? a Study of Childbearing and Induction*, London: Tavistock.

Cartwright, A. and Anderson, R. (1981) *General Practice Revisited: a Second Study of Patients and their Doctors*, London: Tavistock Publications.

Cartwright, S. (1986) 'Hi tech birth without pangs', *Guardian* letters, 22 Feb.

Chalmers, I. (1978) 'Implications of the current debate on obstetric practice', in S. Kitzinger and J. Davis (eds) *The Place of Birth*, Oxford: Oxford University Press.

Charles, N. and Kerr, M. (1985) *Attitudes Towards the Feeding and Nutrition of Young Children*, London: Health Education Council.

——— (1987) 'Just the way it is: gender and age differences in family food consumption', in J. Brannen and G. Wilson (eds) *Give and Take in Families*, London: Allen & Unwin.

Cicourel, A. (1964) *Method and Measurement in Sociology*, New York: The Free Press.

——— (1973) *Cognitive Sociology: Language and Meaning in Social Interaction*, Harmondsworth, Middx: Penguin Books.

Cohen, H., Marmor, M., Des Jarlais, D. C., Spira, T., Friedman, S. R., and Yankowitz, S. (1985) 'Behavioural risk factors for HTLV-111/CAV seropositivity among intravenous drug users', Paper presented at the International Conference on the Acquired Immune Deficiency Syndrome, Atlanta, 14–17 April.

Comaroff, J. (1977) 'Conflicting paradigms of pregnancy: managing ambiguity in antenatal encounters', in A. Davis and G. Horobin (eds) *Medical Encounters: the Experience of Illness and Treatment*, London: Croom Helm.

——— (1978) 'Medicine and culture: some anthropological perspectives', *Social Science and Medicine* 12B: 247–54.

Conrad, P. (1975) 'The discovery of hyperkinesis: notes on the medicalization of deviant behaviour', *Social Problems* 23: 12–21.

——— (1985) 'The meaning of medications: another look at compliance', *Social Science and Medicine* 20(1): 29–37.

Conte, D., Ferroni, G. P., and Aimo, C. (1987) 'HIV and HBV infection in intravenous drug addicts from North Eastern Italy', *Journal of Medical Virology* 22: 299–306.

Cornwell, J. (1984) *Hard Earned Lives: Accounts of Health and Illness from East London*, London, New York: Tavistock Publications.

Court Report (1976) *Fit for the Future*, Report on the Committee on Child Health Services, London: Cmnd 6684, HMSO.

Cousins, M. and Hussain, A. (1984) *Michel Foucault*, London: Macmillan.

Crawford, A. (1987) 'Attitudes about alcohol: a general review', *Drug and Alcohol Dependence* 19: 279–311.

Crawford, R. (1977) 'You are dangerous to your health: the ideology and politics of victim blaming', *International Journal of Health Services* 7: 663–80.

——— (1984) 'A cultural account of "health": control, release and the social body', in J. B. McKinlay (ed.) *Issues in the Political Economy of Health Care*, London: Tavistock Publications.

CSO (1987) *Social Trends* 17, Table 2.1, London: HMSO.

Cunningham-Burley, S. (1984) 'The cultural context of childhood illness', Paper presented to BSA Medical Sociology Group (Scottish Section), Dundee.

———— (1985) 'Rules, roles and communicative performance in qualitative research interviews', *International Journal of Sociology and Social Policy* 5(3): 67–76.

Cunningham-Burley, S. and Irvine, S. (1987) ' "And have you done anything so far?" An examination of lay treatment of children's symptoms', *British Medical Journal* 295: 700–2.

Cunningham-Burley, S. and Maclean, U. (1987a) 'The role of the chemist in primary health care for children with minor complaints', *Social Science and Medicine* 24: 371–7.

———— (1987b) 'Recognising and responding to children's symptoms: mothers' dilemmas', *Maternal and Child Health* (Aug.): 248–56.

Currer, C. and Stacey, M. (eds) (1986) *Concepts of Health, Illness and Disease, a Comparative Perspective*, Leamington Spa, Hamburg, and New York: Berg Publications.

Daly, M. (1979) *Gyn/Ecology: the Metaethics of Radical Feminism*, London: Women's Press.

Davis, A. (1982) *Children in Clinics*, London: Tavistock.

Davis, A. and Horobin, G. (1977) *Medical Encounters: the Experience of Illness and Treatment*, London: Croom Helm.

Davis, F. (1963) *Passage Through Crisis*, New York: Bobbs Merrill.

Dean, K. (1984) 'Influence of health beliefs on lifestyles: what do we know?' *European Monographs in Health Education Research*, Copenhagen and Edinburgh: WHO and Scottish Health Education Group 6: 127–50.

Department of Health and Social Security (1984) *Diet and Cardiovascular Disease: Report of the Panel on Diet in Relation to Cardiovascular Disease*, London: HMSO.

———— (1986) *Social Work Decisions in Child Care. Recent Research Findings and their Implications*, London: HMSO.

Derrida, J. (1976) *Of Gramatology*, translated by G. C. Spivak, Baltimore: Johns Hopkins University Press.

Des Jarlais, D. C. and Friedman, R. D. (1987) 'HIV infection among intravenous drug users: epidemiology and risk reduction', *AIDS* 1: 66–76.

Des Jarlais, D. C., Friedman, S. R., and Stoneburner, R. L. (1988) 'HIV infection and intravenous drug use: critical issues in transmission dynamics, infection outcome and prevention', *Review of Infectious Diseases* 10(1): 151–8.

Dight, S. (1976) *Scottish Drinking Habits*, London: HMSO.

Ditton, J. and Speirits, K. (1981) 'The Rapid Increase of Heroin Addiction in Glasgow during 1981', *Department of Sociology, University of Glasgow Background Paper No. 2*.

Doll, R. and Peto, R. (1982) *The Causes of Cancer*, Oxford: Oxford University Press.

Donnison, J. (1977) *Midwives and Medical Men: a History of Interprofessional*

Rivalries and Women's Rights, London: Heinemann Educational Books.

Douglas, M. (1975) 'Deciphering a meal', in M. Douglas, *Implicit Meanings*, London: Routledge & Kegan Paul.

Douglas, M. and Nicod, M. (1974) 'Taking the biscuit: the structure of British meals', *New Society* 30: 744 – 7.

Doyal, L. (1979) *The Political Economy of Health*, London: Pluto Press.

Draper, J., Field, S., and Thomas, H. (1984) 'The early parenthood project: an evaluation of a community antenatal clinic', Hughes Hall, Cambridge: Cambridge University Mimeo.

Drayton, S. and Rees, C. (1984) 'They know what they're doing', *Nursing Mirror* 159(5): iv – viii.

Dunnell, K. and Cartwright, A. (1972) *Medicine Takers, Prescribers and Hoarders*, London: Routledge & Kegan Paul.

Eco, U. (1979) *The Role of the Reader: Explorations in the Semiotics of Texts*, London: Hutchinson.

Ehrenreich, B. and English, D. (1973) *Witches, Midwives and Nurses: a History of Women Healers*, London: Writers and Readers Publishing Co-op.

———— (1979) *For Her Own Good: 150 Years of the Experts' Advice to Women*, London: Pluto.

Eisenberg, L. (1977) 'Disease and illness: distinctions between professional and popular ideas of sickness', *Culture, Medicine and Psychiatry* 1: 9 – 23.

Erde, E. L. (1979) 'Philosophical considerations regarding defining "health", "disease" etc., and their bearing upon medical practice', *Ethics in Science and Medicine* 6: 31 – 48.

European Atherosclerosis Society (1987) 'Strategy for the prevention of coronary disease', *European Heart Journal* 8: 77 – 8.

Fabrega, H. (1974) *Disease and Social Behaviour: an Interdisciplinary Perspective*, Cambridge, MA: The MIT Press.

———— (1975) 'The need for an ethnomedical science', *Science* 189: 969 – 75.

Family Planning Association Conference (1976) 'The pill on or off prescription?' 23 March, London: Family Planning Association.

Fee, E. (1975) 'Women and health care: a comparison of theories', *International Journal of Health Services* 5(3): 397 – 415.

Field, D. (1976) 'The social definition of illness', in D. Tuckett (ed.) *An Introduction to Medical Sociology*, London: Tavistock.

Field, S., Draper, J., Kerr, M., and Hare, M. J. (1983) 'Babies' illness from the parents' point of view', *Maternal and Child Health* (June): 252 – 6.

Fieldhouse, P. (1986) *Food and Nutrition: Customs and Culture*, London: Croom Helm.

Finch, J. (1984) ' "It's great to have someone to talk to": the ethics and politics of interviewing women', in C. Bell and H. Roberts (eds) *Social Researching. Politics, Problems and Practice*, London: Routledge & Kegan Paul.

Fleury, P. (1967) *Maternity Care: Mothers' Experiences of Childbirth*, London: Allen & Unwin.

Flint, C. (1983) 'Growing in confidence', *Nursing Mirror* 19 Jan: 22.

Follet, E. A. C., McIntyre, A., O'Donell, B., Clements, G. B., and Dusselberger, V. (1986) 'HTLV – III antibody in drug abusers in the west of Scotland: the Edinburgh connection', *Lancet* 8478, vol. 1: 446 – 7.

Foucault, M. (1961) *Histoire de la Folie à l'Age Classique*, Paris: Plou.

————— (1967) *Madness and Civilisation: a History of Insanity in the Age of Reason*, translated by R. Howard, London: Tavistock Publications.

————— (1973) *The Birth of the Clinic*, London: Tavistock.

————— (1977) *Discipline and Punishment*, London: Allen Lane.

————— (1979) *The History of Sexuality*, vol. 1, London: Allen Lane.

————— (1980) 'The eye of power', in M. Foucault, *Power/Knowledge*, C. Gordon (ed.), Brighton: Harvester.

————— (1981) 'Omnes et Singulatum: Towards a Criticism of "Political Reason" ', in S. McMurrin (ed.) *The Tanner lectures on Human Values*, vol. 2, Salt Lake City: University of Utah Press.

Frake, C. O. (1964) 'Notes on queries in ethnography', *American Anthropologist* 66(2): 132 – 45.

Fullerton, W. (1985) 'Statistics given at theoretical course in contraception', (June), Aberdeen University.

Garcia, J. (1981) 'Findings on Antenatal Care from Community Health Council Studies', Radcliffe Infirmary, Oxford, Mimeo, National Perinatal Epidemiology Unit.

Geertz, C. (1975) *The Interpretation of Cultures: Religion as a Cultural System*, London: Hutchinson.

General Register Office (Scotland) (1983) *Multiply-Deprived Household Tables*, Edinburgh: GRO.

Gittins, D. (1985) *The Family in Question: Changing Households and Familial Ideologies*, Basingstoke, London: Macmillan Press.

Glaser, B. G. and Strauss, A. L. (1967) *The Discovery of Grounded Theory*, Chicago: Aldine Publishing Corp.

————— (1970) 'Theoretical sampling', in N. K. Denzin (ed.) *Sociological Methods*, London: Butterworth.

Goffman, E. (1968) *Asylums*, Harmondsworth, Middx: Penguin.

Goldberg, D. (1987) 'Positive intravenous drug misusers in Glasgow up to the end of March 1987', Communicable Diseases (Scotland) Unit, unpublished report.

Gove, W. R. and Hughes, M. (1979) 'Possible causes for the apparent sex differences in physical health: an empirical investigation', *American Journal of Sociology* 44: 126 – 46.

Graham, H. (1982) 'Coping or how mothers are seen and not heard', in S. Friedman and E. Sarah (eds) *On the Problem of Men*, London: Women's Press.

————— (1984) *Women, Health and the Family*, Brighton: Wheatsheaf Books Ltd, Harvester Press Group.

Graham, H. and McKee, L. (1979) 'The First Months of Motherhood', unpublished report of an HEC Project: University of York.

Graham, H. and Oakley, A. (1981) 'Competing ideologies of reproduction: medical and maternal perspectives on pregnancy', in H. Roberts (ed.) *Women Health and Reproduction*, London: Routledge & Kegan Paul.

Gunn, L. (1985) 'In search of excellence: a sceptical view from the public sector', Paper presented at Strathclyde Business School/BKT Publications Seminar (March), Glasgow.

Haavio-Mannila, E. (1986) 'Inequalities in health and gender', *Social Science and Medicine* 22(2): 141–50.

Hall, H., Macintyre, S., and Porter, M. (1985) *Antenatal Care Assessed*, Aberdeen: Aberdeen University Press.

Ham, C. (1981) *Policy-Making in the National Health Service*, London: Macmillan.

Handel, G. (1968) *The Psychosocial Interior of the Family*, London: Allen & Unwin.

Hannay, D. R. (1979) *The Symptom Iceberg: a Study of Community Health*, London: Routledge & Kegan Paul.

―――― (1980) 'The "iceberg" of illness and "trivial" consultations', *Journal of the Royal College of General Practitioners* 30: 551–4.

Harding, S. (ed.) (1987) *Feminism and Methodology*, Milton Keynes: Indiana University Press/Open University Press.

Harris, D. and Guten, S. (1979) 'Health-protective behaviour: an exploratory study', *Journal of Health and Social Behaviour* 20(1): 17–29.

Harrison, S., Mercer, G., and Hedeen-Pohlman, C. (1987) 'A threat to clinical freedom?' in L. H. W. Paine (ed.) *International Hospital Federation Official Yearbook*, London: International Hospital Fund.

Hart, N. (1977) 'Parenthood and patienthood: a dialectical autobiography', in A. Davis and G. Horobin (eds) *Medical Encounters: the Experience of Illness and Treatment*, London: Croom Helm.

Haw, S. (1985) *Drug Problems in Greater Glasgow*, Report of the SCODA Fieldwork Survey in Greater Glasgow Health Board.

Haywood, S. (1983) 'District health authorities in action', Research Report No. 19, Birmingham: Health Services Management Centre, University of Birmingham.

Haywood, S. and Alaszewski, A. (1980) *Crisis in the Health Service*, London: Croom Helm.

Health Education Council (1985) *Eating for a Healthier Heart*, London: HEC.

Heather, N. and Robertson, I. (1985) *Problem Drinking: the New Approach*, Harmondsworth, Middx: Pelican.

Helman, C. (1986) *Culture, Health and Illness*, Bristol: John Wright & Sons.

―――― (1987) ' "Feed a cold and starve a fever": folk models of infection in an English suburban community and their relation to medical treatment', in C. Currer and M. Stacey (eds) *Concepts of Health, Illness and Disease*, Leamington Spa, Hamburg, and New York: Berg Publications.

Henry, J. (1972) *Pathways to Madness*, London: Jonathan Cape.

Henwood, M., Rimmer, L., and Wicks, M. (1987) 'Inside the family: changing roles of men and women', Occasional Paper No. 6, London: Family Policy Studies Centre.

Herzlich, C. (1973) *Health and Illness: a Social Psychological Analysis*, London and New York: Academic Press.

Herzlich, C. and Pierret, J. (1986) 'Illness: from causes to meaning', in C. Currer and M. Stacey (eds) *Concepts of Health, Illness and*

Disease: a Comparative Perspective, Leamington Spa: Berg.

Hill, M. (1981) 'The policy-implementation distinction: a quest for rational control?' in S. Barrett and C. Fudge (eds) *Policy and Action*, London: Methuen.

Himmelstein, D. V., Woolhandler, S., and Bor, D. H. (1988) 'Will cost effectiveness analysis worsen the cost effectiveness of health care?' *International Journal of Health Services* 18(1): 1–9.

Homans, H. (ed.) (1985) *The Sexual Politics of Reproduction*, Aldershot: Gower.

Horobin, G. (1985) Review Essay: 'Medical sociology in Britain: true confessions of an empiricist', *Sociology of Health and Illness* 7, no. 1: 94–107.

Houd, S. and Oakley, A. (1986) 'Alternative perinatal services: report on a pilot survey', in J. Phaff (ed.) *Perinatal Health Services in Europe*, Beckenham: Croom Helm.

Hughes, S. (1987) 'Giving birth by court order', *New Generation* (Dec.): 10.

Hunt, S. M. (1987) 'Subjective indicators for health promotion research', Research Unit in Health and Behavioural Change, Working Paper 18, Edinburgh: RUHBC.

Hunt, S. M. and McLeod, M. (1987) 'Health and behavioural change: some lay perspectives', *Community Medicine* 9: 68–76.

Hunt, S. M. and Martin, C. J. (1988) 'Health related behavioural change: a test of a new model', *Psychology and Health*, in press.

Hunter, D. J. (1980) *Coping with Uncertainty: Policy and Politics in the National Health Service*, Chichester: Research Studies Press/Wiley & Sons.

———— (1984) 'NHS management: is Griffiths the last quick fix?' *Public Administration* 62(1): 91–4.

———— (1986) *Managing the National Health Service in Scotland: Review and Assessment of Research Needs*, Scottish Health Service Studies No. 45, Edinburgh: Scottish Home and Health Department.

Hunter, D. J. and Wistow, G. (1987a) *Community Care in Britain: Variations on a Theme*, London: King Edward's Hospital Fund, London.

———— (1987b) 'The paradox of policy diversity in a unitary state: community care in Britain', *Public Administration* 65(1): 3–24.

———— (1987c) 'Community care in England, Scotland and Wales', *Public Money* 7(3): 27–30.

Illich, I. (1975) *Medical Nemesis: the Expropriation of Health*, London: Calder & Boyars.

Illsley, R. (1980) *Professional or Public Health? Sociology in Health and Medicine*, London: Nuffield Provincial Hospitals Trust.

Inch, S. (1988) 'The Savage suspension: its significance and implications', *Journal of the Royal Society of Medicine* 81: 178–82.

International Journal of Health Services (1975) 5, 2.

Jackson, J. K. (1956) 'The adjustment of the family to alcoholism', *Journal of Marriage and Family Living* 18: 361–9.

Jenkins, B. and Gray, A. (1983) 'Bureaucratic politics and power: developments in the study of bureaucracy', *Political Studies* 31: 177–93.

Katona, C. (1981) 'Approaches to antenatal education', *Social Science and Medicine* 152: 25–33.

Kerr, M. and Charles, N. (1986) 'Servers and providers: the distribution of food within the family', *Sociological Review* 34: 115–57.

Kirke, P. (1980) 'Mothers' views of obstetric care', *British Journal of Obstetrics and Gynaecology* 87: 1029–33.

———— (1980a) 'Mothers' views of care in labour', *British Journal of Obstetrics and Gynaecology* 87: 1034–8.

Kleinman, A. (1981) *Patients and Healers in the Context of Culture: Explorations of the Borderland between Anthropology, Medicine and Psychology*, Berkeley, CA: University of California Press.

La Porte, T. R. (ed.) (1975) *Organised Social Complexity: Challenge to Policy and Politics*, Princeton, NJ: Princeton University Press.

Laws, S., Hey, V., and Eagan, A. (1985) *Seeing Red: the Politics of Pre-Menstrual Tension*, London: Hutchinson.

Levin, L. S., Katz, A. M., and Holst, E. (1977) *Self Care: Lay Initiatives in Health*, London: Croom Helm.

Levine, S. and Sorenson, J. R. (1983) 'Medical sociology and health administration', *The Journal of Health Administration Education* 1(4): 343–82.

Lewis, J. (1980) *The Politics of Motherhood: Child and Maternal Welfare in England 1900–1939*, London: Croom Helm.

Lipsky, M. (1980) *Street Level Bureaucracy*, New York: Russell Sage.

Litman, T. J. and Venters, M. (1979) 'Research on health care and the family: a methodological overview', *Social Science and Medicine* 13a: 379–85.

Locker, D. (1981) *Symptoms and Illness: the Cognitive Organisation of Disorder*, London, New York: Tavistock Publications.

Lofland, J. (1971) *Analysing Social Settings: a Guide to Qualitative Observation and Analysis*, Belmont, CA: Wadsworth.

———— (1976) *Doing Social Life: the Qualitative Study of Human Interaction in Natural Settings*, New York, London: John Wiley & Sons.

Macfarlane, A. and Mugford, M. (1984) *Birth Counts: Statistics of Pregnancy and Childbirth*, London: HMSO.

McIntosh, J. (1986) 'A consumer perspective on the Health Visiting Service', Report to Scottish Home and Health Department and SPORU Occasional Paper, Glasgow: Social Paediatric and Obstetric Research Unit, University of Glasgow.

Macintyre, S. (1976) 'Who wants babies? the social construction of instincts', in D. Barker and S. Allen, *Sexual Divisions and Society*, London: Tavistock Publications.

———— (1977) *Single and Pregnant*, London: Croom Helm.

———— (1980) 'Review article: the sociology of reproduction', in *Sociology of Health and Illness* 2: 215–22.

———— (1981) 'Communications between pregnant women and their medical and midwifery attendants', *Midwives Chronicle and Nursing Notes* (Nov.): 387–94.

———— (1984) 'Consumer reactions to antenatal services', in L. Zander and G. Chamberlain (eds) *Pregnancy Care for the 80s*, London: Macmillan.

Macintyre, S. and Porter, M. (1989) 'Prospects and problems in promoting effective care at the local level', in M. Enkin, M. Keirse, and I. Chalmers (eds) *Effective Care in Pregnancy and Childbirth*, Oxford: Oxford University Press.

246

McKee, I. (1984) 'Community antenatal care: the Sighthill Community Antenatal Scheme', in L. Zander and G. Chamberlain (eds) *Pregnancy Care for the 1980s*, London: Royal Society of Medicine/Macmillan Press.

McKee, L. and O'Brien, M. (1982) *The Father Figure*, London and New York: Tavistock Publications.

McKeganey, N. P. (1987) 'A jab in the wrong direction', *Community Care* (10 Dec.), No. 690.

———— (1988) 'Shadowlands: general practitioners and the treatment of opiate abusing patients', *British Journal of Addiction* 83: 373–86.

———— (1989) 'On the analysis of medical work: general practitioners, opiate abusing patients and medical sociology', *Sociology of Health and Illness*, vol. 11, no. 1: 24–38.

McKeganey, N. P. and Barnard, M. (1988) 'A statistical comparison of the study locale and neighbouring areas', Social Paediatric and Obstetric Research Unit Report.

McKeganey, N. P. and Boddy, F. A. (1988) 'General practitioners and opiate abusing patients', *Journal of the Royal College of General Practitioners* 38: 73–5.

MacKeith, N. (1976) *Women's Health Handook: a Self Help Guide*, 16 Methley Terrace, Leeds.

McKinlay, J. (1975) 'Who is really ignorant — physician or patient?' *Journal of Health and Social Behaviour* 16: 3–11.

McQueen, D. V. (1987) 'Research in health behaviour, health promotion and public health', Research Unit in Health and Behavioural Change Working Paper, Edinburgh: RUHBC.

Major-Poetzl, P. (1983) *Foucault's Archaeology of Western Culture*, Brighton: Harvester Press.

Marlatt, G. A. and Nathan, P. E. (1978) *Behavioral Approaches to Alcoholism*, New Brunswick, NJ: Rutgers Center for Alcohol Studies.

Marmot, M. and McDowall, M. (1986) 'Mortality decline and widening social inequalities', *Lancet* (ii) (Aug.): 274–6.

Mauss, M. (1954) *The Gift*, London: Cohen & West.

Maxwell, R. and Evans, T. (1984) 'Griffiths: challenge and response', Memorandum to House of Commons Social Services Committee, *Griffiths NHS Management Inquiry Report*, First Report Session 1983–4, HC 209. London: HMSO.

Mayall, B. (1986) *Keeping Children Healthy*, London: Allen & Unwin.

Mechanic, D. (ed.) (1980) *Readings in Medical Sociology*, New York: The Free Press.

Ministry of Agriculture, Fisheries and Food (1987) *Household Consumption and Expenditure*. Annual Reports of the National Food Survey Committee, London: HMSO.

Morgan, M., Calnan, M., and Manning, M. (1985) *Sociological Approaches to Health and Medicine*, London: Croom Helm.

Morrell, D. C. and Wade, C. D. (1976) 'Symptoms perceived and recorded by patients', *Journal of the Royal College of General Practitioners* 26: 398.

Morrice, J. K. (1965) 'Permissiveness', *British Journal of Medical Psychology* 38: 247–56.

———— (1979) 'Basic concepts, a critical review', in R. Hinshelwood and N. Manning (eds) *Therapeutic Communities: Reflections and Progress*, London: Routledge & Kegan Paul.

Moser, K. A., Pugh, H., and Goldblatt, P. (1987) 'Inequalities in women's health: developing an alternative approach', Paper presented to the Society for Social Medicine, University College, Dublin.

Moss, A. R. (1987) 'AIDS and intravenous drug use: the real hetero-sexual epidemic', *British Medical Journal* 294: 389–90.

Mulford, H. A. and Miller, D. E. (1960) 'Drinking in Iowa II', *Quarterly Journal of Studies in Alcohol* 21: 279–91.

Mulleady, G. (1987) 'A review of drug abuse and HIV infection', *Psychology and Health* 1: 149–63.

Mullen, K., Blaxter, M., and Dyer, S. (1986) 'Religion and attitudes towards alcohol use in the Western Isles', *Drug and Alcohol Dependence* 18: 51–72.

Murcott, A. (1983) *The Sociology of Food and Eating*, Aldershot, Hants: Gower Publications.

———— (1986) 'Opening the "blackbox": food, eating and household relationships' (unpublished paper).

Nelson, M. (1983) 'Working class women, middle class women and models of childbirth', *Social Problems* 30: 284–97.

NHS Management Inquiry (1983) *Report* (Chairman: Roy Griffiths), London: DHSS.

Nusbaumer, M. R. (1981) 'Religious affiliation and abstinence: a fifteen-year change', *Journal of Studies on Alcohol* 42: 127–31.

Oakley, A. (1975) 'The trap of medicalized motherhood', *New Society* 34(689): 639–41.

———— (1976) 'Wise woman and medicine man: changes in the management of childbirth', in J. Mitchell and A. Oakley (eds) *The Rights and Wrongs of Women*, Harmondsworth: Penguin.

———— (1979) *Becoming a Mother*, Oxford: Martin Robertson.

———— (1980) *Women Confined*, Oxford: Martin Robertson.

———— (1981) 'Interviewing women: a contradiction in terms', in H. Roberts (ed.) *Doing Feminist Research*, London: Routledge & Kegan Paul.

———— (1982) 'The origins and development of antenatal care', in M. Enkin and I. Chalmers (eds) *Effectiveness and Satisfaction in Antenatal Care*, London: Spastics International/Heinemann Medical Books.

———— (1984) *The Captured Womb: a History of the Medical Care of Pregnant Women*, Oxford: Blackwell.

O'Brien, M. and Smith, C. (1981) 'Women's views and experiences of antenatal care', *The Practitioner* 225: 123–6.

OPCS (1985) *OPCS Monitor: Hospital In-patient Enquiry 1985*, OPCS, London: HMSO.

Orbach, S. (1978) *Fat is a Feminist Issue*, London: Hamlyn.

Parker, H., Newcombe, R., and Bakx, K. (1987) 'The new heroin users: prevalence and characteristics in Wirral and Merseyside', *British Medical Journal of Addiction* 82: 147–57.

Parsons, T. (1958) 'Definitions of health and illness in the light of American values and social structure', in E. G. Jaco (ed.) *Patients, Physicians and Illness*, Glencoe, IL: The Free Press.

Parsons, W. and Perkins, E. (1980) 'Why don't women attend for antenatal care?' University of Nottingham: Leverhulme Health Education Project, Occasional Paper No. 23.

Pattison, C. J., Drinkwater, C. K., and Donovan, M. A. P. (1982) 'Mothers' appreciation of their children's symptoms', *Journal of the Royal College of General Practitioners* 32: 149–62.

Pearson, G. (1987) *The New Heroin Users*, Blackwell.

Peters, T. J. and Waterman, R. H. (1982) *In Search of Excellence*, New York: Harper & Row.

Pfeffer, J. (1981) 'Management as symbolic action: the creation and maintenance of organizational paradigms', in L. L. Cummings and B. W. Staw (eds) *Research in Organisational Behavior*, vol. 3. Greenwich, CT: JAI Press.

Pfeffer, N. and Woollett, A. (1983) *The Experience of Infertility*, London: Virago.

Phillips, A. and Rakusen, J. (eds) (1978) *Our Bodies, Ourselves: a Health Book by and for Women*, Harmondsworth: Penguin.

Pierret, J. (1988) 'What social groups think they can do about health', in R. Anderson, J. K. Davies, I. Kickbusch, and D. V. McQueen (eds) *Behavioural Research in Health Promotion*, Oxford: Oxford University Press.

Pill, R. (1985) 'An apple a day . . . Some reflections on working class mothers' views on food and health', in Anne Murcott (ed.) *The Sociology of Food and Eating*, Farnborough: Gower Press.

Pill, R. and Stott, N. (1982) 'Concepts of illness causation and responsibility: some preliminary data from a sample of working class mothers', *Social Science and Medicine* 16: 43–52.

———— (1985) 'Choice or chance: further evidence on ideas of illness and responsibility for health', *Social Science and Medicine* 20(10): 981–91.

Pittman, D. J. (1967) *Alcoholism*, New York: Harper & Row.

Pittman, D. J. and Snyder, C. R. (1962) *Society, Culture, and Drinking Patterns*, New York: John Wiley & Sons.

Pollitt, C., Harrison, S., Hunter, D., and Marnoch, G. (1988) 'The reluctant managers: clinicians and budgets in the NHS', *Financial Accountability and Management* 3: 213–33.

Popay, J. (1986) 'Patterns of health and health care in households with dependent children', Progress Report on a Pilot Study, London: Thomas Coram Institute.

Porter, M. (1980) 'Willing deviants? a study of childlessness', Ph.D. thesis, University of Aberdeen.

———— (1986) 'Free to choose? a study of contraceptive decision making', Report submitted to Family Planning Association, London: FPA.

———— (1987) 'Pre-pregnancy counselling: the patient's perspective', Paper given at Conference on Pre-pregnancy Care for health Professionals (April): Aberdeen University.

Porter, M. and Macintyre, S. (1984) 'The good, the bad and the indifferent: providers of antenatal care', Paper presented at Human Reproduction Study Group meeting, Warwick University.

————— (1984a) 'What is must be best: a research note on conservative or deferential responses to Antenatal Care Provision', *Social Science and Medicine* 19(11): 1197–200.

————— (1989) 'Psychosocial effectiveness of antenatal and postnatal care', in S. Robinson and A. Thomason (eds) *Research in Midwifery/Childbirth Care*, vol. 1, London: Croom Helm.

Potter, J. and Mulkay, M. (1985) 'Scientists' interview talk: interviews as a technique for revealing participants' interpretive practices', in M. Brenner, J. Brown, and D. Canter (eds) *The Research Interview: Uses and Approaches*, London: Academic Press.

Potter, J. and Wetherell, M. (1987) *Discourse and Social Psychology: Beyond Attitudes and Behaviour*, London: Sage.

Prottas, J. M. (1979) *People Processing*, Lexington, MA: Lexington Books.

Prout, A. (1986) ' "Wet children" and "little actresses" ': a primary school's hidden curriculum of the sick role', *Sociology of Health and Illness* 8(2): 111–33.

Rakusen, J. (1981) 'Depo provera: the extent of the problem: a case study in the politics of birth control', in H. Roberts (ed.) *Women, Health and Reproduction*, London: Routledge & Kegan Paul.

Rapoport, R., Rapoport, R. N., and Thiessen, V. (1974) 'Couple symmetry and enjoyment', *Journal of Marriage and the Family* 36(3): 588–91.

Reid, M. (1983) 'Helping those mothers: antenatal care in a Scottish peripheral housing estate', in Glasgow Women's Studies Group (ed.) *Uncharted Lives: Extracts from Scottish Women's Experiences*, Glasgow: Pressgang.

Reid, M. and McIlwaine, G. (1980) 'Consumer opinion of a hospital antenatal clinic', *Social Science and Medicine* 14A: 363–8.

Reid, M., Gutteridge, S., and McIlwaine, G. (1983) 'A comparison of the delivery of antenatal care between hospital and a peripheral clinic', Report submitted to Health Services Research Committee, Scottish Home and Health Department.

Research Unit in Health and Behavioural Change (1988) *Changing the Public Health*, London: John Wiley & Sons. In press.

Richman, J. (1982) 'Men's experiences of pregnancy and childbirth', in L. McKee and M. O'Brien (eds) *The Father Figure*, London and New York: Tavistock Publications.

Rix, K. J. B. and Buyer, M. (1976) 'Public attitudes towards alcoholism in a Scottish city', *British Journal of Addiction* 71: 23–9.

Roberts, H. (1981) 'Male hegemony in family planning', in H. Roberts (ed.) *Women, Health and Reproduction*, London: Routledge & Kegan Paul.

Robertson, J. R., Bucknall, A. B. V., and Wiggins, P. (1986) 'Regional variations in HIV antibody seropositivity in British intravenous drug users', *Lancet* 8478, vol. 1: 1435–6.

Robertson, J. R., Bucknall, A. B. V., Welsby, P. D., Roberts, J. J. K., Inglis, J. M., Peutherer, J. F., and Brettle, R. (1986) 'Epidemic of AIDS related virus (HTLVIII/LAV) infection among intravenous drug abusers', *British Medical Journal* 292: 527–9.

Robinson, D. (1971) *The Process of Becoming Ill*, London: Routledge & Kegan Paul.

———— (1978) *Patients, Practitioners and Medical Care*, London: Heinemann.

Robinson, J. (1974) 'Consumer attitudes to maternity care', *Oxford Consumer* (May).

Romney, M. and Gordon, H. (1981) 'Is your enema really necessary?' *British Medical Journal* 281: 1269.

Rosenbaum, M. (1981) *Women on Heroin*, New Brunswick, NJ: Rutgers University Press.

Royal College of General Practitioners (OPCS 1979) *Studies on Medical and Population Subjects*, No. 36. Morbidity Statistics from General Practice 1971–2, Second National Study, London: HMSO.

Royal College of Obstetricians and Gynaecologists (1975) *Proceedings of the Third Study Group of RCOG on the Management of Labour*, London: Royal College of Obstetricians and Gynaecologists.

———— (1982) *Report of the RCOG Working Party on Antenatal and Intrapartum Care*, London: Royal College of Obstetricians and Gynaecologists.

Rutter, M. and Madge, N. (1976) *Cycles of Disadvantage*, London: Heinemann.

Savage, W. (1986) *A Savage Enquiry: Who Controls Childbirth?* London: Virago.

Schatzman, L. (1973) *Field Research*, Englewood Cliffs, NJ: Prentice-Hall.

Scheff, T. (1968) 'Negotiating reality: notes on power in the assessment of responsibility', *Social Problems* 16: 3–17.

Schilts, R. (1987) *And the Band Played On*, London: Penguin Books.

Schlegel, R. P. and Sandborn, M. D. (1979) 'Religious affiliation and adolescent drinking', *Journal of Studies on Alcohol* 40: 693–703.

Schutz, A. (1972) *The Phenomenology of the Social World*, London: Heinemann Educational Books.

Schwartz, H. and Jacobs, J. (1979) *Qualitative Sociology*, New York: The Free Press.

Scott, M. B. and Lyman, S. M. (1968) 'Accounts', *American Sociological Review* 33: 46–62.

Scottish Home and Health Department (1986) *HIV Infection in Scotland*, Scottish Committee on HIV Infection and Intravenous Drug Misuse.

Scully, D. (1980) *Men Who Control Women's Health*, Boston, MA: Houghton Mifflin.

Secretaries of State for Health, Wales, Northern Ireland and Scotland (1989) *Working for Patients*, London: HMSO.

Sharp, V. (1975) *Social Control in the Therapeutic Community*, Aldershot: Gower.

Short Report (1980) Second Report from the Social Services Committee, Session 1979–1980, *Perinatal and Neonatal Mortality*, vol. 1, London: HMSO.

Shortell, S. M. (1983) 'Organisational theory and health services delivery', Paper presented at Conference on Social Sciences in Health, American Public Health Association Annual Meeting (Nov.), Dallas, Texas.

Shortell, S. M. and Solomon, M. A. (1982) 'Improving health care policy research', *Journal of Health Politics, Policy and Law* 6(4): 684–702.

Silverman, D. (1987) *Communication and Medical Practice*, London: Sage.

Silverman, D. and Bloor, M. (forthcoming) 'Patient-centred medicine: some sociological observations on its constitution, penetration, and cultural assonance', in G. L. Albrecht (ed.) *Advances in Medical Sociology*,

Greenwich, Conn: JAI Pass Inc.

Silverman, D. and Torode, B. (1980) *The Material Word: Some Theories of Language and its Limits*, London: Routledge & Kegan Paul.

Simms, M. and Smith, C. (1982) 'Young fathers: attitudes to marriage and family life', in L. McKee and M. O'Brien, *The Father Figure*, London and New York: Tavistock Publications.

Skolnick, J. H. (1958) 'Religious affiliation and drinking behaviour', *Quarterly Journal of Studies on Alcohol* 19: 452–70.

Smith, D. (1987) 'Women's perspective as a radical critique of sociology', in S. Harding (ed.) *Feminism and Methodology*, Milton Keynes: Indiana University Press/Open University Press.

Smith, G. (1986) 'Service delivery issues', *Quarterly Journal of Social Affairs* 2(3): 265–83.

Smith, G. and Cantley, C. (1985) *Assessing Health Care: a Study in Organisational Evaluation*, Milton Keynes: Open University Press.

Spencer, N. J. (1984) 'Parents' recognition of the ill child', in J. MacFarlane (ed.) *Progress in Child Health*, London: Churchill Livingstone/Longman.

Stacey, M. (1988) *The Sociology of Health and Healing. A Textbook*, London: Unwin Hyman.

Stewart, R. (1985) *The Reality of Organisations*, London: Macmillan.

Stimson, G. (1976) 'General practitioners, "trouble" and types of patient', in M. Stacey (ed.) *Sociology of the National Health Service*, Sociological Review Monograph 22: 43–60.

Stimson, G. and Webb, B. (1975) *Going to See the Doctor: The Communication Process in General Practice*, London: Routledge & Kegan Paul.

———— (1976) 'People's accounts of medical encounters', in M. Wadsworth and D. Robinson (eds) *Studies in Everyday Medical Life*, London: Martin Robertson.

Stimson, G. V., Alldrit, L., Dolan, K., and Donoghoe, M. (1988) 'Syringe exchange schemes for drug users in England and Scotland', *British Medical Journal* 296: 1717–19.

Stivers, R. (1976) *A Hair of the Dog: Irish Drinking and American Stereotype*, Pennsylvania: Pennsylvania State University Press.

Straus, R. (1957) 'The nature and status of medical sociology', *American Sociological Review* 22: 200–4.

Strong, P. and Horobin, G. (1978) 'Medical gentility', Unpublished ms., Aberdeen: Institute of Medical Sociology.

Sugarman, B. (1975) 'Reluctant converts, social control, socialisation, and adaption in therapeutic communities', in R. Wallis (ed.) *Sectarianism*, London: Peter Owen.

Summers, G. F. (1977) *Attitude Measurement*, London: Academic Book Publishers.

Sykes, J. B. (ed.) (1982) *The Concise Oxford Dictionary*, Oxford: Oxford University Press.

Szasz, T. (1971) *The Manufacture of Madness: a Comparative Study of the Inquisition and the Mental Health Movement*, London: Routledge & Kegan Paul.

Taylor, R. (1977) 'The local health system: an ethnography of interest-groups and decision-making', *Social Science and Medicine* 11: 583–92.

———— (1978) 'The local health system: observations on the exercise of professional influence', *Health and Social Service Journal* (21 July), Centre Eight Papers: 27–32.

———— (1981) 'The contribution of social science research to health policy: the Royal Commission on the National Health Service', *Journal of Social Policy* 10(4): 531–48.

———— (1984) 'Community based specialist obstetric services', in L. Zander and G. Chamberlain (eds) *Pregnancy Care for the 1980s*, London: Royal Society of Medicine/Macmillan Press.

Tew, M. (1986) 'Do obstetric intranatal interventions make birth safer?' *British Journal of Obstetrics and Gynaecology* 93: 659–74.

Thompson, F. J. (1986) 'The health policy context', in Carole E. Hill (ed.) *Current Health Policy Issues and Alternatives: an Applied Social Science Perspective*, Athens, GA: University of Georgia Press.

Townsend, P. and Davidson, N. (eds) (1982) *The Black Report on Inequalities in Health*, Harmondsworth: Penguin.

Toynbee, P. (1985) 'A woman who is enjoying her labour . . .' *Guardian* (29 May).

———— (1986) letter, *Guardian* (12 May).

———— (1987) *Options* (Nov.).

Tuckett, D. and Kaufert, J. M. (eds) (1978) *Basic Readings in Medical Sociology*, London: Tavistock Publications.

Unit for Continuing Education (1983) *District Food Health Policies*, Manchester: University of Manchester.

Verbrugge, L. M. (1985) 'Gender and health: an update on hypotheses and evidence', *Journal of Health and Social Behaviour* 26: 156–82.

Versluysen, M. (1981) 'Midwives, medical men and poor women labouring of child: Lying-in hospitals in eighteenth-century London', in H. Roberts (ed.) *Women, Health and Reproduction*, London: Routledge & Kegan Paul.

Wadsworth, M. E. J. and Robinson, D. (1976) *Studies in Everyday Medical Life*, London: Martin Robertson.

Wadsworth, M. E. J., Butterfield, W. J. H., and Blaney, R. (1971) *Health and Sickness: the Choice of Treatment*, London: Tavistock Publications.

Waugh, N. (1987) 'Proteinuria prevalence in insulin-treated patients: predictions of need for end-stage renal failure', *Diabetic Medicine*, 4: 151–5.

Waxler, N. E. (1981) 'Learning to be a leper: a case study in the social construction of illness', in E. G. Mishler *et al.* (eds) *Social Contexts of Health, Illness and Patient Care*, Cambridge: Cambridge University Press.

Welsh Office (1983) *All Wales Strategy for the Development of Services for Mentally Handicapped People*, Cardiff: Welsh Office.

West, P. (1976) 'The physician and the management of childhood epilepsy', in M. Wadsworth and D. Robinson (eds) *Studies in Everyday Medical Life*, London: Martin Robertson.

Whitehead, M. (1987) *The Health Divide: Inequalities in Health in the 1980s*, London: Health Education Council.

Williams, G. H. (1984) 'The genesis of chronic illness: narrative reconstruction', *Sociology of Health and Illness* 6: 175–200.

Williams, R. G. A. (1983) 'Concepts of health: an analysis of lay logic', *Sociology* 17: 182–205.

———— (1985) 'The salt of the earth: ideas linking diet, exercise and virtue among elderly Aberdonians', in A. Murcott (ed.) *The Sociology of Food and Eating*, Farnborough: Gower Press.

Williamson, A. and Room, G. (eds) (1983) *Health and Welfare States of Britain*, London: Heinemann.

Willis, P. (1977) 'The cultural meaning of drug abuse', in S. Hall and J. Jefferson (eds) *Resistance through Rituals — Youth Subculture in Post-war Britain*, London: Hutchinson University Library.

Worm, A. M. (1986) 'Incidence of HIV antibodies in IV drug abusers and prostitutes in Copenhagen', Paper presented at Workshop in Epidemiological Surveys on AIDS — Epidemiology of HIV Infection in Europe — Spread among Intravenous Drug Users and the Heterosexual Population, Berlin (12–14 Nov.).

Young, A. (1981) 'When rational men fall sick: an inquiry into some assumptions made by medical anthropologists', *Culture Medicine and Psychiatry* 5: 317–35.

Young, K. and Mills, L. (1980) *Public Policy Research: a Review of Qualitative Methods*, London: Social Science Research Council.

Zander, L. and Chamberlain, G. (eds) (1984) *Pregnancy Care for the 1980s*, London: Royal Society of Medicine/Macmillan Press.

Zola, I. (1963) 'Problems of communication, diagnosis and patient care', *Journal of Medical Education* 38: 829.

NAME INDEX

SUBJECT INDEX

259